At no time in history has public diplomacy played a more significant role in world affairs and international relations. As a result, global interest in public diplomacy has escalated, creating a substantial academic and professional audience for new works in the field.

The *Global Public Diplomacy Series* examines theory and practice in public diplomacy from a global perspective, looking closely at public diplomacy concepts, policies, and practices in various regions of the world. The purpose is to enhance understanding of the importance of public diplomacy, to advance public diplomacy thinking, and to contribute to improved public diplomacy practices.

This series is indexed in Scopus.

Palgrave Macmillan Series in Global Public Diplomacy

Niedja de Andrade e Silva Forte dos Santos

Anticorruption Public Diplomacy

A Comparative Perspective on Denmark, New Zealand, the United States and South Korea

palgrave
macmillan

Niedja de Andrade e Silva Forte dos Santos
University of Coimbra Institute for Legal Research (UCILeR)
Faculty of Law
Coimbra, Portugal

ISSN 2731-3883 ISSN 2731-3891 (electronic)
Palgrave Macmillan Series in Global Public Diplomacy
ISBN 978-3-032-28667-3 ISBN 978-3-032-28668-0 (eBook)
https://doi.org/10.1007/978-3-032-28668-0

This Palgrave Macmillan imprint is published by the registered company Springer Nature Switzerland AG, part of Springer Nature.
The registered company address is: Gewerbestrasse 11, 6330 Cham, Switzerland

To Caio, Tatiana and Luíza,
who show, through every gesture,
that the truest form of diplomacy
builds bridges across worlds, generations, and hearts.

To Antonio,
a companion in every negotiation with time and with destiny,
whose quiet presence embodies a distinctive form of soft power,
patiently reshaping paths and transforming environments,
always showing
that influence is strongest when rooted in care,
that standing for what one loves is the noblest of commitments,
that the most enduring transformations often begin in silence, and
that the deepest forms of change emerge not from force, but from constancy.

Foreword

Niedja Santos has written a worthy new addition to the distinguished Palgrave series in Global Public Diplomacy. Her book is insightful, innovative, and timely. As one would expect, in the years since Palgrave launched this series the field of public diplomacy studies has evolved. It is now common for scholars to argue that the dominant theoretical framework within the field – that of Joseph Nye's concept of Soft Power – has reached a limit either in theory or in practice. For my part in this process, I proposed it was time to embrace a wider concept, less dominated by the experience of the most successful Western nations, which I called Reputational Security.

Reputational Security referred to the enhancement to a country's physical well-being that comes from being well-thought of in the world, which might include the willingness of others to support that country in the event of a crisis. When applied to policy, the essence of this idea was that it was important not only to accentuate the positive aspects of one's own society through distributing an image (typically the heart of a Soft Power strategy) but also to do what one can to eliminate the negative aspects of that society (typically missing from a Soft Power strategy). The key was to actually being better as a result of reform. I argued a country's reputation (and thereby its security) could be enhanced by anticorruption work and cited Ukraine's efforts in this field in the years between the initial Russian incursions of 2014 and the full-scale invasion of 2022 as a prime case of this. I also argued that while Soft Power posited a vision of the world as a mix of a beauty contest and battle royale of all against all, the reality was that reputations were often considered collectively by region, cultural affinity (say religion) or political system. The extension of this was the argument that a public diplomacy initiative to enhance an ally's reputation by helping them share a positive or eliminate a negative was a wise investment in collective Reputational Security. This is exactly the territory and set of policies outlined in this book.

Niedja Santos, currently a scholar based in Portugal, is originally from Brazil where her previous career included practice as a city diplomat engaging through such platforms as the UNESCO Creative Cities Network. Her book reflects both a practitioner's eye for the practicalities of the policies she considers and a scholar's eye for detail and broader implications. She also does our field a tremendous favor by presenting a thorough exploration of a hitherto neglected case – Anticorruption Public Diplomacy – though the experience of four countries: Denmark, New Zealand, South Korea, and the United States. Non-American cases are always welcome in a field that has been dominated by the US experience and theoretical language best suited to discussing it.

Denmark is a great case not least because its commitment to anticorruption has required the management of the involvement of its own Danske Bank in perhaps Europe's largest ever money-laundering scandal in 2017–18. New Zealand brings an important new dimension – ethical principles derived from indigenous sources – namely the Tikanga Māori or indigenous ethics/practices/protocols that now inform that country's approach to its presence in the world beside the settler ethics derived from the Westminster democracy/British common law. South Korea's chapter also widens our vocabulary by introducing the Korean concept of Jeokpye Cheongsan or deep-rooted bad practices, a metaphor that borrows from the idea of society as a garden.

We should recall that the English concept of 'corruption' is also a metaphor, drawing a parallel between civic malpractice and the idea of an object or organism rotting into debased form. South Korea's challenge is to be its best self even as it manifestly wrestles with the persistence of entrenched exploitation of self-interest within some of its leadership class. Its answer, as Santos relates, includes combining moral communication with strategic design across regional platforms such as the OECD, UNCAC, and the Open Government Partnership.

Santos's treatment of the United States is similarly instructive and includes a worrying picture of an actor headed in the opposite direction and turning away from past efforts in AntiCorruption Public Diplomacy. The second Trump Administration has soft-pedalled anticorruption work, just as it has neglected so many aspects of public diplomacy. The suspension of the Foreign Corrupt Practices Act was a shock. My own feeling is that the U.S. has long-standing vulnerabilities in the area of anticorruption and courts accusations of double standards in its public diplomacy. Foreign-born observers find it ironic that embassies delivering anticorruption leadership and messages are so often led by people who owe their appointment to having made lavish financial contributions to the incumbent president's election campaign, whatever that president's political stripe.

Santos's concluding chapters show the commonalities between her cases: shared struggles for integrity and partnerships based on norms. She shows how integrity has become an element in strategic public diplomacy or in my terms, an extended and collective pursuit of Reputational Security. It is a pleasure to read this book and to encounter, within it, the distinctive voice of Niedja Santos to the collective conversation about the present and future of public diplomacy.

University of Southern California
Los Angeles, CA, USA

Nicholas J. Cull

Preface

The origins of this book lie in a question that gradually took shape over many years before finding expression in a formal research endeavour. What began as an intellectual curiosity eventually developed into doctoral research in International Relations at the Institute of Social and Political Sciences (ISCSP), University of Lisbon, where I sought to understand how anticorruption efforts shape international credibility, legitimacy, and influence.

Yet it was during my years in Brazil in the 2010s that I encountered a phenomenon that would profoundly reshape my understanding of the relationship between governance and international engagement. As the country launched major anticorruption operations, strengthened investigative capacities, and prosecuted high-profile corruption cases, I expected its international image to improve. Instead, Brazil's standing in international assessments of corruption often deteriorated. At the same time, South Korea, despite facing recurrent corruption scandals of its own, gradually improved its standing in global assessments. Although this observation did not constitute the empirical focus of the research itself, it raised questions that would lead me to investigate the broader international dimensions of anticorruption.

The contrast suggested that the effective control of corruption was, in itself, insufficient to transform international perceptions. Rather, the translation of domestic integrity efforts into international recognition appeared to depend on additional processes that remained poorly understood. This observation challenged the assumption that accountability automatically generates reputational gains. More importantly, it revealed an underexplored relationship between integrity and international standing that deserved scholarly attention.

As international politics evolved, the significance of this question became increasingly difficult to ignore. Over recent decades, corruption has moved from the margins of global governance to become a prominent concern of international organisations, development agencies, multinational corporations, and diplomatic institutions. Integrity is now measured, ranked, monitored, and debated through international conventions, governance indicators, transnational advocacy networks, and digital communication environments. States increasingly operate within a context in which international credibility affects investment flows, economic partnerships, development cooperation, and political influence. As a result, corruption can no longer be understood solely as a domestic governance challenge. Its consequences extend across borders, affecting international business, development assistance, regulatory cooperation, security agendas, and diplomatic relations. In this environment, questions of integrity have become increasingly visible as an international concern and, consequently, as a matter of diplomacy.

The puzzle I had encountered was not entirely unfamiliar. My previous professional experiences in public diplomacy had already sensitised me to the ways institutions seek legitimacy, recognition, and influence in international environments. In the steel industry, corporate diplomacy revealed how organisations engage with diverse stakeholders and cultivate legitimacy, while my involvement in city diplomacy through the UNESCO Creative Cities Network demonstrated how places construct identities and project themselves internationally. These experiences familiarised me with the processes through which institutions seek to shape their international standing.

Turning to the academic literature, I encountered a striking omission. Public diplomacy scholarship offered sophisticated explanations of communication, soft power, relationship-building, reputation, and international engagement. Corruption studies, meanwhile, had generated extensive knowledge regarding governance reforms, policy effectiveness, compliance mechanisms, and accountability frameworks. Yet the intersection between these two fields remained largely unexplored. Public diplomacy scholars rarely treated anticorruption as a meaningful dimension of international engagement, while corruption scholars seldom considered the international projection of integrity as a subject worthy of analytical attention. What remained insufficiently explained was how states communicate, negotiate, and institutionalise anticorruption commitments internationally, and how these processes influence their credibility and standing within global governance. Existing approaches could illuminate either corruption control or diplomatic communication, but not the relationship between them.

It was this analytical lacuna that ultimately prompted the formulation of Anticorruption Public Diplomacy. Existing concepts captured important aspects of the phenomenon but failed to fully explain it. Soft power highlighted attraction but not necessarily integrity. Nation branding focused on reputation but often overlooked the normative dimensions of governance. Governance promotion addressed the diffusion of standards but not the broader diplomatic dynamics through which anticorruption commitments are projected and recognised. At the same time, most corruption research remained predominantly focused on domestic institutions and policy outcomes. Anticorruption Public Diplomacy emerged as a way of bringing these strands together. It provides a framework for understanding how states project, communicate, institutionalise, and negotiate anticorruption commitments internationally, treating integrity not merely as a policy outcome but also as a strategic, normative, and socialising resource within international relations.

As the research progressed, constructivism emerged as a particularly fruitful lens through which to understand how identities, norms, meanings, and legitimacy shape international behaviour. The phenomenon I had observed could not be adequately explained through material incentives alone. It involved the ways in which states construct understandings of integrity, how these understandings are recognised by others, and how they become embedded within international practices. The concept of socialisation became especially useful because it allowed me to explore how anticorruption norms are learned, internalised, reproduced, and projected across international contexts. This perspective also encouraged me to look beyond communication, image, and reputation as explanatory categories. While messaging remains important, the evidence suggested that Anticorruption Public Diplomacy concerns deeper processes involving credibility, identity formation, normative alignment, and international legitimacy.

The comparative design of this study reflected a desire to explore these dynamics across markedly different contexts. Denmark and New Zealand were selected because they have consistently occupied leading positions in global anticorruption assessments and are frequently regarded as international references for integrity. The United States offered a different perspective, particularly through its pioneering role in internationalising anticorruption enforcement via the Foreign Corrupt Practices Act (FCPA) and its broader efforts to shape global anticorruption governance. South Korea presented yet another trajectory, demonstrating a remarkable improvement in international perceptions despite experiencing recurrent corruption scandals and political crises. Together, these four cases represent different political systems, diplomatic traditions, geographical regions, historical experiences, and pathways towards international anticorruption credibility. Examining them comparatively allowed me to investigate whether multiple routes exist towards international legitimacy and how different states transform integrity into influence within global governance.

This book seeks to contribute to an emerging conversation about the place of integrity within contemporary international relations. More specifically, it aims to establish Anticorruption Public Diplomacy as a distinct field of inquiry and to provide an analytical framework capable of explaining its operation across different contexts. In doing so, it engages with debates not only in public diplomacy, but also in international relations, global governance, and corruption studies. The book proposes that anticorruption should be understood not only as a domestic governance concern but also as a dimension of international engagement. Viewed from this perspective, anticorruption becomes an intersubjective and diplomatic process through which states seek recognition, credibility, legitimacy, and influence. In this sense, integrity functions not merely as a policy objective but also as a resource through which states position themselves within global governance.

Ultimately, the significance of Anticorruption Public Diplomacy extends well beyond the confines of this book. It speaks to a broader transformation in international politics, one in which states increasingly compete not only through military capabilities, economic resources, or cultural attraction, but also through their capacity to cultivate credibility, reputation, integrity, transparency, and responsible governance. Understanding this transformation helps us better appreciate the relationship between legitimacy and influence in contemporary world politics. It also invites reflection on whether integrity has become one of the defining currencies of international credibility and on how such credibility is constructed, communicated, and contested. As global governance becomes more interconnected and reputational assessments become more visible and immediate, these questions are likely to become even more significant. It is my hope that the pages that follow will contribute to this emerging conversation and stimulate further reflection on the role that Anticorruption Public Diplomacy may play in shaping the future of diplomacy and global governance.

University of Coimbra Institute
for Legal Research (UCILeR)
CoimbraPortugal
June 2026

N. de A.e S. F. dos Santos

Acknowledgments This book is the culmination of a long intellectual journey shaped by the guidance, generosity, and insight of many individuals and institutions. Although it is impossible to acknowledge everyone who contributed along the way, I wish to express my sincere gratitude to those whose support made this work possible. Above all, I am grateful to my family, whose unwavering patience, encouragement, and support sustained me throughout. Their presence, often quiet, yet enduring, has been a form of everyday collaborative power, creating the ideal conditions in which this project could emerge, evolve, and ultimately find expression in this book.

Although my engagement with public diplomacy and my interest in anticorruption pre-dated this research, sustained processes of intellectual engagement with Professors Heitor Romana, Jónatas Machado and Nuno Canas Mendes first enabled me to situate these interests within a coherent scholarly framework bridging public diplomacy and anticorruption. This marked not a beginning, but a reorientation: a shift from professional practice to analytical enquiry that gradually transformed empirical observation and experience into scholarly reflection. Under the careful supervision of Sandra Balão and José Luís Jacinto at the Institute of Social and Political Sciences (ISCSP), University of Lisbon, this transition was further develolped, enabling me to consolidate a coherent and rigorous research agenda.

Exchanges with Professors Carla Costa, Claudia Vaz, Jorge Manuel Coutinho de Abreu, Juan Luis Manfredi, Maria João Antunes, Maria João Ferreira, and Teresa Almeida e Silva helped me to refine my methodological choices and deepen my engagement with theoretical debates and the practices of academic publishing. These interactions were not merely supportive but constitutive of the work itself, reflecting processes of intellectual co-construction and shared learning through which many of the ideas developed in this book were tested, challenged, and refined. I am also particularly grateful to Professors Dulce Lopes and Alexandra Aragão, whose encouragement played a decisive role in bringing this book to fruition.

Over the years, this work has been enriched through a broad transnational network of scholars, editors, and project coordinators, whose advices, critical insights, and collaboration provided invaluable spaces for academic reflection, relational learning, and knowledge production. I would particularly like to acknowledge Professors Eduardo Figueiredo,

Efe Sevin, Fernando Carbajo Cascón, Giles Scott-Smith, Isaías Hipólito, Kenneth Weisbrode, Michael Johnston, Mihalis Kavaratzis, Nicholas Cull, Sean Aday, Sohaela Amiri, and Sónia Sebastião. I am equally grateful to the colleagues and co-authors who accompanied me on this journey with expertise, generosity, and intellectual clarity, including Cícero Ricci Cavini, Dulce Del Santoro, Luísa Barbosa, Marcelly Gullo, Paula Nunes, Rodrigo Corrêa, and Rui Lora. I also wish to acknowledge the institutions that supported my academic work—the Institute of Social and Political Sciences (ISCSP) and the Centre for Public Administration and Public Policies (CAPP) at the University of Lisbon, the University of Coimbra Institute for Legal Research (UCILeR), and the Portuguese Foundation for Science and Technology (FCT). Their support fostered the institutional environments in which scholarly communities, intellectual exchange, and knowledge production could flourish.

This book also owes much to the practitioners and scholars who generously shared their time, expertise, and perspectives, thereby significantly enriching the comparative analysis. Their contributions embody the dialogic character of public diplomacy itself. Through attentive listening and exchange, they helped transform this project from an individual endeavour into a genuinely collaborative exercise in knowledge production. For the Danish case, I thank Professor Arne Strand and Ana Revuelta. For the United States, I am grateful to Professors Michael Johnston, Nancy Boswell, Andrew Spalding, and Arvind Kumar Jain, as well as Gary Kalman and Annalise Burkhart from Transparency International. For New Zealand, I thank Professors Robert Gregory and Karin Lasthuizen, together with Julie Haggie from Transparency International New Zealand. For South Korea, I extend my appreciation to Professors Choong-Sik Chung (정충식), Jungoh Son (손정오), Hyelim Lee (이혜림), and Han-Beom You (유한범), as well as colleagues from Transparency International South Korea.

I would also like to acknowledge those who accompanied the earlier stages of my professional career and whose influence shaped the way I understand and critically engage with social phenomena. In this regard, I am grateful to Eugenia Granja, Italo Quidicomo, José Manuel Tavares, Jyoti Hosagrahar, Madalena Nitz, Marcia Oliveira, Marco Paulo Cabral, and Omar Silva Júnior.

Finally, I am deeply grateful to the editors of the *Palgrave Macmillan Series in Global Public Diplomacy*, Kathy Fitzpatrick and Vivian Walker, for recognising the potential of this project and welcoming it to this distinguished series. I am also grateful to the editorial teams at Palgrave

Macmillan and Springer Nature, particularly Isobel Cowper-Coles, Suriya Ilangovan and Kirthika Sanjivi, whose professionalism, guidance, and support were instrumental in bringing this book to publication.

Competing Interests The author has no competing interests to declare that are relevant to the content of this manuscript.

About the Book

This book offers the first systematic and theoretically grounded analysis of Anticorruption Public Diplomacy (ACPD) as a distinct domain within contemporary international relations. By bringing anticorruption into the analytical core of public diplomacy, it addresses a significant gap in the literature, where anticorruption has traditionally been treated as a domestic governance issue rather than as a meaningful dimension of international engagement.

Conceptually, the book advances an interpretivist–constructivist framework that understands ACPD as a process of international socialisation through which states construct, communicate, and negotiate integrity within global governance. Moving beyond instrumental and communication-based approaches, the book demonstrates how identities, interests, and norms are co-produced through diplomatic practice. From this perspective, anticorruption becomes not only a policy field but also a strategic and normative resource through which states seek legitimacy, credibility, and influence.

Empirically, the book develops a comparative analysis of four cases—Denmark, New Zealand, the United States, and South Korea—demonstrating that, despite differences in political systems and geopolitical positions, ACPD follows a consistent processual logic. Across these cases, integrity emerges as a shared diplomatic language through which states position themselves within international society. Building on these findings, the book proposes an original analytical framework structured around the interaction of strategic orientations, actor constellations, modes of action, and the resource–power nexus. This framework offers a transferable model for analysing governance-based diplomacy across issue areas.

Bridging public diplomacy, international relations theory, and governance studies, the book will appeal to scholars, practitioners, and policymakers engaged with public diplomacy, corruption studies, and global governance, particularly readers seeking to understand how ethical commitments evolve into instruments of power through Anticorruption Public Diplomacy in contemporary world politics.

Contents

About the Author

Niedja de Andrade e Silva Forte dos Santos is a jurist and interdisciplinary researcher whose work bridges international relations, law, public policy, and management. She holds a PhD in International Relations from the Institute of Social and Political Sciences (ISCSP), University of Lisbon, and is currently pursuing a PhD in Law at the University of Coimbra. She also holds bachelor's and master's degrees in Law and an MBA, and is admitted to the Brazilian Bar Association (OAB).

Based in Portugal, she is a researcher at the University of Coimbra Institute for Legal Research (UCILeR) and at the Centre for Public Administration and Public Policies (CAPP), at the University of Lisbon. Her research examines public diplomacy, corporate diplomacy, anticorruption, democracy, and governance, with particular emphasis on the relationship between governance and international engagement.

Within this broader research agenda, her scholarship investigates the diplomatic and normative dimensions of anticorruption, alongside questions of global governance, international cooperation, and corporate governance. She has authored numerous peer-reviewed articles and book chapters published by leading academic publishers, including Palgrave Macmillan, Edward Elgar, Routledge, Taylor & Francis, and Mare & Martin. She has also presented her work at major international conferences, including those convened by the International Studies Association (ISA), the International Political Science Association (IPSA), and other leading scholarly associations.

Her academic career is complemented by extensive professional experience across both the private and public sectors in Brazil. Before entering academia full-time, she pursued a career in management, corporate diplomacy, and institutional relations. She subsequently served as Deputy Secretary for Economic Development and Director of Economic Innovation for the Municipality of Santos, Brazil, where she led initiatives in innovation, economic development, creative economy, city diplomacy, and international cooperation. Internationally, she served as a Cluster Coordinator within the UNESCO Creative Cities Network and advised on city diplomacy initiatives in China. This combination of academic and professional experience lends her research interdisciplinary, policy-relevant, and practice-oriented character.

Abbreviations

ACPD	Anticorruption Public Diplomacy
ACRC	Anti-Corruption and Civil Rights Commission (South Korea)
AI	artificial intelligence
APEC	Asia–Pacific Economic Cooperation
ARIN-AP	Asset Recovery Interagency Network Asia-Pacific
ASEAN	Association of Southeast Asian Nations
BRICS	Brazil, Russia, India, China, South Africa, Egypt, Ethiopia, Iran, United Arab Emirates, and Indonesia
CIA	Central Intelligence Agency (United States)
CIO	Corruption Investigation Office for High-Ranking Officials (South Korea)
CSR	corporate social responsibility
DANIDA	Danish International Development Agency
DIIS	Danish Institute for International Studies
DoD	Department of Defense (United States)
DoJ	Department of Justice (United States)
DoS	Department of State (United States)
ECO	New Zealand Export Credit Office
EITI	Extractive Industries Transparency Initiative
EKF	Export Credit Agency (Denmark)
ERCAS	European Research Centre for Anti-Corruption and State-Building
Eximbank	Export–Import Bank of Korea
FATF	Financial Action Task Force
FBI	Federal Bureau of Investigation (United States)
FCPA	Foreign Corrupt Practices Act (United States)
FinCEN	Financial Crimes Enforcement Network

FKI	Federation of Korean Industries
G8	Group of Eight
GDP	gross domestic product
GFP	Global Firepower
GNI	gross national income
GRECO	Group of States against Corruption
IACA	International Anti-Corruption Academy
IEEPA	International Emergency Economic Powers Act (United States)
IFU	Investment Fund for Developing Countries
IMF	International Monetary Fund
INTERPOL	International Criminal Police Organizaton
K-Pact	Korean Pact for Anti-Corruption and Transparency
KICAC	Korea Independent Commission Against Corruption
KOICA	Korea International Cooperation Agency
MFAD	Ministry of Foreign Affairs of Denmark
MOFA	Ministry of Foreign Affairs (South Korea)
NATO	North Atlantic Treaty Organization
NGO(s)	non-governamental organisation(s)
NORAD	Norwegian Agency for Development Cooperation
NZFAT	New Zealand Foreign Affairs and Trade
OAS	Organization of American States
ODA	official development assistance
OECD	Organisation for Economic Co-operation and Development
OGP	Open Government Partnership
RICO	Racketeer Influenced and Corrupt Organizations Act (United States)
SEC	Securities and Exchange Commission (United States)
SFO	Serious Fraud Office (New Zealand)
SØIK	Prosecutor for Serious Economic and International Crime (Denmark)
SPO	Supreme Prosecutors' Office (South Korea)
TI Danmark	Transparency International Danmark
TINZ	Transparency International New Zealand
UN	United Nations
UNCAC	United Nations Convention against Corruption
UNDP	United Nations Development Programme
UNODC	United Nations Office on Drugs and Crime
USAID	Agency for International Development (United States)
WIPO	World Intellectual Property Organization
WJP	World Justice Project

List of Figures

CHAPTER 1

Introduction: Rethinking Public Diplomacy Through the Anticorruption Lens

1.1 Globalising Integrity: The New Face of Public Diplomacy

In recent years, integrity has quietly become a language of diplomacy. From summit declarations to development partnerships, terms such as transparency, accountability, and anticorruption now stand alongside peace and security in world affairs. The global contest for credibility increasingly unfolds less through military alliances or trade agreements than through claims to ethical governance. When governments invoke honesty, fairness, or respect for the rule of law internationally, they are not merely addressing domestic audiences, they are performing diplomacy. In this evolving landscape, embassies, aid agencies, and international organisations compete to be recognised as powerful and as trustworthy.

This shift is reflected in recent national anticorruption strategies and international engagements. In 2021, the United States Strategy on Countering Corruption framed corruption as "a core United States national security interest" and committed to elevating it "as a priority within its diplomatic and public diplomacy efforts" (White House, 2021, p. 34). Likewise, in 2025, the United Kingdom anticorruption strategy identified corruption as a threat to national interests, particularly economic growth, security, and democracy (Government of the United Kingdom, 2025). At the supranational level, the European Union

N. de A. e S. F. dos Santos, *Anticorruption Public Diplomacy*, Palgrave Macmillan Series in Global Public Diplomacy,
https://doi.org/10.1007/978-3-032-28668-0_1

reinforced this trend through Directive (EU) 2026/1021, which strengthened the Union's anticorruption framework and further consolidated integrity, transparency, and accountability as shared governance priorities across member states (Santos, 2026). South Korea offers another illustrative case: its Anti-Corruption and Civil Rights Commission (ACRC) has engaged international organisations, including the Organisation for Economic Co-operation and Development (OECD) and Transparency International, while actively promoting national performance in the Corruption Perceptions Index (ACRC, 2022, para. 1). Taken together, these initiatives demonstrate how anticorruption has become a form of strategic signalling in contemporary public diplomacy.

Comparable dynamics can be observed elsewhere. In Europe, Denmark and the European Union launched a €16 million programme to strengthen anticorruption reforms in Ukraine (European Union External Action, 2016, para. 1). Meanwhile, New Zealand's Serious Fraud Office expanded anticorruption cooperation with regional and international partners across the Asia-Pacific. This included participation in the Hong Kong Independent Commission Against Corruption Symposium to foster knowledge exchange and professional networks (Asia-Pacific Economic Cooperation, 2012, p. 152). Collectively, these initiatives illustrate how states operationalise anticorruption through outward-facing engagement combining cooperation, communication, and international positioning.

This pattern points to an emerging practice conceptualised here as anticorruption public diplomacy (ACPD). It refers to processes through which governments communicate commitments to integrity abroad while negotiating recognition and legitimacy in international society. This understanding reflects the broader constructivist insight that legitimacy and influence emerge through shared meanings rather than material capabilities alone.

Corruption has become one of the defining challenges of contemporary global governance. It erodes democratic legitimacy, distorts economic competition, undermines social trust, and weakens the rule of law (Mungiu-Pippidi, 2023; Rothstein, 2021). Once treated primarily as a domestic issue, corruption is now widely recognised as a transnational problem with far-reaching consequences (Hough, 2013). Estimates suggest that corruption drains up to US$2.6 trillion annually from the global economy (International Monetary Fund [IMF], 2019). This reinforces its status as both a development and a security concern, as reflected in Sustainable Development Goal 16.5.

International institutions have played a central role in consolidating anticorruption as a global norm. The United Nations Convention against Corruption (UNCAC) and the Organisation for Economic Co-operation and Development (OECD) Anti-Bribery Convention have institutionalised integrity commitments across national jurisdictions. Multilateral organisations, including the IMF and the World Bank, have embedded anticorruption within broader frameworks of sustainable development and good governance (IMF, 2019; Kaufmann et al., 2010). Through these processes, anticorruption has been normalised as an expected standard of legitimate conduct, increasingly structuring global expectations of governance and state behaviour.

In parallel, public diplomacy has undergone a profound transformation. Moving beyond Cold War paradigms, it now emphasises relationship-building, dialogue, and sustained engagement with foreign publics as part of foreign policy practice (Cull, 2024; Gilboa, 2008; Melissen & Wang, 2019; Taplin, 2025). Public diplomacy connects domestic values with international perceptions, enhancing legitimacy, standing, and mutual understanding (Cull, 2024; Manfredi-Sánchez, 2025; Sevin, 2017). As power diffuses and non state agents gain prominence, the ability to shape global narratives has become a central source of influence (Miller, 2025; Nye, 2019). This book contributes to understanding a broader shift towards governance-centred diplomacy, in which internal standards of integrity, accountability, transparency, and institutional credibility increasingly inform external recognition.

Despite their parallel evolution, anticorruption and public diplomacy are rarely analysed together. Anticorruption is typically approached as a matter of governance and law (Mungiu-Pippidi, 2023), while public diplomacy is often understood as strategic communication and influence directed at foreign publics, and, increasingly, as an integral dimension of diplomacy more broadly defined (Snow & Cull, 2020; Gregory, 2025). Yet both are fundamentally concerned with legitimacy, trust, and the projection of values in the international arena (Bukovansky, 2015; Cull, 2024; Nye, 2019). From this perspective, anticorruption can be seen as a diplomatic process involving norm diffusion, international socialisation, and identity construction (Finnemore & Sikkink, 2001; Mccoy & Heckel, 2001). Exploring this intersection opens new analytical ground for understanding the relational foundations of credibility and influence in contemporary international relations.

Beyond addressing this theoretical gap, this book contributes to debates on ethics, values, and morality in public diplomacy. Drawing on Cull's (2024) concept of reputational security, integrity emerges not merely as a moral aspiration but as strategic capital and a condition of international security, shaping how states are trusted, supported, and protected within global politics (Manfredi-Sánchez, 2025; Nye, 2011; Vukovic, 2020). At the same time, and in line with critical perspectives on public diplomacy, morality is not neutral: it is embedded in relations of power and often mobilised as a form of strategic communication through which actors seek to project virtue and legitimacy in the international sphere (Alexander, 2021). By bringing together anticorruption and public diplomacy, the book addresses an issue that extends well beyond academic debates. Corruption and anticorruption increasingly influence development assistance, foreign investment, and the credibility of international partnerships (Bauhr et al., 2013). The ability of states to project integrity therefore shapes their practical capacity to cooperate and lead.

The notion of reputational security proposed by Cull (2024) further clarifies this dynamic. From this perspective, international reputation is more than an intangible asset or an instrument of attraction; it is a condition that may enhance a state's physical security by increasing the willingness of others to provide support in times of crisis. Crucially, reputational security is built not solely through the projection of positive images, as in a soft power logic, but also through efforts to address and reduce the negative features that undermine credibility. Reform, therefore, becomes part of international positioning. The case of Ukraine is particularly illustrative: anticorruption efforts undertaken between 2014 and 2022 contributed to strengthening its international standing and to fostering a broader climate of external support. Cull (2024) further suggests that assisting allies in improving their reputation can be understood as an investment in collective reputational security. This insight is especially relevant to ACPD, as it connects domestic integrity reform, international recognition, and security outcomes within a single analytical framework.

This book examines how states use public diplomacy to construct and project integrity as part of their foreign policy identities. By comparing Denmark, New Zealand, the United States, and South Korea, it shows that integrity is more than a moral aspiration, operating as a strategic resource. It underpins reputational security, cooperation, and influence in global politics. Against this backdrop, a more precise understanding of what constitutes corruption becomes essential, as the meanings attributed to it shape both its communication and its role within diplomatic practice.

1.2 What Counts as Corruption?

Corruption resists a single, universally accepted definition (Heywood, 2015; Johnston, 2001). Its meaning varies across disciplinary traditions, legal frameworks, institutional practices, and cultural contexts. Despite this plurality, many analyses rely on Transparency International's definition of corruption as the abuse of entrusted power for private gain. This understanding has gained considerable influence across academic and policy-oriented debates.

International institutional and legal frameworks generally adopt a more circumscribed approach. The UNCAC, for instance, defines corruption through codified offences such as bribery, trading in influence, and abuse of functions. This legalistic perspective undoubtedly provides necessary standards for compliance and international cooperation. However, it privileges formal illegality and often overlooks lawful practices that nevertheless distort public purpose. As a result, legal definitions struggle to capture how corruption operates in practice, particularly in transnational settings.

From a systemic standpoint, corruption is rooted in incentive structures, principal–agent relationships, and institutional designs (Johnston, 2005; Rose-Ackerman, 2025). It is understood not merely as rule-breaking, but as an outcome of governance arrangements characterised by discretion, weak accountability, and information asymmetries. Building on this logic, the quality of government perspective locates corruption in the absence of impartiality in the exercise of public power, regardless of formal legal compliance (Rothstein, 2021). Consequently, corruption signals not only illegality, but a broader failure of fairness and institutional trust.

These definitional debates are particularly relevant for ACPD. Beyond legal or governance failure, corruption also constitutes a reputational security issue (Cull, 2023). The way it is framed shapes how states communicate integrity, normative legitimacy, and commitment to global norms. Accordingly, corruption is conceptualised here as a relational and normative phenomenon embedded in social processes. It refers to the instrumentalisation of public resources or representational ties for private or particularistic purposes. Such practices violate social norms such as integrity, impartiality, and the public interest (Johnston, 2005;

Mungiu-Pippidi, 2023; Rothstein, 2021). From this angle, corruption may distort the public purpose even when the practices involved remain formally legal.

The decisive criterion for identifying corruption lies not in the means employed, but in the purposes served and the normative context within which influence is exercised. More broadly, diplomatic incentives and influence strategies may be legitimate when transparent and oriented towards recognised public goals. However, they become corrupt when they generate hidden asymmetrical dependencies, suppress criticism, or erode shared norms of integrity. Corruption is thereby approached as a systemic failure of normative socialisation rather than an individual moral deviation.

Accordingly, and in connection with concerns about reputational security, this book engages with refinements to the smart power framework, particularly the concept of sharp power (Nye, 2019, 2021), by adopting an explicit normative criterion for assessing influence. The focus is not only on effectiveness, but also on whether influence sustains or corrodes norms upon which legitimate authority depends (Nye, 2019; Cull, 2024). Strategies that purchase silence, obscure corrupt practices, or manipulate accountability mechanisms may yield short-term gains, yet remain normatively corrosive, undermining both credibility and long-term legitimacy. In this sense, corruption can be understood as a process that is shaped, contested, and reproduced across domestic and international arenas marked by power asymmetries and competing moral claims.

1.3 Opening the Field: Public Diplomacy Meets Anticorruption

Since the end of the Cold War, both public diplomacy and anticorruption have gained prominence alongside international debates on governance, legitimacy, and power. Yet their trajectories have largely unfolded separately, with limited conceptual or analytical integration.

Public diplomacy evolved within a broader reconfiguration of statecraft under conditions of interdependence (Aday, 2025; Melissen et al., 2023). As communication became inseparable from foreign policy, governments expanded their engagement with external audiences beyond traditional diplomatic channels (Gilboa, 2008; Gregory, 2025; Nye, 2011; Zaharna, 2022). Dialogue, credibility, and long-term relationship-building increasingly complemented, and often displaced, one-way persuasion as dominant logics (Cull, 2019, 2024; Melissen, 2005). In this context, reputation emerged not merely as an outcome of diplomatic action, but as a strategic condition shaping how states are perceived, trusted, and supported in the international arena (Cull, 2024). Non-state agents, including civil society, business, and media, became increasingly central in mediating these processes, influencing how states project values and construct their identities abroad (Hocking et al., 2012; Snow & Cull, 2020). These developments repositioned public diplomacy as a relational practice centred not only on engagement and value projection, but also on the cultivation and maintenance of reputational security.

In parallel, anticorruption consolidated as a global governance concern. Initially framed as a domestic issue, corruption gained international salience through instruments such as the OECD Anti-Bribery Convention and the UNCAC (Hough, 2013; Heywood, 2015). These conventions marked a shift towards shared standards and transnational governance regimes (Harris, 2019). Global indices, notably Transparency International's Corruption Perceptions Index, rendered integrity visible, comparable, and politically consequential (Heywood & Rose, 2014). Over time, anticorruption evolved into a marker of reliability and reputational security in world politics.

Despite this practical convergence in policy and discourse, including emerging efforts to link anticorruption to reputational security (Cull, 2023), the two fields remain weakly connected analytically. Anticorruption research tends to privilege institutional design, public sector decision-making, and policy reform (Johnston, 2001; Rose-Ackerman, 2025). Public diplomacy scholarship, by contrast, centres on communication, image construction, legitimacy, reputational security, and relationship-building (Aday, 2025; Cull, 2024; Melissen & Wang, 2019). Even recent analyses of country images and expectations across foreign publics and communication environments (Ingenhoff & Chariatte, 2025) overlook corruption as a substantive concern. Similarly, within approaches emphasising value and norm diffusion processes (Ayhan, 2019; Cull, 2024; Durrani, 2025), anticorruption remains marginal rather than analytically central.

Studies that mention the term anticorruption diplomacy usually denote intergovernmental negotiation with limited attention to engagement with foreign publics (Tourinho, 2016). Such studies raise two issues. First, they tend to imply a more rigid binary between traditional diplomacy and public diplomacy. However, recent research increasingly understands public diplomacy as an integral component of diplomacy (Gregory, 2024, 2025; Melissen et al., 2023; Wiseman & Scott, 2026). Second, they give little attention to how states use public diplomacy instruments to promote integrity and anticorruption as part of their global identity.

Bringing together the public diplomacy and anticorruption literatures highlights a shared concern with credibility as power (Nye, 2019; Brown, 2025; Bukovansky, 2015). In an environment of information abundance, reputational security has become a form of strategic capital (Cull, 2023, 2024; Nye, 2019). Just as democracy or human rights narratives have become defining features of foreign policy identities (Miller, 2025), anticorruption increasingly performs a similar signalling function. It communicates ethical commitment and institutional reliability to foreign publics and partners.

This convergence invites a reconsideration of integrity as a diplomatic resource. Public diplomacy research reveals that attraction and credibility derive from perceived values as much as from policy outcomes (Nye, 2011; Cull, 2024; Pamment et al., 2025). Anticorruption scholarship likewise demonstrates that institutional trust depends on shared norms rather than legal enforcement alone (Johnston, 2005; Rothstein, 2021). Viewed through this lens, ACPD operates at the intersection of governance, legal studies, policy practice, strategic communication, and international relations. It describes how states promote integrity as both a domestic value and an international asset, diffusing norms and building legitimacy through dialogue, persuasion, and example.

The expression *anticorruption public diplomacy* first appeared in the American Department of State documents (US Department of State [DoS], 2001, 2015). It referred to outreach efforts promoting accountability abroad. This was an early institutional recognition of anticorruption as a communicative and diplomatic, rather than purely legal, domain. The United States was also the first country to consider public diplomacy in an anticorruption strategy (White House, 2021), thereby signalling the gradual integration of integrity concerns into the strategic and communicative dimensions of foreign policy.

From this synthesis, ACPD has come to constitute an embryonic yet increasingly visible dimension of global public diplomacy. States have incorporated anticorruption narratives into foreign policy, positioning integrity as a hallmark of national identity and a source of international influence. Integrity operates as a substrate for public diplomacy and as a cornerstone of reputational security. By exploring four comparative case studies, this book develops a first systematic comparative account of ACPD. It shows how integrity becomes a language of influence in contemporary international relations.

1.4 Understanding Anticorruption Public Diplomacy Through Constructivism

Building on the conceptual synthesis developed above, this section situates the analysis of ACPD within a constructivist and interpretive framework. This perspective foregrounds the relational, communicative, and normative ways in which integrity is articulated, contested, and projected in international contexts. The book aligns with modernist constructivism (Finnemore & Sikkink, 2001), understood as an epistemologically moderate position (Finnemore & Wendt, 2024) that emphasises empirically grounded processes of norm diffusion, socialisation, and identity formation in world politics. These theoretical foundations allow ACPD to be understood as a socially embedded process through which states construct meaning, legitimacy, and international standing.

Ontologically, this book adopts an anti-foundationalist position that recognises the social construction of international reality. From this standpoint, international politics is not an objective structure to be discovered, but a constellation of meanings produced through social interaction (Thomas, 2017, p. 122). Institutions, norms, and interests possess no independent causal power beyond the understandings attributed to them by social agents (Marsh et al., 2018). Reality is thus relational, contingent, and historically situated. This has direct implications for how anticorruption norms are interpreted and enacted across contexts.

Although states may formally endorse comparable anticorruption standards, the meanings attached to these norms vary across political cultures and historical trajectories. For instance, while both New Zealand and the United States promote integrity, the former tends to interpret it through a communitarian ethos of fairness and inclusiveness, whereas the latter embeds it within a discourse of leadership and global responsibility. Accordingly, anticorruption is understood here as a socially embedded and communicatively constituted concept, rather than a universally agreed standard.

Epistemologically, this stance corresponds to interpretivism, which examines how social phenomena are understood and given meaning by agents and researchers (Porta & Keating, 2013). A central assumption is the existence of a double hermeneutic, whereby researchers interpret meanings already produced by social actors (Marsh et al., 2018). As a result, knowledge is partial and context-bound, shaped by values, traditions, and discursive environments.

At the same time, constructivism retains a commitment to analytical rigour and objectivity in an intersubjective sense, producing claims constrained by evidence, whether oriented towards causal mechanisms, interpretive meanings, or both (Finnemore & Wendt, 2024). Meanings, identities, and norms are not fixed; they are constructed and contested through interaction (Checkel, 2026). This perspective is particularly relevant to the study of public diplomacy. In this domain, meanings are actively constructed, communicated, and challenged through dialogue, representation, and symbolic practices (Adler, 2013; Gilboa, 2008). Accordingly, understanding public diplomacy requires close attention to how agents frame issues, narrate values, and interpret the responses of foreign publics.

Constructivism provides a suitable analytical framework for examining how norms, identities, and meaning are socially constructed and sustained in world politics (Adler, 2013; Finnemore & Sikkink, 2001). Emerging in the 1990s, it responded to the limitations of realism and liberalism by introducing a sociological understanding of international relations. A core constructivist premise is that international behaviour is shaped by shared ideas and intersubjective understandings, rather than solely by material capabilities (Katzenstein, 1996; Wendt, 1999). In this scenario, state interests and identities are not pre-given; they are socially produced through interaction (Adler, 2013; Wendt, 1999). Ideas and norms influence political behaviour, while political practice simultaneously reinforces and reproduces those norms and identities, shaping how agents understand who they are and what roles they perform in international society (Finnemore & Sikkink, 2001). The relationship between agents and structures is co-constitutive: structures shape what agents can plausibly do, while agents reproduce and transform those structures through practice (Finnemore & Wendt, 2024). In this structurationist sense, interests and identities are mutually constituted rather than exogenously given.

Applied to public diplomacy, this constructivist logic implies that states engage in communicative practices through which they articulate who they are and what they value, thereby shaping perceptions and expectations within international society (Melissen, 2005; Sevin, 2017). Hence, public diplomacy operates not merely as an instrument of influence, but as a site where norms and identities are performed, interpreted, and contested. It typically operates through persuasion, relationship-building, advocacy, and mutual adjustment, but may also involve other means, such as material incentives (Nye, 2019; Vukovic, 2020). Importantly, norms are not simply transmitted unchanged; they are interpreted, adapted, and negotiated across different contexts.

When states engage in ACPD, they are performing their identities and actively reshaping normative expectations. By projecting narratives of transparency, fairness, and accountability, they seek to position themselves as credible and legitimate agents within global governance (Bukovansky, 2015; Nye, 2011). In this way, the promotion of integrity becomes part of the ongoing social construction of international order (Adler, 2013; Finnemore & Sikkink, 2001). This performative dimension was evident in the United States' Summit for Democracy initiative, where public diplomacy campaigns intertwined anticorruption discourse with narratives of leadership and moral authority, projecting integrity as desirable in the international order and constitutive of national character.

Seen through this lens, ACPD cannot be assumed to be normatively neutral or inherently benign. It constitutes a contested social space in which integrity narratives, power relations, strategic interests, and reputational claims intersect, making it as much an arena of negotiation and struggle as one of ethical projection. Claims of integrity can function as instruments of reputational management and international positioning, while also serving as a moral façade for political projects whose goals, beneficiaries, and consequences are contested (Alexander, 2021). Importantly, dynamics of internalisation and instrumentalisation are not mutually exclusive; they often coexist within the same diplomatic practices. ACPD therefore warrants analysis not only for what it promotes, but also for what it legitimises, obscures, or normalises in the making of international order.

Against this backdrop, ACPD can be understood as a process of norm diffusion and socialisation embedded within the broader anticorruption normative environment, often described as a global anticorruption regime (Harris, 2019). Anchored primarily in the OECD Anti-Bribery Convention and the UNCAC, this regime possesses not only material but also ideational dimensions, as it reflects a shared global anticorruption norm (Mccoy & Heckel, 2001), interpreted differently across contexts and progressively shaping global expectations regarding appropriate state behaviour.

From a constructivist perspective, states internalise norms not only through coercion, external pressure, or material incentives, but also through identification with the values those norms express. This internalisation process has significant implications for state identity. As anticorruption norms become embedded within domestic institutions and foreign policy, compliance may evolve from obligation to self-understanding. Anticorruption thus becomes not merely a regulatory requirement, but a marker of moral credibility and trustworthiness. This transformation is particularly consequential for public diplomacy, as internalised norms shape how states narrate themselves abroad.

Through this process, integrity acquires symbolic value, reinforcing reputational security and diplomatic legitimacy. Denmark's alignment with global anticorruption norms illustrates this dynamic. Over time, compliance shifted into an element of national identity, where maintaining the image of the world's least corrupt state became a source of pride and international recognition. This internalisation shaped both domestic reform trajectories and Denmark's external self-presentation, embedding integrity within its diplomatic narrative. States that successfully internalise anticorruption norms are better positioned to project credibility, reliability, and legitimacy in international affairs, rather than merely demonstrating compliance with external expectations.

1.5 The Architecture of Anticorruption Public Diplomacy

Building on the theoretical framework discussed above, ACPD may be provisionally defined as the process through which states and non state agents communicate and institutionalise integrity as part of their identities, foreign policy practices, and international self-presentation in pursuit of strategic interests. Situated at the intersection of public diplomacy and anticorruption, ACPD combines the communicative and relational logics of the former with the normative substance of the latter. Rather than constituting a distinct policy domain or operating outside diplomacy, it designates a way in which integrity is framed, projected, and negotiated in international contexts.

At its core, ACPD centres on engagement with foreign publics, diffusion of anticorruption norms, and co-construction of meanings through processes of international socialisation. It encompasses interactions with other states, civil society organisations, think tanks, and media actors, whose participation shapes perceptions of legitimacy, credibility, and transparency beyond formal diplomatic channels (Snow & Cull, 2020; Hocking et al., 2012). This emphasis reflects the broader transformation of diplomacy towards more plural, networked, and audience-oriented forms of international engagement.

For empirical research purposes, the chapters that follow approach ACPD through six interrelated analytical aspects. Four of these constitute its core dimensions: (1) identities and interests, capturing the normative and strategic motivations underpinning the international promotion of anticorruption (Finnemore & Sikkink, 2001); (2) objectives and strategic orientations, referring to foreign policy goals guiding anticorruption-related engagement (Banks, 2020); (3) agents, encompassing state and non state entities involved in the diffusion and socialisation of integrity norms through public diplomacy practices (Ayhan, 2019; Gregory, 2025; Porte, 2012); and (4) activities, including diplomatic, communicative, cultural, relational, and educational initiatives directed towards foreign publics (Cull, 2019; Martino, 2020). Two cross-cutting elements complement these dimensions: (5) material and immaterial factors, referring to resources whose value and meaning are constituted through public diplomacy processes (Nye, 2011); and (6) ideational factors, or smart power configurations, capturing the combination of soft, collaborative, hard, and sharp power (Nye, 2011, 2021; Slaughter, 2011; Vukovic, 2020) mobilised to position anticorruption as a source of global influence.

Taken together, this analytical framing allows ACPD to be examined not as a fixed model, but as a dynamic process consistent with a constructivist understanding of social reality as produced and stabilised through practice (Finnemore & Wendt, 2024; Adler-Nissen, 2023). In this scenario, anticorruption contributes to state identity formation and global norm articulation. It underscores how the meanings of anticorruption are continuously negotiated between national identities, interests, and international expectations, reinforcing the constructivist insight that ACPD is as much about international socialisation as it is about persuasion, compliance, communication, and relationship-building.

1.6 Designing an Analytical Framework for Anticorruption Public Diplomacy

This study adopts a research design that explores how ACPD relates to state interests and identities. It does not seek to measure causal effects. The analysis traces how integrity acquires meaning and operates as a diplomatic resource through communicative practice and socialisation within public diplomacy. The central research question—*How is anticorruption public diplomacy related to state interests and identities?*—reflects this epistemological stance by linking the communicative and relational dimensions of diplomacy to the social construction of international self-representation. From this question follows the broader goal of mapping how states socialise and project anticorruption and integrity internationally as part of their identities.

The comparative structure comprising these six interrelated dimensions (identities and interests, objectives, agents, activities, material and immaterial factors, and ideational factors/smart power) translates the constructivist approach. This structure allows the interaction among dimensions to be observed across diverse contexts, showing how integrity operates as a diplomatic resource. Each case functions as a bounded system examined individually before contributing to a comparative synthesis (Stake, 2006). Thus, the comparative model explores how meanings and practices are co-produced across distinct political cultures (Adler, 2013; Marsh et al., 2018). The aim is to achieve contingent generalisations (Finnemore & Sikkink, 2001) regarding ACPD, following the interpretivist logic of theory-building through comparison.

The four cases were selected for their combined relevance to both anticorruption and public diplomacy. Denmark and New Zealand serve as high integrity benchmarks, consistently leading global transparency and governance rankings. The United States represents a major power with a long-standing tradition of norm entrepreneurship. South Korea illustrates a post-reform trajectory marked by efforts at reputational recovery. Together, these cases span Europe, Oceania, North America, and East Asia. They combine normative convergence with contextual diversity, allowing for the identification of common mechanisms of norm diffusion across varied political and cultural environments. Nevertheless, while the comparative framework captures important variations across four regions, it does not aim to provide a globally representative account of anticorruption public diplomacy. Important experiences from Africa and Latin

America fall beyond the scope of the present study and warrant dedicated future research.

This interpretive-constructivist framework aligns method and theory coherently, positioning the analysis of ACPD at the intersection of meaning and practice. It shows how states pursue interests through the socialisation of narratives and how the projection of integrity through public diplomacy shapes identities. Moving beyond the procedural structure of the author's doctoral thesis (Santos, 2025), the book advances an analytical narrative that integrates theory and evidence, establishing ACPD as both an emerging field of study and a dynamic practice of international relations, in which the socialisation of values and the construction of norms serve as sources of power and identity.

1.7 Reframing Anticorruption as Power in Public Diplomacy

Anticorruption and integrity, once approached primarily as moral virtues or administrative principles (Doig & McIvor, 2003), have become strategic resources through which states build legitimacy, reputational security, and influence in the global arena (Cull, 2023; Pozsgai-Alvarez & Lang, 2025). The central argument of this book is that ACPD constitutes a process and an outcome of the social construction of integrity in international relations, illustrating how power operates not only through material capabilities but through the structuring of shared meanings, expectations, and norms (Finnemore & Wendt, 2024). In this sense, integrity becomes a medium through which power is exercised and recognised internationally.

Within this normative environment, states negotiate who they are and how they wish to be recognised internationally (Bukovansky, 2015; Finnemore & Sikkink, 2001; Nye, 2019), aligning external narratives with evolving global anticorruption norms. ACPD is thus treated not merely as a policy instrument but as a relational practice through which identity, legitimacy, and influence are co-produced.

The book advances a theoretical contribution demonstrating that public diplomacy provides the relational and communicative infrastructure through which anticorruption norms are diffused, internalised, and legitimised. In doing so, it extends prevailing understandings of soft power beyond attraction and persuasion to include recognition, ethical consistency, and reputational reliability as core sources of influence (Cull, 2024; Nye, 2011). Integrity and anticorruption thereby constitute forms of symbolic capital, increasingly central in an international system where legitimacy is mediated through trust and reputation (Rothstein, 2021; Vukovic, 2020). Seen in this way, anticorruption operates as a link between normative commitment and the practical exercise of influence in contemporary public diplomacy.

From this perspective, anticorruption comes to operate as a diplomatic idiom through which states pursue both ethical and strategic goals. The consistent communication of integrity can generate symbolic authority, enhancing recognition and shaping international agendas (Adler, 2013; Finnemore & Sikkink, 2001). Conversely, the normalisation of corruption or the absence of credible integrity narratives undermines reputational security and constrains diplomatic reach. ACPD thus illuminates how ethical performance and public diplomacy intersect in the ongoing production of global order.

The study further contributes to rethinking the nature of power in public diplomacy. Rather than opposing soft and hard power, ACPD highlights how multiple power styles, namely soft, collaborative, hard, and sharp, interact within broader smart power strategies (Nye, 2019, 2021; Slaughter, 2011; Vukovic, 2020). Anticorruption functions as a connective element through which these resources can be mobilised coherently. For instance, development assistance, multilateral cooperation, and corporate accountability programmes serve not only policy aims but also reputational purposes, reinforcing the credibility of states as promoters of ethical governance (Harris, 2019; Hough, 2013). In this sense, integrity and anticorruption can enhance moral authority while generating diplomatic advantage.

By integrating theory and empirical analysis, the book reinforces the constructivist understanding of international politics in three ways. First, it shows that norms such as integrity do not diffuse automatically; they are actively communicated, interpreted, contested, and adapted across different political and cultural contexts (Checkel, 1998, 2026; Johnston, 2001). Second, it demonstrates that the socialisation of anticorruption norms through public diplomacy reshapes state identities, influencing both domestic reform trajectories and international self-representation (Adler, 2013; Adler-Nissen, 2023). Third, it provides empirical evidence that anticorruption has become a key dimension of contemporary global governance, linking internal accountability to external legitimacy (Heywood,

2015; Mungiu-Pippidi, 2023). In combination, these findings confirm the centrality of international socialisation in the contemporary politics of integrity.

The analytical framework developed in this book is not confined to the cases examined here. Although the study focuses on Denmark, New Zealand, the United States, and South Korea, the dynamics of anticorruption public diplomacy are also observable across other regions and governance contexts. In recent decades, countries in Latin America have advanced important transparency, accountability, and open government initiatives (Ramírez-Alujas & Cruz-Rubio, 2025; Teixeira et al., 2025), while regional organisations and policy frameworks in Africa have increasingly incorporated anticorruption norms into broader governance agendas (Suleiman et al., 2026). Likewise, South–South cooperation mechanisms provide additional spaces through which integrity-related norms, practices, and narratives may be communicated, negotiated, and socialised internationally (Waisbich, 2025). These developments suggest that ACPD extends beyond the geographical scope of the present study and offer promising avenues for future comparative research.

Ultimately, this book establishes ACPD as a distinct analytical category within the broader field of global public diplomacy. It shows that the international projection of integrity is simultaneously an expression of state identity and a mechanism of power. By treating integrity as a shared language of legitimacy, the study demonstrates how moral credibility and strategic influence converge in diplomatic practice, advancing an integrated perspective on governance, communication, and identity in international relations.

1.8 Mapping the Journey of the Book: A Roadmap for Readers

This book is organised to guide the reader from concept to comparison, and from theory to implication. Following this introductory chapter, Chap. 2 lays the conceptual and theoretical groundwork. It clarifies how identities, interests, and norms are socially constructed and diffused, and it defines ACPD. It introduces the analytical dimensions that recur throughout the book, including identities and interests, objectives, agents, activities, material and immaterial factors, and smart power. These dimensions provide the basis for the country chapters that follow. Readers who wish to focus on a particular case will benefit from first engaging with this analytical architecture.

Chapter 3 turns to Denmark, examining how its reputation as one of the world's least corrupt countries is not simply inherited. It is actively constructed and maintained through strategic investment, development cooperation, and global partnerships. Rather than portraying integrity as an intrinsic moral attribute, the analysis approaches it as a politically and economically mediated resource embedded in foreign policy practice. The chapter demonstrates how this approach transforms integrity into a form of smart power, combining credibility, financial capacity, and policy innovation. It also underscores that this reputation is not immune to tension or contestation. The chapter shows how Denmark's integrity functions simultaneously as a foreign policy asset and as a site of ongoing negotiation shaped by practice, perception, and public scrutiny.

Chapter 4 focuses on New Zealand and its articulation of integrity as a core component of national identity. The analysis explores how transparency, accountability, and inclusive governance are projected externally through public diplomacy. It shows how partnerships with civil society and engagement with diverse communities inform the country's international voice on integrity. Rather than relying on coercive tools, New Zealand privileges listening, collaboration, and persuasion, framing integrity as a relational practice. The chapter elaborates how ethical coherence at home underpins credibility abroad, highlighting moral consistency as a distinctive source of international standing for a state with modest material capabilities.

Chapter 5 examines how the United States has framed anticorruption within public diplomacy as a normative commitment and a strategic policy practice. It traces the articulation of integrity through key initiatives, including the Denying Safe Haven Policy and enforcement of the Foreign Corrupt Practices Act. While focusing primarily on the evolution of United States anticorruption public diplomacy up to December 2024, the chapter also considers recent developments associated with the 2025 policy recalibration, including debates surrounding the temporary pause in the United States Foreign Corrupt Practices Act (FCPA) enforcement and their implications for norm leadership and international credibility. By situating these dynamics within the longer trajectory of American leadership and reputation management, the chapter highlights the enduring tension between idealism and pragmatism that characterises major-power

ACPD. Ultimately, it provides a framework for understanding both the continuities and the prospective reconfigurations of United States ACPD.

Chapter 6 explores South Korea, where ACPD is entwined with processes of cultural reform and institutional renewal. The chapter analyses how state bodies, civil society, and media participate in reshaping public culture while projecting integrity abroad. It considers cooperation with international organisations and the mobilisation of education, cultural initiatives, and digital tools in sustaining reform. By tracing how domestic transformation feeds into external communication, the chapter illustrates ACPD as a bridge between internal coherence and external influence, and as a means of reconstructing legitimacy after episodes of scandal and public disillusionment.

Chapter 7 synthesises the four cases comparatively to identify patterns, differences, and mechanisms of socialisation. Using the common analytical framework, it examines how the four countries translate integrity into diplomatic strategy and how agents, activities, and factors interact across contexts. The chapter illuminates different ACPD approaches, distinguishing between models centred on development cooperation, relational credibility, leadership entrepreneurship, and cultural reform. Rather than seeking universal generalisations, it offers contingent insights into how states communicate who they are through what they champion.

Finally, Chap. 8 draws together the conceptual, methodological, and empirical strands of the book. Revisiting the cases, it reflects on the conditions under which integrity strengthens standing, how reputations are sustained, and how values and interests coexist within diplomatic processes. It concludes by outlining implications for research and practice, and by suggesting avenues for examining ACPD across additional regions, institutions, and policy domains, as well as within regional organisations and South–South cooperation frameworks.

Taken together, the chapters advance a cohesive argument: anticorruption has become a communicative resource in world politics, and ACPD is a social process through which states negotiate identities, pursue interests, and shape norms. The book thus offers a structured analytical journey, providing readers with a coherent lens for understanding how the politics of integrity is communicated, socialised, and leveraged in public diplomacy. Readers are invited to follow the book's progression, moving from theory to practice and recognising the role of ACPD in world politics.

References

Aday, S. (2025). Introduction to the handbook on public diplomacy. In S. Aday (Ed.), *Handbook on public diplomacy* (pp. 1–6). Elgar. https://doi.org/10.4337/9781803926568.00008

Adler, E. (2013). Constructivism in international relations: Sources, contributions, and debates. In W. Carlsnaes, T. Risse, & B. Simmons (Eds.), *Handbook of international relations* (2nd ed., pp. 112–144). Sage. https://doi.org/10.4135/9781446247587

Adler-Nissen, R. (2023). Practice. In S. Goddard, G. Lawson, & J. Sending (Eds.), *The Oxford handbook of international political sociology* (pp. 177–198). Oxford University Press.

Alexander, C. (2021). Hegemony, morality and power: A Gramscian theoretical framework for public diplomacy. In C. Alexander (Ed.), *The frontiers of public diplomacy* (pp. 9–24). Routledge.

Anti-Corruption and Civil Rights Commission (ACRC). (2022, June 14). *ACRC actively promotes anti-corruption policy achievements in international community.* Retrieved February 9, 2026, from https://acrc.go.kr/board.es?mid=a20301000000&bid=62&list_no=39725&act=view

Asia-Pacific Economic Cooperation. (2012). *Interim reports on implementation of APEC anti-corruption commitments.* Retrieved February 9, 2026, from https://www.apec.org/docs/default-source/Groups/ACT/ACTWG-InterimReport-Anticorruption-Commitments_28052012.pdf

Ayhan, K. (2019). The boundaries of public diplomacy and nonstate actors: A taxonomy of perspectives. *International Studies Perspectives, 20*(1), 63–83. https://doi.org/10.1093/isp/eky010

Banks, R. (2020). Public diplomacy evaluation. In N. Snow & N. Cull (Eds.), *Routledge handbook of public diplomacy* (2nd ed., pp. 64–75). Routledge. https://doi.org/10.4324/9780429465543

Bauhr, M., Charron, N., & Nasiritousi, N. (2013). Does corruption cause aid fatigue? Public opinion and the aid-corruption paradox. *International Studies Quarterly, 57*(3), 568–579. https://doi.org/10.1111/isqu.12025

Brown, K. (2025). Losing hearts and minds: Unpacking the legacy of US public diplomacy in Afghanistan, 2001–2021. In S. Aday (Ed.), *Handbook on public diplomacy* (pp. 462–474). Elgar. https://doi.org/10.4337/9781803926568.00049

Bukovansky, M. (2015). Corruption rankings: Constructing and contesting the global anti-corruption agenda. In A. Cooley & J. Snyder (Eds.), *Ranking the world* (pp. 60–84). Cambridge University Press. https://doi.org/10.1017/CBO9781316161555

Checkel, J. (1998). The constructivist turn in international relations theory. *World Politics, 50*(2), 324–348. https://doi.org/10.1017/s0043887100008133

Checkel, J. (2026). Identity politics and deep contestations of the liberal international order. In A. Wiener, D. Lake, & T. Risse (Eds.), *Deep contestations of the liberal international order* (pp. 179–203). Oxford University Press.

Cull, N. (2019). *Public diplomacy: Foundations for global engagement in the digital age*. Polity.

Cull, N. (2023). The war for Ukraine: Reputational security and media disruption. *Place Branding and Public Diplomacy, 19*(2), 195–199. https://doi.org/10.1057/s41254-022-00281-3

Cull, N. (2024). *Reputational security*. Polity.

Doig, A., & McIvor, S. (2003). The National Integrity System: Assessing corruption and reform. *Public Administration and Development, 23*(4), 317–332. https://doi.org/10.1002/pad.287

Durrani, S. (2025). Schisms in nation brands. In S. Aday (Ed.), *Handbook on public diplomacy* (pp. 391–406). Elgar. https://doi.org/10.4337/9781803926568.00042

European Union External Action. (2016, September 23). *EU and Danish government announce major anti-corruption initiative in Ukraine*. Retrieved February 9, 2026, from https://www.eeas.europa.eu/node/10946_en

Finnemore, M., & Sikkink, K. (2001). Taking stock: The constructivist research program in international relations and comparative politics. *Annual Review of Political Science, 4*, 391–416. https://doi.org/10.1146/annurev.polisci.4.1.391

Finnemore, M., & Wendt, A. (2024). When "old" constructivism was new: Reflections on classical constructivism. *Perspectives on Politics, 22*(4), 1248–1268. https://doi.org/10.1017/S1537592724001464

Gilboa, E. (2008). Searching for a theory of public diplomacy. *The Annals of the American Academy of Political and Social Science, 616*(1), 55–77. https://doi.org/10.1177/0002716207312142

Government of the United Kingdom. (2025, December). *UK Anti-Corruption Strategy 2025*. Retrieved February 9, 2026, from https://assets.publishing.service.gov.uk/media/6932caa7375aee4a15ee8c8c/36.37_HO_JACU-Strategy_v12b_FINAL_WEB.pdf

Gregory, B. (2024). *American diplomacy's public dimension*. Palgrave Macmillan.

Gregory, B. (2025). Diplomacy's public dimension. In S. Aday (Ed.), *Handbook on public diplomacy* (pp. 8–21). Elgar. https://doi.org/10.4337/9781803926568.00010

Harris, H. (2019). *The global anti-corruption regime*. Routledge.

Heywood, P. (2015). Introduction: Scale and focus in the study of corruption. In P. Heywood (Ed.), *Routledge handbook of political corruption* (pp. 1–13). Routledge.

Heywood, P., & Rose, J. (2014). Close but no cigar: The measurement of corruption. *Journal of Public Policy, 34*(3), 507–529. https://doi.org/10.1017/S0143814X14000099

Hocking, B., Melissen, J., Riordan, S., & Sharp, P. (2012, October). *Futures for diplomacy* (Clingendael—Report 1). Clingendael. Retrieved February 9, 2026, from https://www.clingendael.org/sites/default/files/pdfs/20121030_research_melissen.pdf

Hough, D. (2013). *Political corruption & governance*. Palgrave Macmillan. https://doi.org/10.1057/9781137268716

Ingenhoff, D., & Chariatte, J. (2025). Reframing public diplomacy. In S. Aday (Ed.), *Handbook on public diplomacy* (pp. 360–377). Elgar. https://doi.org/10.4337/9781803926568.00040

International Monetary Fund (IMF). (2019, April). *Fiscal monitor: Curbing corruption*. IMF. Retrieved February 9, 2026, from https://www.imf.org/en/Publications/FM/Issues/2019/03/18/fiscal-monitor-april-2019

Johnston, M. (2001). The definitions debate: Old conflicts in new guises. In A. Jain (Ed.), *The political economy of corruption* (pp. 11–31). Routledge.

Johnston, M. (2005). *Syndromes of corruption*. Cambridge University Press.

Katzenstein, P. (1996). *Cultural norms and national security*. Cornell University Press.

Kaufmann, D., Kraay, A., & Mastruzzi, M. (2010). *The Worldwide Governance Indicators* (Working paper - 5430). World Bank. Retrieved February 9, 2026, from https://papers.ssrn.com/sol3/papers.cfm?abstract_id=1682130

Manfredi-Sánchez, J. (2025). *How disinformation ruins public diplomacy*. Routledge. https://doi.org/10.4324/9781032650524

Marsh, D., Ercan, S., & Furlong, P. (2018). A skin, not a sweater: Ontology and epistemology in political science. In V. Lowndes, D. Marsh, & G. Stoker (Eds.), *Theory and methods in political science* (4th ed., pp. 177–198). Palgrave Macmillan.

Martino, L. (2020). The spectrum of listening. In N. Snow & N. Cull (Eds.), *Routledge handbook of public diplomacy* (2nd ed., pp. 21–29). Routledge. https://doi.org/10.4324/9780429465543

Mccoy, J., & Heckel, H. (2001). The emergence of a global anti-corruption norm. *International Politics, 38*(1), 65–90. https://doi.org/10.1057/palgrave.ip.8892613

Melissen, J. (2005). The new public diplomacy: Between theory and practice. In J. Melissen (Ed.), *The new public diplomacy* (pp. 3–27). Palgrave Macmillan.

Melissen, J., Du, S., & Goswami, A. (2023). Public diplomacy. In P. James (Ed.), *Oxford bibliographies in international relations*. Oxford University Press.

Melissen, J., & Wang, J. (2019). Introduction: Debating public diplomacy. *The Hague Journal of Diplomacy, 14*(1), 1–5. https://doi.org/10.1163/1871191X-14101064

Miller, T. (2025). Lessons from Zelensky: The power of narrative alignment. In S. Aday (Ed.), *Handbook on public diplomacy* (pp. 519–531). Elgar. https://doi.org/10.4337/9781803926568.00054

Mungiu-Pippidi, A. (2023). *Rethinking corruption*. Elgar. https://doi.org/10.4337/9781800379831
Nye, J. (2011). *The future of power*. Public Affairs.
Nye, J. (2019). Soft power and public diplomacy revisited. *The Hague Journal of Diplomacy, 14*(1–2), 7–20. https://doi.org/10.1163/1871191X-14101013
Nye, J. (2021). Soft power: The evolution of a concept. *Journal of Political Power, 14*(1), 196–208. https://doi.org/10.1080/2158379X.2021.1879572
Pamment, J., Smedberg, M., & Isaksson, E. (2025). National security and public diplomacy. In S. Aday (Ed.), *Handbook on public diplomacy* (pp. 449–461). Elgar. https://doi.org/10.4337/9781803926568.00048
Porta, D. d., & Keating, M. (2013). How many approaches in the social sciences? An epistemological introduction. In D. della Porta & M. Keating (Eds.), *Approaches and methodologies in the social sciences* (5th ed., pp. 19–39). Cambridge University Press.
Porte, T. l. (2012). The impact of "intermestic" non-state actors on the conceptual framework of public diplomacy. *The Hague Journal of Diplomacy, 7*(4), 441–458. https://doi.org/10.1163/1871191X-12341241
Pozsgai-Alvarez, J., & Lang, B. (2025). Getting "strategic corruption" right: Mapping contested meanings in a changing geopolitical landscape. *Public Integrity*, 1–19. https://doi.org/10.1080/10999922.2025.2495366
Ramírez-Alujas, A. V., & Cruz-Rubio, C. N. (2025). Design and implementation of open government policies and strategies in Latin America (2012–2022). In L. Secchi & C. N. Cruz-Rubio (Eds.), *Handbook of public policy in Latin America* (pp. 372–386). Elgar. https://doi.org/10.4337/9781035310197.00032
Rose-Ackerman, S. (2025). Corruption as a problem in public choice. In R. Jong-a-Pin & C. Bjørnskov (Eds.), *Elgar encyclopedia of public choice* (pp. 175–180). Elgar. https://doi.org/10.4337/9781802207750
Rothstein, B. (2021). *Controlling corruption*. Oxford University Press. https://doi.org/10.1093/oso/9780192894908.001.0001
Santos, N. de A. e S. F. dos. (2025). *Diplomacia pública anticorrupção: uma análise comparativa* (Doctoral thesis in International Relations). University of Lisbon. http://hdl.handle.net/10400.5/102696.
Santos, N. de A. e S. F. dos. (2026). From regulation to reputation: *The EU's anticorruption directive as public diplomacy. Eastern Journal of European Studies, 17*(1). Forthcoming. https://ejes.uaic.ro/archive.htm
Sevin, E. (2017). A multilayered approach to public diplomacy evaluation: Pathways of connection. *Politics & Policy, 45*(5), 879–901. https://doi.org/10.1111/polp.12227
Slaughter, A.-M. (2011, November 30). A new theory for the foreign-policy frontier: Collaborative power. *The Atlantic*. Retrieved February 9, 2026, from https://tinyurl.com/TheAtlantic2011Nov

Snow, N., & Cull, N. (2020). Preface and introduction. In N. Snow & N. Cull (Eds.), *Routledge handbook of public diplomacy* (2nd ed., pp. X–XIV). Routledge. https://doi.org/10.4324/9780429465543

Stake, R. E. (2006). *Multiple case study analysis*. Guilford.

Suleiman, M. R., Slighoua, M., & Yahaya, A. (2026). From regionalism to resilience: Assessing Africa's progress on SDG 16 through regional cooperation. *Sustainable Development*, 1–19. https://doi.org/10.1002/sd.71162

Taplin, M. (2025). Diplomacy comma public: The triumph and tribulations of American PD. In S. Aday (Ed.), *Handbook on public diplomacy* (pp. 532–542). Elgar. https://doi.org/10.4337/9781803926568.00055

Teixeira, M. A. C., Zuccolotto, R., Spinelli, M. V. C., & Rodrigues, R. V. (2025). Transparency in Latin America: Argentina, Brazil, Colombia, and Mexico. In L. Secchi & C. N. Cruz-Rubio (Eds.), *Handbook of public policy in Latin America* (pp. 224–242). Elgar. https://doi.org/10.4337/9781035310197.00023

Thomas, G. (2017). *How to do your research project* (3rd ed.). Sage.

Tourinho, M. (2016). Diplomacia anticorrupção. In M. Specktor (Ed.), *Dez desafios da política externa brasileira* (pp. 61–72). Konrad Adenauer Stiftung, CEBRI.

US Department of State (DoS). (2001). *Report to congress pursuant to the International Anticorruption and Good Governance Act*. Retrieved February 9, 2026, from https://2009-2017.state.gov/j/inl/rls/rpt/c6698.htm

US Department of State (DoS). (2015, June). *INL guide to anticorruption policy and programming*. Retrieved February 9, 2026, from https://2009-2017.state.gov/documents/organization/244730.pdf

Vukovic, S. (2020). The many faces of power in diplomatic negotiations. *SAIS Review of International Affairs, 40*(1), 45–57. https://doi.org/10.1353/sais.2020.0004

Waisbich, L. T. (2025). *Southern powers and global development: Responsible but different*. Bristol University Press. https://doi.org/10.51952/9781529247954

Wendt, A. (1999). *Social theory of international politics*. Cambridge University Press.

White House. (2021, December). *United States Strategy on Countering Corruption*. Retrieved February 9, 2026, from https://bidenwhitehouse.archives.gov/wp-content/uploads/2021/12/United-States-Strategy-on-Countering-Corruption.pdf

Wiseman, G., & Scott, A. (2026). Engaging citizens in a polarised society: The choices for US diplomacy. In J. Melissen, H. Kim, & G. Chandrasekara (Eds.), *Home engagement in diplomacy* (pp. 210–248). Brill. https://doi.org/10.1163/9789004738324_010

Zaharna, R. S. (2022). *Boundary spanners of humanity*. Oxford University Press. https://doi.org/10.1093/oso/9780190930271.001.0001

CHAPTER 2

Understanding Anticorruption Public Diplomacy: From Conceptual Foundations to an Analytical Lens

2.1 Public Diplomacy as a Process of International Socialisation

Public diplomacy unfolds within an intersubjective sphere where self-understandings encounter external perceptions through communicative logics that shape meaning (Zaharna, 2022). This process follows a recursive sequence: interaction generates understandings; understandings reshape identities; identities reconfigure interests; and interests orient behaviour (Finnemore, 1996; Finnemore & Sikkink, 2001; Wendt, 1999). These dynamics constitute processes of international socialisation involving sustained engagement with foreign publics, the negotiation of behavioural expectations, routine contestation, co-creation, and the gradual internalisation of norms (Adler-Nissen, 2024). Collectively, these features render international socialisation observable as a structured social phenomenon.

Public diplomacy constitutes a visible arena in which this sequence unfolds. It gives form to long-standing interpretive frameworks and to patterns of engagement, disruption, and dissent that are continually transformed through culturally and historically situated practices (Adler-Nissen, 2024; Cull, 2025a; Pingeot & Pouliot, 2024). These practices privilege certain voices, competences, and forms of recognition rather than relying solely on abstract rule-following. From a practice-oriented perspective,

N. de A. e S. F. dos Santos, *Anticorruption Public Diplomacy*, Palgrave Macmillan Series in Global Public Diplomacy,
https://doi.org/10.1007/978-3-032-28668-0_2

public diplomacy is thus composed of patterned performances and shared repertoires (Adler & Pouliot, 2011; Adler-Nissen, 2023). It is through such practices that meaning, legitimacy, and expectations are incrementally stabilised, making public diplomacy observable and analytically tractable.

The socialisation promoted by anticorruption public diplomacy (ACPD) centres on the negotiation of shared expectations underpinning the global anticorruption norm. This unfolds through engagement with foreign publics via diplomatic routines, symbolic gestures, strategic communication, promotion of integrity narratives, participation in cooperative structures, and sustained relationships. In doing so, states enact and project identities associated with integrity, often mobilising moral language that frames virtue and goodness as components of broader strategies of legitimacy and recognition (Alexander, 2021). At the same time, states adjust narratives and representational practices in response to external perceptions. In this way, ACPD shapes both domestic identity and international standing by structuring how meanings of integrity are co-produced, contested, and recognised across audiences. Contestation is increasingly embedded in routine practices and institutional cultures (Adler-Nissen, 2024). This positioning situates integrity and anticorruption as relational and continuously negotiated attributes of statehood.

2.2 Socialisation Mechanisms of Anticorruption Public Diplomacy

Four interrelated mechanisms structure the international socialisation process through which ACPD operates: cognitive, normative, relational, and ethical. Together, they capture how meanings and expectations are formed, transformed, and stabilised across borders. The cognitive mechanism concerns how material and immaterial anticorruption resources, such as laws, reputations, economic assets, and performance indicators, acquire meaning. This is an ideational process in which such resources are valued, contested, or rendered salient within specific communicative contexts (Finnemore & Sikkink, 2001). ACPD influences this space by communicating reforms, governance models, and historical trajectories, reflecting the role of shared interpretations in constructing international politics (Adler, 2013). Resources become effective only when recognised as credible or exemplary by target audiences (Nye, 2011, p. 62), underscoring that cognitive change is inherently relational and dialogical.

The normative mechanism involves the internalisation of standards of rightful conduct. Instruments such as the United Nations Convention against Corruption (UNCAC), the Organisation for Economic Co-operation and Development (OECD) Anti-Bribery Convention, and the evaluation tools of the Group of States against Corruption (GRECO) establish expectations of legitimate behaviour (Harris, 2019; Hough, 2013), thereby reinforcing the global anticorruption norm (Mccoy & Heckel, 2001). Anticorruption also carries moral undertones (Bukovansky, 2015) when framing corruption as a threat to global public goods (Bhargava, 2006) and integrity as a marker of responsible statehood (Hough, 2013; Jakobi, 2013). Through ACPD, states publicly perform adherence to, or contestation of, these standards (Mccoy & Heckel, 2001), thereby contributing to the stabilisation of the normative content of anticorruption.

The relational mechanism concerns the practices through which trust, recognition, and cooperation are generated. ACPD is inherently relational, involving diplomats, ministries, oversight bodies, non-governmental organisations (NGOs), multilateral institutions, and foreign publics in the creation of shared repertoires, symbols, gestures, and expectations (Adler & Pouliot, 2011; Bjola & Kornprobst, 2018; Jakobi, 2013). Through its activities, ACPD supports collective identities linked to integrity and strengthens the social infrastructure that enables anticorruption norms to circulate.

Finally, the ethical mechanism concerns the ethical quality of influence practices and how this quality shapes legitimacy, trust, and receptivity within socialisation processes, specifically whether ACPD practices sustain or corrode the integrity norms on which legitimate authority depends. This question becomes particularly salient when influence practices deliberately exploit cognitive and emotional vulnerabilities in target publics (Grahn & Pamment, 2024), or function primarily as moral performances that mask strategic or reputational objectives (Alexander, 2021). These ethical tensions are intensified in communicative environments increasingly shaped by generative artificial intelligence, where agency, responsibility, and attribution become structurally blurred (Miskimmon & O'Loughlin, 2025). The ethical mechanism thus highlights that ACPD is not inherently virtuous; rather, the ethical quality of its influence practices directly conditions socialisation outcomes by enabling or undermining trust, recognition, and normative alignment. In this sense, ACPD may involve instrumentalisation, reputational management, or coercive and manipulative practices that contradict the very standards being promoted, turning integrity into a moral façade embedded in power relations (Alexander, 2021; Nye, 2019; Cull, 2024). This perspective foregrounds ethics as an integral, rather than ancillary, aspect of ACPD.

Viewed through these four mechanisms, ACPD appears as a cumulative cycle in which identities shape interests, interests define objectives, objectives mobilise agents, agents undertake activities, and these activities generate meanings that feed back into identities and expectations (Finnemore & Sikkink, 2001; Wendt, 1999). ACPD can therefore be understood as a co-constitutive set of practices through which states and foreign agents mutually transform their understandings of integrity.

National trajectories exemplify diverse pathways of socialisation. Illustratively, Denmark and New Zealand tend to engage in identity-driven ACPD rooted in reputations for high integrity, while the United States adopts a more strategic and interest-oriented approach linking anticorruption to security, commerce, and democracy. South Korea combines an identity-building strategy based on domestic reforms with competitiveness-driven goals. Multilateral organisations further amplify these dynamics through cooperative mechanisms and peer-review processes that generate transnational communities of practice (Adler & Pouliot, 2011). These brief references are illustrative and serve solely to signal the diversity of socialisation pathways, anticipating the systematic comparative analysis developed in the empirical chapters that follow.

2.3 The Anatomy of Anticorruption Public Diplomacy: Constitutive Dimensions

Conceptualising public diplomacy as a process of international socialisation provides the processual lens through which ACPD is analysed in this book. However, its analytical examination requires a distinct set of constitutive dimensions that specify the constituent elements of the ACPD process. These dimensions reflect the cognitive, normative, relational, and ethical mechanisms through which states engage foreign publics on integrity matters and contribute to producing, contesting, stabilising, and diffusing the global anticorruption norm.

ACPD operates as a constellation of interconnected components that function simultaneously and recursively, shaping how states project identities, pursue interests, articulate commitments, and interact with international audiences. The following sections examine in depth six constitutive dimensions that together form the analytical anatomy of ACPD: (1) identities and interests; (2) objectives; (3) agents; (4) activities; (5) material and immaterial factors; and (6) ideational factors (smart power). Taken together, these dimensions provide a coherent model for the comparative analysis of ACPD across national contexts. They illustrate how motivations, structures, practices, and meanings interact, revealing how anticorruption commitments and narratives are articulated and negotiated in the international arena.

2.4 Identities and Interests

This dimension captures the motivational foundations of ACPD. It examines how states understand who they are, what they seek to achieve, and how these self-conceptions shape their engagement with foreign publics on matters of integrity. Identities and interests constitute the conceptual anchor of ACPD. They express the deeper orientations through which states define themselves, articulate their aspirations, and interact with international audiences. This dimension therefore focuses on the motivations that precede and guide diplomatic engagement. Narratives rooted in historical experiences, institutional traditions, and normative commitments provide the backdrop against which states determine what is desirable, appropriate, or necessary in their external conduct. Public diplomacy becomes one of the principal arenas in which these orientations take visible form.

Identity answers what a state is, while interest concerns what it wants; the latter cannot be understood independently of the former (Wendt, 1999). Identity comprises self-understandings rooted in domestic governance traditions, legitimacy principles, societal expectations, and systemic understandings shaped by external perceptions (Wendt, 1999). ACPD mediates this latter aspect by enabling states to influence how they are perceived in anticorruption terms while internalising feedback that gradually reshapes their own sense of self. This process reinforces identity as a situated and enacted practice rather than a fixed attribute (Finnemore & Wendt, 2024). In this process, ministries of foreign affairs play an active role by articulating and performing national identity through their ongoing engagement with foreign publics (Wiseman, 2022), thereby embedding identity work within the everyday practice of public diplomacy.

Wendt's typology provides a useful heuristic for analysing identity production within ACPD. It distinguishes between corporate, type, role, and collective identities, each capturing a different dimension of how states understand themselves and their place in the international system (Wendt, 1999). *Corporate identity* encompasses enduring institutional features, such as legal systems, administrative traditions, oversight bodies, and historical experiences of reform, that underpin a state's integrity architecture. *Type identity* groups states according to governance models and normative commitments. High-trust democracies often draw on reputations for professionalism and rule-of-law traditions, whereas states in transition may employ ACPD to reposition themselves by foregrounding reform trajectories and anti-impunity efforts. *Role identity* concerns the positions states adopt within the global integrity landscape, whether as norm entrepreneurs, reform leaders, or capacity-building partners. ACPD provides the communicative arena in which these roles are enacted and recognised. Finally, *collective identity* emerges when states perceive themselves as part of a wider anticorruption community grounded in shared expectations of integrity. The global anticorruption norm contributes to the formation of such a community (Mccoy & Heckel, 2001) in which integrity functions as a symbolic marker of belonging.

Interaction with norms reinforces this identity–interest nexus by defining legitimate forms of behaviour (Adler, 2013; Finnemore, 1996). Instruments such as UNCAC and the OECD Anti-Bribery Convention have produced a dense integrity regime in which anticorruption becomes not only a domestic priority but a symbol of international credibility (Harris, 2019; Hough, 2013). As these norms diffuse and are stabilised through rankings and peer-review mechanisms (Mccoy & Heckel, 2001), they support the emergence of collective identities grounded in expectations of transparency and accountability.

Interests derive from these identities and emerge from how states interpret who they are and how they understand their role in the international system (Adler, 2013; Finnemore & Sikkink, 2001). From this perspective, identities and interests are mutually constitutive and enacted through practice rather than existing as fixed or exogenous attributes (Finnemore, 1996; Finnemore & Wendt, 2024). Power becomes a foreign policy interest when autonomy or prestige is integral to a state's sense of self, while prosperity becomes an interest where economic wellbeing is closely linked to legitimacy. Interests thus reflect socially constructed understandings of national purpose and responsibility and may vary widely across issue areas and political contexts.

A useful point of departure for mapping types of interests within ACPD is provided by the global issue areas identified by Bjola and Kornprobst (2018) as structuring contemporary diplomatic agendas. Among these, three are particularly salient in anticorruption contexts: security (war and peace), economics, and development. Corruption threatens security by facilitating external interference, undermining reputational security, and fuelling conflicts (White et al., 2025). It jeopardises economic performance and development by distorting markets, deterring investment, and eroding institutional trust (Rothstein, 2018). It also affects governance and collective self-esteem, as global reputational indicators, such as the Corruption Perceptions Index (Transparency International) and the Control of Corruption indicator (World Bank), together with international assessment mechanisms, including those of the GRECO and the Open Government Partnership (OGP), shape perceptions of credibility, reliability, and institutional quality.

Recent public diplomacy scholarship further conceptualises reputation itself as a dimension of security (Cull, 2024), insofar as states perceived as corrupt or unreliable become more vulnerable to coercion, marginalisation, and strategic pressure in international arenas. This shift is reinforced by recent analyses of public diplomacy and national security, which show that reputational standing has become a condition for autonomy, predictability, and resilience in contexts marked by hybrid threats and foreign information manipulation (Pamment et al., 2025). States that identify as transparent or reform-oriented likewise integrate anticorruption into their external engagement, while those undergoing governance transitions may use ACPD to signal credibility, attract investment, and reduce perceived risk. Together, these developments illustrate how identities shape interpretations of risk and opportunity.

In sum, identities and interests provide the motivational foundations of ACPD. They determine how states enter the global arena, and define their priorities, performance, and position in the evolving integrity community. The next section examines how these orientations are translated into strategic objectives that guide ACPD internationally.

2.5 Objectives

Objectives translate identity- and interest-based motivations into purposeful international action, guiding how states communicate with foreign publics and allocate ACPD resources, albeit within contested institutional and political contexts. They also function as implicit causal assumptions about how specific communicative interventions are expected to produce desired effects, making clarity and alignment on objectives a precondition for strategic coherence, even though achieving such alignment is often challenging (Arsenault, 2025). Clear objectives ensure coherence by aligning messaging and activities with broader foreign policy aims (Banks, 2020; Sevin, 2017), thereby strengthening strategic consistency across ACPD initiatives.

Leonard et al. (2002), alongside Nye (2008), suggest that public diplomacy objectives can be understood along three temporal horizons: short, medium, and long term, each reflecting distinct functions. Short-term objectives are essentially reactive and time-sensitive, unfolding over hours or days. Their primary purpose is to manage reputational risk and prevent the crystallisation of negative narratives. Rapid communication following corruption scandals, the correction of misinformation, or the highlighting of favourable developments, such as improved anticorruption rankings, is common practice. These swift interventions stabilise perceptions by signalling responsiveness (Fitzpatrick, 2017) and reaffirming a commitment to transparency.

Medium-term objectives operate over months or years. At this temporal horizon, ACPD focuses on shaping normative contexts and strengthening international cooperation. States advocate global standards, support reform processes, and seek to influence transnational policy debates (Pamment, 2020). Examples include campaigns banning facilitation payments in international commerce, support for extraterritorial enforcement in corruption cases, and contributions to the diffusion of global anticorruption conventions (Boswell, 1997; Hough, 2013). Medium-term objectives thus reflect proactive engagement with the global anticorruption regime and reinforce role identities as reformers or norm entrepreneurs.

Long-term objectives span several years and emphasise institutional consistency and sustained normative performance. Their aim is to consolidate an anticorruption identity (Sparling, 2021) and cultivate enduring trust within the international community (Cull, 2019). These objectives seek reputational security, understood as occupying "the high ground of the global imagination", where isolated scandals are more likely to be interpreted as anomalies rather than systemic failures (Cull, 2019, p. 135). Reputation functions here as a form of protection against political and informational harm, preserving a state's room for manoeuvre and credibility over time (Cull, 2024). This logic resonates with Nye's metaphor of the "city on the hill" (2011, p. 94), which captures how credibility can generate attraction, sustain influence, and reduce reputational vulnerability during moments of crisis. In the long run, credibility and trust become the core assets of ACPD.

To sum up, short-term goals protect credibility; medium-term aims shape norms, alliances, and agendas; and long-term objectives build durable reputational authority and shared expectations. Together, they illustrate that ACPD is future-oriented and relational: states do not merely pursue interests but participate in defining and contesting the standards and values that sustain the global anticorruption norm.

2.6 Agents and Representational Ties

Agents are those who carry, contest, interpret, and perform integrity-related narratives in the ACPD arena. As diplomacy's public dimension has become integral to contemporary diplomatic practice (Gregory, 2025), ACPD is increasingly produced by a wider constellation of agents across government and society. Through their actions, norms circulate, expectations are shaped, and commitments become visible. These agents translate abstract principles of integrity into concrete diplomatic practices, linking foreign policy to wider processes of international socialisation (Finnemore & Sikkink, 2001; Jakobi, 2013). They operate across multiple levels of governance and within distinct communities of practice characterised by durable routines and professional identities (Gregory, 2025), which shape how integrity is communicated and enacted across borders. This constellation includes traditional diplomatic services, specialised ministries, anticorruption and oversight bodies, international organisations, NGOs, businesses, subnational representatives, diasporas, and influential individuals.

What distinguishes these agents is not only their institutional nature, but the ties that confer legitimacy on their representation. These ties are treated here as an internal analytical component of the agents' dimension. They include formal and fixed forms of representation, such as institutional mandates, as well as ties enacted and negotiated through everyday diplomatic practices (Adler-Nissen, 2023). Grounded in delegation, participation, or relational legitimacy, these ties shape how agents are recognised as credible and effective. Understanding ACPD therefore requires attention both to the diversity of agents involved and to the distinct forms of authority that underpin their roles.

State Agents and the National Diplomatic System

State agents constitute the historical core of public diplomacy (Hocking, 2005) and remain central to anticorruption diplomatic engagement abroad. Public diplomacy has traditionally been carried out by career diplomats (Melissen, 2005), consular services (Cooper, 2019), and foreign ministers, who act as the institutional face of the state in the international arena and mediate between domestic political authority and external representation (Wiseman, 2022). These agents perform classical functions of representation by articulating official positions, conveying national values, negotiating interests, and maintaining communication channels with foreign target audiences. Their authority derives from formal state structures and international legal frameworks, notably the Vienna Convention on Diplomatic Relations. At the same time, this authority is shaped by the interaction between political leadership and professional diplomatic expertise within ministries of foreign affairs (Wiseman, 2022). These elements position state agents as the primary custodians of legitimacy and continuity in ACPD.

Over recent decades, state participation in public diplomacy has broadened as issues once confined to domestic governance have become globalised, contributing to the transversalisation of foreign policy (Hocking et al., 2012). Public diplomacy now operates through a "national diplomatic system" (Hocking, 2005, p. 35), reflecting the wider scale of whole-of-government diplomacy in contemporary practice (Gregory, 2025). Within this system, multiple state organs engage collaboratively in external action, increasingly drawing on the technical expertise of sectoral ministries and specialised agencies. In the anticorruption domain, the credibility and technical competence required for effective international engagement are distributed across a wide range of actors. These include ministries of justice, judicial authorities, electoral courts, anticorruption agencies, enforcement bodies, oversight and audit institutions, regulatory authorities, police forces, and central banks (Hopkinson & Pelizzo, 2006; Marcus,

2019; McDevitt, 2020). Their participation provides thematic legitimacy that complements, and in some cases exceeds, the representational authority of traditional diplomatic services.

Heads of state and government also play an increasingly visible role (Santos, 2021). In addition to engaging foreign publics directly through speeches, they increasingly use digital communication, particularly social media. Their anticorruption statements often set the tone for national commitments and shape international expectations of integrity. At the same time, this visibility exposes states to heightened scrutiny, especially when domestic practices and external narratives diverge.

Subnational actors, such as provinces and municipalities, function as state agents when they are formally integrated into the national diplomatic system (Santos, 2025b). When authorised by the central government or granted a role in foreign affairs under national law, their participation acquires a distinctive representational status. Debates surrounding the City and State Diplomacy Act in the United States illustrate this dynamic. By formally recognising subnational diplomacy, such legislation would shift cities and states from autonomous nonstate actors to state agents exercising delegated authority.

Taken together, these developments reveal a plural and interconnected state apparatus. ACPD emerges from a set of formal state institutions whose combined activities shape how integrity is projected and negotiated internationally. Within this system, representational ties are predominantly grounded in formal delegation through elections, appointments, statutory mandates, and hierarchical instructions.

Non State Agents: Diversity, Credibility, and Collaborative Roles

Non state agents communicate, interpret, and mobilise around integrity-related norms in ways that complement, extend, and at times challenge state-led efforts. Their involvement reflects the growing pluralisation of global governance, in which authority is dispersed across networks of actors whose legitimacy derives from expertise, practice, societal trust, organisational capacity, and narrative influence rather than formal delegation.

At the international level, examples include international NGOs such as Transparency International and advocacy networks such as the UNCAC Coalition and the U4 Anti-Corruption Resource Centre. These agents exercise normative authority by devising public understandings of corruption, monitoring state performance, and pressuring for reform (Bukovansky, 2015; Grass & Seiter, 2020). Intergovernmental organisations such as the UN, the OECD, and the Council of Europe often operate through hybrid bureaucratic structures that resemble non state agents, insofar as they pursue agendas and exercise influence beyond direct state control (Goff, 2015; Langhorne, 2005). In doing so, they blur the boundaries between diplomacy and other forms of transnational influence (Gregory, 2025), extending the reach of ACPD beyond the state.

With regard to domestic actors, these comprise multinational enterprises, industry associations, chambers of commerce, and stock exchanges that project norms of integrity abroad (Langhorne, 2005; Nye, 2019; Riordan, 2005). They shape external perceptions of national governance standards through initiatives related to compliance, due diligence, and corporate responsibility. Alongside them, NGOs such as national chapters of Transparency International and OGP perform advocacy, public education, and watchdog functions that resonate beyond national borders. Similarly, through narratives, information flows, and epistemic cooperation, cultural institutions, media organisations, and universities (Zaharna, 2019; Nye, 2019) also influence anticorruption perceptions.

Subnational authorities hold a hybrid position when acting autonomously. Their initiatives in areas adjacent to anticorruption, such as ethics and sustainability, may reinforce or complicate national narratives (Santos, 2025b), illustrating the porous boundaries between state and non state agency in ACPD. As meso-level governance environments, subnational arenas shape how integrity-related norms are perceived, enacted, and contested, with local institutional practices (Korosteleva et al., 2020) generating effects that may extend beyond national borders.

Individuals are also relevant, often acting as boundary spanners who operate between communities, translating meanings and enabling connections that traditional diplomatic channels cannot easily replicate (Zaharna, 2022). Activists, opinion leaders, intellectuals, journalists, religious leaders, and celebrities can mobilise emotions, shape narratives, and frame public debates across borders (Adler-Nissen, 2024; Keck & Sikkink, 1998; Neff & Jemielniak, 2024). Anticorruption scholars, such as Susan Rose-Ackerman and Michael Johnston, similarly function as epistemic agents whose policy insights travel transnationally and inform institutional reform. Diasporas add another layer to this ecosystem (Cull, 2024), acting as transnational bridges that influence perceptions of their home countries through professional, cultural, and civic networks, increasingly forming part of broader strategies of reputational security.

Across this diverse landscape, credibility, including interdependent expertise, trustworthiness, and goodwill, shapes perceptions of competence, honesty, and commitment to the public interest (Grass & Seiter, 2020). Independent agents often enjoy higher public trust than governmental institutions, enabling them to reach audiences resistant to official communication (Riordan, 2005, p. 182). In ACPD, where integrity functions as both the subject and a moral horizon, credibility is therefore pivotal yet fragile. It may be undermined when non state actors appear overly dependent on state funding or politically instrumentalised, making transparency in governance, funding, and partnerships essential to sustaining legitimacy (Riordan, 2005). As participation expands, so too do risks of fragmentation, inconsistency, and reputational harm.

Non state agents expand the communicative, technical, and normative reach of ACPD and may also act as sources of disruption and dissent that reshape reputational dynamics beyond state control (Cull, 2025a). Their influence remains conditioned by their position within hierarchical fields of expertise and recognition (Pingeot & Pouliot, 2024). While diversity enables states to mobilise complementary forms of authority, such as moral credibility, cultural resonance, social trust, and expertise, it also introduces coordination challenges and reputational risks, underscoring the importance of situating non state roles within wider architectures of representation.

International Actors as Audiences and Co-Producers of Anticorruption Norms

In ACPD, international actors may occupy multiple roles simultaneously, operating as audiences, validators, peer-review interlocutors, and co-producers of the norms under consideration, depending on the setting. In this chapter, the focus is on their audience-facing role and their capacity to co-produce integrity meanings through feedback, assessment, and engagement. Public diplomacy targets “foreign societies and specific groups” (Melissen, 2005, p. 5), including diplomatic circles, political elites, business coalitions, academic communities, and international media. These publics interpret anticorruption messages through distinct interests and logics, making strategic audience segmentation essential (Banks, 2011; Riordan, 2005). Far from passive recipients, they interpret, contest, and internalise integrity messages, shaping how anticorruption norms circulate and consolidate. By responding to and reframing the standards articulated in international arenas, foreign audiences contribute to the global anticorruption norm (Jakobi, 2013). Their reactions feed back into socialisation processes that influence how states assess performance and adjust external communication.

This dual role is particularly evident in contexts of technical assistance, capacity-building, and peer review. In these settings, interlocutors act simultaneously as recipients and as agents, absorbing, reinterpreting, and adapting the anticorruption identities of assisting actors. Influence flows in both directions: donors seek to diffuse standards, while recipients localise and reshape them within specific institutional and cultural contexts. International actors therefore operate not only as audiences but also as partners in constructing the global anticorruption norm. Their engagement highlights the relational and dialogical character of ACPD and underscores the importance of analysing how legitimacy and authority are negotiated across borders.

Representational Ties: Formal, Social, and Relational Legitimacy

The plurality of agents involved in ACPD renders questions of legitimacy central: Who has the authority to represent whom, and on what basis? Public diplomacy is not merely a communicative practice but an exercise in representation, in which actors speak and act in the name of a state, cause, or constituency. Such representational authority is not automatically conferred; it is enacted through situated practices combining functional roles, symbolic performance, and social recognition (Adler-Nissen, 2016). Agents therefore exercise varying degrees of influence depending on resources, access, and credibility, as well as on their position within hierarchical communities of practice that structure recognition and authority (Adler-Nissen, 2023). These hierarchies are sustained through everyday diplomatic practices that confer or withhold recognition among actors operating within shared professional and normative fields (Adler-Nissen, 2016). Effectiveness depends heavily on the perceived credibility and legitimacy of those who claim representational authority (Buchanan & Keohane, 2006, p. 419), particularly in a normatively charged domain such as anticorruption.

For state actors, legitimacy primarily derives from formal delegation embedded in the institutional architecture of the state. Elections, civil service recruitment, political appointments, and statutory mandates establish legally recognised bonds of representation that authorise officials to act on behalf of the state. Diplomats, for instance, derive representational authority from public office and from the international legal framework of the Vienna Convention on Diplomatic Relations (Adler-Nissen, 2016), which codifies their rights, privileges, and obligations.

Grant and Keohane (2005) distinguish two main models of delegation. In the principal-agent model, representatives act under instructions from a mandating authority and are expected to demonstrate loyalty and accountability. In the trustee model, representatives enjoy greater autonomy, exercising judgement grounded in expertise and ethical responsibility. Heads of government, central bank governors, or supreme audit officials often operate as trustees when representing national commitments to integrity in multilateral forums. In both models, legitimacy rests on legal-rational procedures that define who may legitimately speak for the state.

Non state agents, by contrast, lack such formal delegation and must derive legitimacy from socially constructed forms of authority. Three practical criteria are particularly salient. First, organisational capacity refers to clear objectives, governance structures, and sustained activities (Porte, 2012). Second, political relevance concerns the ability to set agendas or contribute meaningfully to public-interest issues, grounded in credibility, competence and honesty (Langhorne, 2005; Porte, 2012). Third, communicative capacity (Jönsson & Hall, 2002) enables sustained participation in transnational dialogues.

These criteria intersect with broader theoretical traditions. Weber's (1978) typology of authority, including traditional, charismatic, and legal-rational authority, remains visible in ACPD, ranging from historic universities and influential individuals to formalised NGOs. Relational approaches (Slaughter, 2011; Zaharna, 2013) further highlight hybrid forms of legitimacy rooted in trust, reciprocity, and belonging. Diasporas exemplify such hybrid authority, deriving legitimacy from embeddedness in host societies and from symbolic ties to countries of origin.

Representational ties also vary in stability. State agents generally possess stable ties grounded in formal acts of delegation, including appointments, legal provisions, treaties, or official invitations (Santos, 2025a). Non state agents may similarly acquire stable ties when formally mandated by the state through agreements, memoranda of understanding, or contracts. By contrast, precarious ties arise when agents assume representational roles unilaterally. Such cases reflect the contingent, contestable, and situational nature of diplomatic agency beyond formal delegation (Adler-Nissen, 2016). A journalist publishing an investigative article abroad or an organisation attending an international workshop without a mandate may influence perceptions of integrity, but without durable representational authority or clear accountability. In ACPD, representational ties therefore cannot be presumed; they must be assessed on a case-by-case basis, considering the source of authority, the stability of the mandate, and the credibility they command.

Synthesis: Agents in Anticorruption Public Diplomacy

ACPD operates as a multilayered ecosystem encompassing a wide array of agents. Diplomatic services, governmental bodies, international organisations, cities, businesses, NGOs, individuals, and diasporas all participate in projecting and negotiating anticorruption commitments across borders. Their effectiveness is closely tied to representational legitimacy, as distinct patterns of delegation, participation, and relational trust generate differentiated roles and degrees of credibility.

2.7 Activities: The Operational Dimension of Anticorruption Public Diplomacy

A repertoire of activities translates identities, interests, and representational roles into concrete practices of ACPD. This book draws on Cull's (2019) five widely recognised core activities: listening, advocacy, cultural diplomacy, exchange, and broadcasting. It also incorporates subsequent scholarship that expands this repertoire to include dialogical engagement (Martino, 2020) and three supporting functions: action planning (Gregory, 2005; Maronkova, 2018), evaluation, and institutional learning (Butler et al., 2017). For the purposes of this analytical framework, these elements are operationalised as a nine-part repertoire through which anticorruption norms are communicated, interpreted, contested, and internalised through ACPD in international contexts.

Listening: Diagnostic Foundations

Listening constitutes the foundation of ACPD, providing the diagnostic intelligence required for effective engagement and enabling a shift from message-centred persuasion to more relational and collaborative approaches (Zaharna, 2022). It involves the systematic collection and analysis of information to understand foreign publics' perceptions and behaviours (Cull, 2019) while taking into account linguistic hierarchies and unequal capacities to be heard in global politics (Pouliot, 2025). Listening encompasses traditional tools such as conversations, interviews, focus groups, opinion surveys, listening tours, and media monitoring, increasingly complemented by digital instruments such as social media analysis and data mining. These practices respond to the growing need to detect coordinated information influence operations and psychologically targeted manipulation in complex online environments (Sörensen & Pamment, 2023; Pamment et al., 2025), reinforcing listening as an adaptive and contested practice.

In ACPD, listening is particularly important in politically sensitive environments characterised by complex local norms and opaque practices. By identifying reputational vulnerabilities, expectations of reform, and reactions to policy developments, listening shapes how anticorruption messages are framed and which partners are prioritised. At the same time, it raises ethical and legal concerns when practices approach espionage or intrusive data collection (Coward & Bjola, 2016), concerns that may undermine credibility in a field centred on integrity. More than a technical exercise, listening establishes the ground on which ACPD initiatives are built and functions as a prerequisite for reputational security under conditions of media disruption and intensified competition (Cull, 2024), anchoring subsequent activities in contextual awareness and legitimacy.

Dialogical Engagement: Negotiating Norms

Dialogical engagement entails sustained, bidirectional communication with international publics because the effectiveness of public diplomacy depends on a deep understanding of audiences' interests and perspectives (Martino, 2020). It relies on continued interaction through face-to-face meetings and relationship-building practices (Ingenhoff & Chariatte, 2025), complemented by mediated channels such as email, digital platforms, and social media (Golan et al., 2019). Dialogue presupposes regular contact, mutual responsiveness, and openness to adaptation, reflecting a relational logic grounded in empathy, trust, and durable bonds (Zaharna, 2022). In ACPD, such dynamics create the conditions for sustained cooperation and contextualised norm negotiation.

Dialogical engagement is therefore central to negotiating the meaning and implementation of integrity norms across different legal and political contexts. It facilitates cooperation on joint investigations, asset recovery, and multijurisdictional case resolution (Borlini & Peters, 2024), while also exposing tensions rooted in power asymmetries. Funding arrangements that encourage self-censorship (Walker, 2018) and the extraterritorial reach of anticorruption legislation (Biersteker, 2020), including the United States Foreign Corrupt Practices Act (FCPA), France's Loi Sapin II, and the United Kingdom Bribery Act, sometimes criticised as overreaching (Leibold, 2015), illustrate how dialogue may be shaped by unequal leverage. Even under such constraints, dialogical engagement remains a key mechanism for adapting ACPD strategies to local sensitivities.

Advocacy: Promoting Anticorruption Norms and Reforms

Advocacy involves the promotion and defence of norms, policies, and reform agendas before international audiences (Cull, 2019). It relies on narratives, strategic messaging, speeches, press releases, campaigns, reports, and digital content to influence opinion and policy debates (Pamment, 2016). As a persuasive practice, advocacy depends critically on credibility (Cull, 2019), requiring agents to project expertise, honesty, and commitment to the public interest (Grass & Seiter, 2020). Within ACPD, advocacy elevates anticorruption as a foreign policy priority, frames specific reforms as legitimate, and positions states as norm entrepreneurs or reform-oriented agents. Both state and non state agents participate in this activity (Cull, 2019). Yet the same instruments may also be misused: practices such as caviar diplomacy, disinformation, covert campaigns, or instrumental sanctions risk eroding trust and undermining the ethical foundations of ACPD (Nye, 2023). Effective advocacy therefore rests on maintaining a balance between strategic communication and normative consistency.

Cultural Diplomacy: Embedding Integrity Through Symbolic Practices

Cultural diplomacy mobilises cultural expressions and shared values to foster understanding and long-term relationships (Cull, 2019). It operates through events, artistic productions, educational programmes, and cultural exchanges that communicate identities indirectly, often appealing to emotions and shared experiences rather than explicit political argument. Within ACPD, cultural diplomacy embeds integrity themes in symbolic and accessible forms. Initiatives such as anticorruption film festivals or creative contests translate complex governance issues into compelling narratives. Large-scale events such as the OECD Global Anti-Corruption & Integrity Forum and Transparency International's Anti-Corruption Conference function as cultural platforms that combine expertise, public communication, and symbolic rituals of commitment. Given the historical association of cultural diplomacy with covert influence, perceptions of manipulation can quickly undermine trust, making transparency and authenticity essential to its credibility.

International Exchange: Learning, Exposure, and Socialisation

International exchanges immerse participants in foreign institutional environments, fostering interpersonal ties, exposure, and mutual learning (Cull, 2019; Scott-Smith, 2023). They function as boundary-spanning mechanisms that connect actors across cultural, institutional, and normative divides (Zaharna, 2022) and include technical missions, study visits, fellowships, training programmes, and residencies, often organised by states, international organisations, or specialised institutes such as the International Anti-Corruption Academy (IACA). Within ACPD, exchanges are powerful mechanisms of socialisation into integrity norms. Participants engage directly with institutional designs, enforcement practices, and policy communities, gaining practical insight into how anticorruption frameworks function in different contexts. Such experiences may generate emulation effects, support reform coalitions, and sustain long-term professional networks. At the same time, exchanges must avoid instrumentalisation, ideological manipulation, or opaque selection processes, which risk reputational damage and perceptions of bias. When transparently designed, exchanges translate abstract standards into lived practice and durable professional learning.

International Broadcasting: Mass Communication for Integrity

International broadcasting disseminates anticorruption messages across borders through radio, television, digital platforms, podcasts, and social media (Arceneaux & Powers, 2020; Cull, 2019). It is particularly relevant when states seek to reach dispersed audiences rapidly, such as during major scandals, high-profile prosecutions, or the launch of international strategies. Once largely unidirectional, broadcasting increasingly incorporates interactive elements, such as online feedback and social media engagement, allowing limited audience response.

Within ACPD, international broadcasting frames national narratives on integrity for global audiences, explaining domestic reforms, clarifying contested cases, and countering disinformation. It operates in fragmented digital diplomatic environments that complicate coherence, authority, and audience alignment (Wiseman, 2024). At the same time, the information space is increasingly shaped by AI-assisted content generation, synthetic media, and coordinated influence campaigns, which challenge attribution and credibility (Fredheim & Pamment, 2025). Because competing accounts circulate easily, broadcaster credibility becomes pivotal in an environment marked by media disruption, weakened gatekeeping, and heightened reputational risk (Cull, 2024). While the same tools may also serve propaganda, censorship, or digital information control (Cull, 2019), responsible broadcasting grounded in verifiable information and transparent sourcing remains essential to sustaining trust in anticorruption communication.

Strategic Design, Evaluation, and Institutional Learning

Beyond the core communicative and relational activities of ACPD, three supporting practices, namely planning, evaluation, and institutional learning, underpin coherence, accountability, and long-term sustainability. These practices structure how ACPD initiatives are planned, assessed, and adapted over time.

Strategic design provides the framework that links intentions to concrete action. It involves defining objectives, identifying target audiences, allocating responsibilities, and aligning resources with short-, medium-, and long-term priorities (Gregory, 2005; Nye, 2008). In many countries, ACPD is embedded within broader public diplomacy or anticorruption strategies coordinated by ministries of foreign affairs or specialised agencies. Effective planning reduces fragmentation and promotes consistency between domestic reforms and external messaging.

Evaluation examines whether activities plausibly contribute to intended outcomes. Measuring ACPD is inherently challenging due to multiple causal pathways, diffuse influence, and temporal delays (Banks, 2020; Maronkova, 2018), challenges compounded in the anticorruption field by political volatility and transnational criminal dynamics. Evaluation therefore draws on a combination of qualitative and quantitative tools, including surveys, interviews, media monitoring, digital metrics, and stakeholder feedback, informed by international benchmarks such as global scores and indices, governance indicators, or external assessments. Although causal precision is rarely attainable, evaluation supports judgements about plausibility, the direction of change, and alignment between goals and observed effects.

Institutional learning converts evaluation into durable capacity. Lessons learned, understood as structured reflections on successes, failures, and their underlying causes (Milton, 2010), remain underutilised in diplomacy (Butler et al., 2017) but are particularly salient in anticorruption, where domestic politics, international expectations, and criminal innovation intersect. Integrating insights from national experience with those generated by the OECD, regional bodies, or peer countries strengthens institutional memory and helps prevent repeated mistakes. In this way, institutional learning links evaluation to future planning and contributes to the sustainability of ACPD.

Taken together, strategic design, evaluation, and institutional learning form a reinforcing cycle that complements the core operational activities of ACPD, enhancing coherence, adaptability, and long-term credibility.

2.8 Material and Immaterial Factors

ACPD operates through material and immaterial resources whose significance is shaped by intersubjective interpretation. Influence derives not only from what states possess, but also from how these assets are socially understood (Finnemore & Sikkink, 2001; Vukovic, 2020). Adapting Nye's (2004, pp. 33–72) classification, this section identifies six categories of resources relevant to ACPD: (1) anticorruption culture and values; (2) anticorruption policy frameworks; (3) economic resources; (4) technology; (5) information and ideas; and (6) participation in international anticorruption networks. Although analytically distinct, these resources may overlap in concrete situations.

Culture and values, such as ethical universalism, transparency, meritocracy, and the rejection of undue privilege, constitute core immaterial anti-corruption resources (Bhargava, 2006; Rotberg, 2020). Their diplomatic significance depends not only on projection, but also on vulnerability to reputational challenge and erosion by external actors (Cull, 2025b). When consistently reflected in practice, such values shape perceptions of credibility and underpin integrity narratives. High-trust societies, professional bureaucracies, and coherent democratic traditions tend to project greater attractiveness in ACPD (Hopkinson & Pelizzo, 2006; Mungiu-Pippidi, 2018), as values become influential particularly when foreign publics perceive them as authentic and stable.

Policy frameworks institutionalise values. National strategies, legal instruments, anticorruption agencies, audit bodies, and regulations governing political finance, lobbying, conflicts of interest, whistleblowing, or access to information signal commitment to integrity standards (Hopkinson & Pelizzo, 2006). Their diplomatic relevance depends not on formal adoption alone, but on perceived independence, effectiveness, and enforcement capacity; weak implementation can quickly undermine credibility.

Economic resources shape the scope and sustainability of ACPD. Financial capacity enables technical assistance, training, exchanges, and participation in multilateral mechanisms (Brinkerhoff, 2000; Bhargava, 2006), while also supporting long-term engagement. Economic strength thus reinforces perceptions of reliability and sustained commitment.

Technology constitutes both a functional and symbolic resource. Digital reporting systems, AI-based tools, blockchain applications, and e-government platforms support prevention, detection, and enforcement (Rotberg, 2020), while also signalling modernisation and transparency. At the same time, technology may generate negative effects when associated with surveillance, manipulation, or cyber intrusions (Diamond, 2021; Walker, 2018), making its impact in ACPD heavily dependent on narratives of ethics and accountability.

Information and ideas operate as immaterial resources. The organisation of data, the framing of achievements, and the circulation of narratives contribute to constructing integrity norms, but may also be used to distort evidence or exert pressure (Walker, 2018). Reports, speeches, campaigns, and digital diplomacy efforts acquire relevance when they are referenced, adopted, or emulated by others, thereby reinforcing an actor's position within the global anticorruption regime.

Finally, participation in networks, such as the UN Global Compact, the OGP, the Financial Action Task Force, or the Extractive Industries Transparency Initiative, provides both material opportunities, including access to platforms, learning, and monitoring, and immaterial benefits, such as credibility and peer recognition (Cole, 2015; Harris, 2019). Network participation enables states to co-produce standards, undergo peer review, and project integrity through collectively validated practices.

Across these categories, resources acquire influence only through the meanings attributed to them in social interaction. ACPD therefore depends not simply on the possession of material or immaterial assets, but on how these assets are interpreted, valued, and integrated into broader narratives of integrity within the international system.

2.9 Ideational Factors: Smart Power

Possessing material or immaterial resources is insufficient to generate influence; their impact depends on how they are interpreted and rendered meaningful through processes of international socialisation. Resources produce effects only when they are recognised by others as attractive, legitimate, or relevant (Nye, 2011). Meaning-making is not automatic but emerges from interaction among multiple agents who validate, contest, or reinterpret these resources (Finnemore & Sikkink, 2001). Such processes may also involve disruption and dissent that undermine official reputational narratives (Cull, 2025b), particularly in contexts of fragmented multilateralism and contested institutional authority (Wiseman, 2025). Domestic integrity standards or anticorruption programmes, for example, become consequential internationally only when foreign audiences recognise their significance. Outcomes therefore depend less on the mere existence of policies than on how they are shared, perceived, and reframed across borders.

This conversion of resources into outcomes relies on "skillful conversion strategies" (Nye, 2011, p. 99), through which domestic assets are selected, framed, and projected in ways that resonate with foreign publics. This strategic work of interpretation and alignment with the expectations and identities of external audiences constitutes the ideational dimension of ACPD. Smart power provides the analytical lens for examining this process, linking resources to influence through distinct logics of action.

The Strategic Role of Smart Power

Nye defines power as the capacity to act and influence others (2021, p. 197), while Vukovic emphasises the link between resources, ideas, and outcomes (2020, p. 46). Taken together, these perspectives highlight that influence depends not on resources alone but on the strategic skills through which they are mobilised. In ACPD, this implies that assets such as anticorruption legislation, meritocratic values, or investments in training acquire diplomatic relevance only when they are actively organised and perceived as enablers or reinforcers of integrity.

Smart power operates across three interconnected levels (Fig. 2.1) (Nye, 2011, 2021; Vukovic, 2020). At the national level, basic resources, such as values, policy frameworks, and economic capacities, reflect identities and interests guiding foreign policy, constituting power-in-being (Treverton & Jones, 2005). At the second level, these resources are adapted to external contexts and transformed into instruments of action, representing power-in-doing (Nye, 2004; Treverton & Jones, 2005). At the third level, these shaped resources contribute to the achievement of ACPD objectives, constituting power-in-getting. This process rests on "the nexus of will (interests and resources) and skill (ability to translate the resources into a desired outcome)" (Vukovic, 2020, p. 45). It unfolds

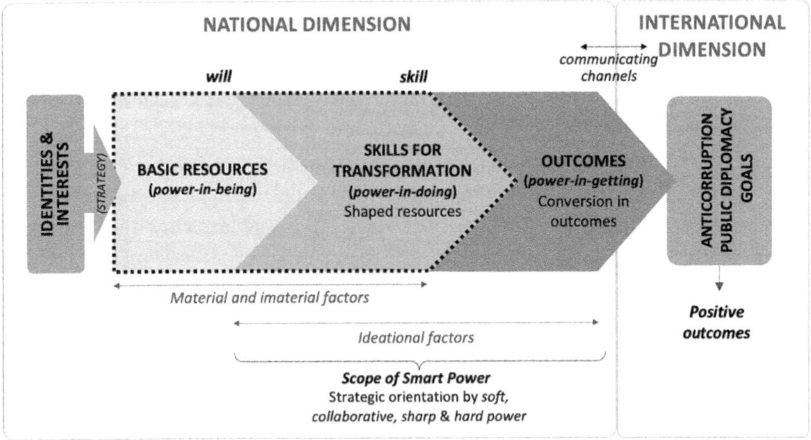

Fig. 2.1 Smart power across three interconnected levels of power. Source: Author's elaboration based on references mentioned in this section

within social environments where meanings are intersubjectively negotiated, as emphasised by Finnemore and Sikkink (2001), and where legitimacy and authority are continuously constructed through interaction.

Within this framework, smart power functions as the mechanism through which ideational factors guide the movement from national assets to international achievements (Nye, 2011, pp. 218–231). It underscores that anticorruption values, institutional safeguards, or reputational capital generates influence only when articulated through styles of power attuned to specific audiences and contexts.

Styles of Power as Ideational Mechanisms of Meaning-Making

The concept of smart power emerged from Nye's recognition that complex foreign threats, such as organised crime, require a combination of capabilities rather than reliance on a single form of influence (Nye, 2011). It denotes the strategic combination of different styles of power, originally conceived as the combination of soft and hard power, through which resources are assigned meaning and converted into preferred outcomes. Subsequent scholarship highlighted networked forms of influence (Zaharna, 2013), giving rise to the concept of collaborative power (Slaughter, 2009, 2011). In parallel, the notion of sharp power was introduced (Nye, 2019; Walker, 2018) to capture manipulative and constraining practices that operate through distortion, coercion, or reputational pressure.

Some scholars argue that sharp power should be excluded from public diplomacy due to its anti-democratic tendencies (Manfredi-Sánchez, 2025). Analytically, however, this book treats sharp power not as "good" or normatively desirable public diplomacy, but as an empirically observable mode of influence that may overlap with public diplomacy practices when integrity narratives are strategically instrumentalised. Acknowledging sharp power therefore offers a more accurate account of the empirical overlap that emerges in contemporary ACPD. Because no country is entirely free from corruption (UN General Assembly, 2021), governments face incentives to deploy manipulative techniques to project integrity where it is fragile.

This dynamic reflects the moralisation of power through communicative spectacles (Alexander, 2021) and may be operationalised, for instance, through economic dependencies that induce self-censorship within international organisations responsible for anticorruption rankings. Recognising sharp power is therefore essential for analysing ACPD as a contested practice rather than an inherently virtuous one. From this perspective, claims to moral authority may function as instruments of hegemonic stabilisation rather than expressions of ethical commitment (Alexander, 2021), reinforcing the argument advanced in Chap. 1 that integrity narratives can operate simultaneously as normative commitments and as forms of reputational power.

Because ACPD unfolds in heterogeneous and contested environments, the attribution of meaning requires continuous strategic adaptation (Finnemore & Sikkink, 2001, p. 394). Taken together, these four styles—soft, hard, sharp, and collaborative power—constitute distinct behavioural logics through which states adapt, frame, and project their resources in ACPD.

Soft Power

Soft power is anchored in co-opting behaviour, operating through attraction, persuasion, and the voluntary internalisation of values (Nye, 2011, 2021). Its behavioural spectrum spans arguing, attracting, engaging, influencing, inspiring, securing acquiescence, communicating, negotiating, and listening (Nye, 2011). Rather than imposing obligations, soft power presents domestic practices as models to be admired and emulated.

In ACPD, the principal sources of soft power are cultural, value-based, and policy-related resources that signal a credible commitment to integrity (Nye, 2011). Through soft power, integrity reforms, open government policies, whistleblower protections, and high-trust social environments are framed as desirable and legitimate reference points. This framing adds ideational value to resources that might otherwise carry limited diplomatic weight. Meritocratic recruitment systems, independent oversight bodies, and traditions of ethical public service acquire global resonance when articulated as exemplars of good governance, reinforcing attraction and normative alignment.

Soft power effects tend to be long-term and depend on consistency between projected messages and perceived realities (Nye, 2011). They are also highly context-sensitive: shared values facilitate voluntary adherence, whereas abusive or controversial practices undermine attraction and persuasion (Nye, 2011, 2021). Respect for human rights and the rule of law is therefore central to moral credibility (Buchanan & Keohane, 2006). A structural constraint in ACPD is that soft power relies heavily on external perceptions of integrity; high-level scandals or weak enforcement can erode credibility and limit persuasive potential. In such contexts, states often complement soft power with more assertive strategies, shifting towards hard or sharp power to offset reputational vulnerabilities.

Hard Power

Hard power operates by creating incentives or disincentives, shaping behaviour through material capabilities rather than voluntary alignment. In ACPD, it relies predominantly on economic instruments rather than military force, mobilised through commanding behaviour (Nye, 2011, pp. 25–80). Its capacities include determining, deterring, controlling, sanctioning, intervening, conditioning, protecting, incentivising, rewarding, and enabling influence by structuring the environments in which foreign actors make decisions.

The operational repertoire of hard power in ACPD includes capacity-building investments, funding for international exchanges and conferences, development assistance conditioned on anti-bribery reforms, due diligence clauses in trade agreements, and restrictions on financial cooperation with jurisdictions that facilitate illicit flows. Although such measures may be experienced as coercive by recipients, they signal strategic priorities and alter partners' cost-benefit calculations. The United States, for example, often links foreign assistance or access to markets to governance benchmarks and corruption performance.

Because hard power reduces voluntarism, its effects tend to be short or medium term. It is more readily deployed where political corruption is perceived as a threat to national interests and where complex interdependence increases vulnerability to economic leverage (Nye, 2011). Conversely, symmetrical markets limit its impact (Nye, 2011). Institutional weakness poses a further constraint: without robust monitoring and enforcement mechanisms, material assets are difficult to convert into credible anticorruption influence. Perceptions of political manoeuvring or biased assessments can also undermine attempts to deploy hard power in ACPD.

While both hard power and sharp power may rely on leverage, conditionality, or economic pressure, they are analytically distinguished by their underlying mechanisms. Hard power operates through incentives and material structuring that shape cost-benefit calculations while preserving formal agency and transparency. Sharp power, by contrast, emerges when leverage or conditionality is combined with deception, distortion, coercive information control, or autonomy-reducing dependency, thereby constraining choice rather than merely influencing it.

Sharp Power

Sharp power is characterised by constraining behaviour that limits the autonomy of other actors through legal, informational, or political mechanisms (Nye, 2023, pp. 113–114). It is increasingly enacted through information influence operations that exploit vulnerabilities in digital and psychological environments (Grahn & Pamment, 2024). By exposing tensions between reputational strategies and the integrity norms that public diplomacy purports to uphold, understood as ethically charged claims (Alexander, 2021), this dynamic foregrounds the ethical dimension of ACPD.

In the anticorruption domain, sharp power encompasses practices such as extraterritorial enforcement, cross-border investigations, naming-and-shaming, and economically induced dependencies that secure reputational compliance where integrity is fragile. These practices typically operate under conditions of reduced voluntarism (Nye, 2021) and are largely implemented by state agents embedded in diplomatic, regulatory, and security structures. Their behavioural logic relies on manipulating, confusing, disorienting, deceiving, controlling, pressuring, threatening, coercing, banning, suppressing, spying, surveilling, interfering, censoring, corrupting, and constraining.

Within ACPD, sharp power draws primarily on technological and informational resources, including algorithmic tools, artificial intelligence, and digital platforms, combined with information strategies that exploit cognitive biases, emotional triggers, and attention dynamics to manipulate narratives or amplify selective interpretations of integrity (Biersteker, 2020; Diamond, 2021; Fredheim & Pamment, 2025). Economic leverage and sanctions complement these mechanisms, while anticorruption laws with extraterritorial reach, such as the FCPA or global Magnitsky-type provisions, exert pressure on foreign elites by exposing them to legal and financial risks. In this context, such measures operate as sharp power when they are deployed alongside reputational pressure, informational distortion, or dependency-inducing strategies that constrain autonomy. Potential outcomes include agenda-setting, the neutralisation of criticism, and the monopolisation of ideas (Diamond, 2021; Walker, 2018; Wu, 2019), depending on how technological, informational, and economic instruments are combined.

The key distinction between soft and sharp power lies in voluntarism (Nye, 2021). While soft power preserves audiences' capacity to choose, sharp power distorts or restricts that choice through coercion, manipulation, or dependency (Nye, 2021). Political and social asymmetries, particularly between democratic and non-democratic systems (Nye, 2019; Walker, 2018), as well as weak institutions, increase vulnerability to sharp power. In the contemporary international environment, enabling conditions tend to outweigh constraints, and sharp power effects are often short term. Effective countermeasures therefore require integrated strategies, societal awareness, and institutional resilience (Nye, 2019; Ördén & Pamment, 2021; Walker, 2018). For ACPD, recognising sharp power is essential both for assessing its strategic utility and for delineating the ethical limits of anticorruption norm promotion.

Collaborative Power

Collaborative power rests on coordinating behaviour to enable joint problem-solving and the co-production of norms (Slaughter, 2011). It depends on communicative environments that privilege relational and holistic logics over purely instrumental persuasion (Zaharna, 2022). Defined as "the power of many to do together what no one can do alone" (Slaughter, 2011, para. 6), it differs from soft power's power over by operating as power with others (Slaughter, 2011; Nye, 2011). In ACPD, collaborative power materialises through multilateral engagement, peer-review mechanisms, capacity-building, knowledge sharing, and network orchestration, as illustrated by initiatives such as the OGP, the UNCAC Implementation Review Mechanism, and OECD integrity forums.

Collaborative power derives from network dynamics. Networks consist of nodes, which are individuals, organisations or institutions, and links, understood as the relationships among them (Fisher, 2013). The density and quality of these connections shape the capacity for collective action (Slaughter, 2009). Its behavioural repertoire includes connection, negotiation, engagement, and coordination (Slaughter, 2011), supported by capabilities such as sharing, adapting, cooperating, mediating, listening, and orchestrating. In ACPD, collaborative power mobilises resources rooted in values, policy frameworks, and network participation, collectively validating governance models that may diffuse across jurisdictions. At the same time, it remains vulnerable, as Cull (2025a) observes, to reputational disruption when collaborative narratives are contested by organised non state networks.

Shared interests, transparency, and mutual trust facilitate collaboration, whereas self-centred goals or manipulation hinders it (Arquilla & Ronfeldt, 1999; Fisher, 2013; Slaughter, 2009; Zaharna, 2013, 2022). Outcomes may unfold over the short, medium, or long term, ranging from agenda-setting effects to the consolidation of durable integrity initiatives (Fisher, 2013; Slaughter, 2009). For ACPD, collaborative power is particularly significant because it anchors anticorruption commitments in cooperative structures rather than unilateral claims, thereby reinforcing both legitimacy and sustainability.

2.10 Concluding Remarks: From Concept to Analysis

This chapter has operationalised ACPD as a process of international socialisation through which states construct, negotiate, and project meanings of integrity in an environment where expectations, identities, and reputations are continuously shaped by interaction. Understood in this way, ACPD resides at the intersection of public diplomacy, global governance, and the evolving global anticorruption norm.

The chapter has identified six constitutive dimensions that together form the analytical anatomy of ACPD. Identities and interests provide the motivational grounding through which states interpret their integrity commitments. Objectives translate these motivations into strategic direction. Agents define who acts in the name of integrity, while representational ties shape the authority through which such action is exercised. Activities constitute the operational repertoire through which ACPD is enacted. Material and immaterial factors constitute the assets states mobilise, and ideational factors determine how these assets acquire meaning and are converted into influence. Taken together, these dimensions offer a structured and coherent way of examining how states communicate, perform, and institutionalise their anticorruption agendas.

A central insight of the chapter is that ACPD is constitutive rather than merely instrumental. It does not simply promote pre-existing norms but actively participates in their production. Cognitive interpretations, normative expectations, and relational trust are all shaped through sustained engagement with foreign publics. Identities and interests evolve through this process; activities and material and immaterial factors gain significance when socially recognised; and the four styles of power operate as ideational mechanisms that give meaning to anticorruption practices. ACPD thus functions as a recursive cycle in which states articulate who they are, what they value, and how they seek recognition within an emerging integrity community.

This conceptualisation provides the analytical foundation for the comparative inquiry that follows. Denmark, New Zealand, the United States, and South Korea represent distinct pathways through which ACPD is mobilised, each combining the six dimensions in different configurations. Their trajectories reveal how variations in identities, institutional capacities, power styles, and resource endowments shape the practice of ACPD. Applying the model developed here, the subsequent chapters examine how these states construct integrity narratives, respond to international expectations, and participate in the co-production of the global anticorruption norm.

The movement from concept to analysis therefore marks a shift from theoretical construction to empirical assessment. The framework presented in this chapter offers both the lens and the criteria for identifying patterns, divergences, and hybrid forms of ACPD, as well as for analysing how domestic integrity frameworks are transformed into internationally meaningful influence. Grounded in socialisation, meaning-making, and power, this analytical architecture enables systematic comparison across political, institutional, and cultural contexts. If Chap. 1 established the need to rethink anticorruption through a public diplomacy lens, this chapter has provided the conceptual and analytical foundations through which that rethinking becomes empirically observable.

References

Adler, E. (2013). Constructivism in international relations: Sources, contributions, and debates. In W. Carlsnaes, T. Risse, & B. Simmons (Eds.), *Handbook of international relations* (2nd ed., pp. 112–144). Sage. https://doi.org/10.4135/9781446247587

Adler, E., & Pouliot, V. (2011). International practices. *International Theory, 3*(1), 1–36. https://doi.org/10.1017/S175297191000031X

Adler-Nissen, R. (2016). Diplomatic agency. In C. Constantinou, P. Kerr, & P. Sharp (Eds.), *The SAGE handbook of diplomacy* (pp. 92–103). Sage.

Adler-Nissen, R. (2023). Practice. In S. Goddard, G. Lawson, & J. Sending (Eds.), *The Oxford handbook of international political sociology* (pp. 177–198). Oxford University Press.

Adler-Nissen, R. (2024). The normalization of contestation: The sociology of knowledge and the challenges to the liberal international order. *Global Studies Quarterly, 4*(2), 1–5. https://doi.org/10.1093/isagsq/ksae020

Alexander, C. (2021). Hegemony, morality and power: A Gramscian theoretical framework for public diplomacy. In C. Alexander (Ed.), *The frontiers of public diplomacy* (pp. 9–24). Routledge.

Arceneaux, P., & Powers, S. (2020). International broadcasting public diplomacy as a game in a marketplace of loyalties. In N. Snow & N. Cull (Eds.), *Routledge handbook of public diplomacy* (2nd ed., pp. 50–63). Routledge. https://doi.org/10.4324/9780429465543

Arquilla, J., & Ronfeldt, D. (1999). *The emergence of noopolitik: Toward an American information strategy*. RAND.

Arsenault, A. (2025). The measurement dilemma in public diplomacy. In S. Aday (Ed.), *Handbook on public diplomacy* (pp. 348–359). Elgar. https://doi.org/10.4337/9781803926568.00039

Banks, R. (2011). *A resource guide to public diplomacy evaluation*. Figueroa Press.

Banks, R. (2020). Public diplomacy evaluation. In N. Snow & N. Cull (Eds.), *Routledge handbook of public diplomacy* (2nd ed., pp. 64–75). Routledge. https://doi.org/10.4324/9780429465543

Bhargava, V. (2006). Curing the cancer of corruption. In V. Bhargava (Ed.), *Global issues for global citizens* (pp. 341–370). World Bank.

Biersteker, T. (2020). The potential of Europe's sharp and soft power. *Global Policy, 11*(3), 384–387. https://doi.org/10.1111/1758-5899.12815

Bjola, C., & Kornprobst, M. (2018). *Understanding international diplomacy* (2nd ed.). Routledge.

Borlini, L., & Peters, A. (2024). Three decades of international cooperation against corruption: Looking ahead. *International Journal of Constitutional Law, 22*(2), 469–486. https://doi.org/10.1093/icon/moae031

Boswell, N. (1997). An emerging consensus on controlling corruption. *University of Pennsylvania Journal of International Law, 18*(4), 1165–1176.

Brinkerhoff, D. (2000). Assessing political will for anti-corruption efforts: An analytic framework. *Public Administration and Development, 20*(3), 239–252. https://doi.org/10.1002/1099-162X(200008)20:3<239::AID-PAD138>3.0.CO;2-3

Buchanan, A., & Keohane, R. (2006). The legitimacy of global governance institutions. *Ethics & International Affairs, 20*(4), 405–437. https://doi.org/10.1111/j.1747-7093.2006.00043.x

Bukovansky, M. (2015). Corruption rankings: Constructing and contesting the global anti-corruption agenda. In A. Cooley & J. Snyder (Eds.), *Ranking the world: Grading states as a tool of global governance*. Cambridge University Press. https://doi.org/10.1017/CBO9781316161555

Butler, D., Bohman, A., Burnett, C., Thompson, J., Kadlec, A., & Hanauer, L. (2017). *Enhancing next-generation diplomacy through best practices in lessons learned*. RAND. Retrieved February 6, 2026, from https://www.rand.org/pubs/research_reports/RR1930.html

Cole, W. (2015). Institutionalizing a global anti-corruption regime: Perverse effects on country outcomes, 1984–2012. *International Journal of Comparative Sociology, 56*(1), 53–80. https://doi.org/10.1177/0020715215578885

Cooper, A. (2019). Adapting public diplomacy to the populist challenge. *The Hague Journal of Diplomacy, 14*(1–2), 36–50. https://doi.org/10.1163/1871191X-14101011

Coward, A., & Bjola, C. (2016). Cyber-intelligence and diplomacy: The secret link. In C. Bjola & S. Murray (Eds.), *Secret diplomacy* (pp. 201–228). Routledge.

Cull, N. (2019). *Public diplomacy: Foundations for global engagement in the digital age*. Polity.

Cull, N. (2024). *Reputational security*. Polity.

Cull, N. (2025a). Reputational insecurity and breaking apartheid: Non-governmental networks of disruption and dissent and the case of South Africa. In A. Popkova (Ed.), *Disruption and dissent in public diplomacy* (pp. 59–80). Palgrave Macmillan.

Cull, N. (2025b). What's past is prologue. In S. Aday (Ed.), *Handbook on public diplomacy* (pp. 22–33). Elgar. https://doi.org/10.4337/9781803926568.00011

Diamond, L. (2021). Democratic regression in comparative perspective: Scope, methods, and causes. *Democratization, 28*(1), 22–42. https://doi.org/10.1080/13510347.2020.1807517

Finnemore, M. (1996). *National interests in international society*. Cornell University Press.

Finnemore, M., & Sikkink, K. (2001). Taking stock: The constructivist research program in international relations and comparative politics. *Annual Review of Political Science, 4*, 391–416. https://doi.org/10.1146/annurev.polisci.4.1.391

Finnemore, M., & Wendt, A. (2024). When "old" constructivism was new: Reflections on classical constructivism. *Perspectives on Politics, 22*(4), 1248–1268. https://doi.org/10.1017/S1537592724001464

Fisher, A. (2013). *Collaborative public diplomacy: How transnational networks influenced American studies in Europe*. Palgrave Macmillan.

Fitzpatrick, K. (2017). Public diplomacy in the public interest. *Journal of Public Interest Communications, 1*, 78–93.

Fredheim, R., & Pamment, P. (2025). Assessing the risks and opportunities posed by AI-enhanced influence operations on social media. *Place Branding and Public Diplomacy, 21*(3), 319–326. https://doi.org/10.1057/s41254-023-00322-5

Goff, P. (2015). Public diplomacy at the global level: The alliance of civilizations as a community of practice. *Cooperation and Conflict, 50*(3), 402–417. https://doi.org/10.1177/0010836715574915

Golan, G., Manor, I., & Arceneaux, P. (2019). Mediated public diplomacy redefined: Foreign stakeholder engagement via paid, earned, shared, and owned media. *American Behavioral Scientist, 63*(12), 1665–1683. https://doi.org/10.1177/0002764219835279

Grahn, H., & Pamment, J. (2024). *Exploitation of psychological processes in information influence operations* (Psychological Defence Research Institute—Working Paper 2024:4). Lund University.

Grant, R., & Keohane, R. (2005). Accountability and abuses of power in world politics. *The American Political Science Review, 99*(1), 29–43. https://doi.org/10.1017/S0003055405051476

Grass, R., & Seiter, J. (2020). Credibility and public diplomacy. In N. Snow & N. Cull (Eds.), *Routledge handbook of public diplomacy* (2nd ed., pp. 155–168). Routledge. https://doi.org/10.4324/9780429465543

Gregory, B. (2005, August 31). *Public diplomacy and strategic communication: cultures, firewalls and imported norms* (Conference paper). APSA Conference on International Communication and Conflict. Retrieved February 6, 2026, from https://universityofleeds.github.io/philtaylorpapers/pmt/exhibits/2468/gregory.pdf

Gregory, B. (2025). Diplomacy's public dimension. In S. Aday (Ed.), *Handbook on public diplomacy* (pp. 1–6). Elgar. https://doi.org/10.4337/9781803926568.00010

Harris, H. (2019). *The global anti-corruption regime: The case of Papua New Guinea*. Routledge.

Hocking, B. (2005). Rethinking the "new" public diplomacy. In J. Melissen (Ed.), *The new public diplomacy* (pp. 28–46). Palgrave Macmillan.

Hocking, B., Melissen, J., Riordan, S., & Sharp, P. (2012, October). *Futures for diplomacy* (Clingendael—Report 1). Clingendael. Retrieved February 6, 2026, from https://www.clingendael.org/sites/default/files/pdfs/20121030_research_melissen.pdf

Hopkinson, N., & Pelizzo, R. (2006). WBI-CPA conferences at Wilton Park: Reports. In R. Stapenhurst, N. Johnston, & R. Pelizzo (Eds.), *The role of parliament in curbing corruption* (pp. 251–263). World Bank.

Hough, D. (2013). *Political corruption & governance.* Palgrave Macmillan. https://doi.org/10.1057/9781137268716

Ingenhoff, D., & Chariatte, J. (2025). Reframing public diplomacy. In S. Aday (Ed.), *Handbook on public diplomacy* (pp. 360–377). Elgar. https://doi.org/10.4337/9781803926568.00040

Jakobi, A. (2013). The changing global norm of anti-corruption: From bad business to bad government. *Zeitschrift für Vergleichende Politikwissenschaft (ZfVP)*, *7*(1), 243–264. https://doi.org/10.1007/s12286-013-0160-y

Jönsson, C., & Hall, M. (2002). *Communication: An essential aspect of diplomacy* (Conference paper). 43rd Annual ISA Convention. Retrieved February 6, 2026, from https://cuts-citee.org/pdf/CDS02-Session7-03.pdf

Keck, M., & Sikkink, K. (1998). *Activists beyond borders*. Cornell University Press.

Korosteleva, J., Mickiewicz, T., & Stępień-Baig, P. (2020). It takes two to tango: Complementarity of bonding and bridging trust in alleviating corruption in cities. *Regional Studies, 54*(6), 851–862. https://doi.org/10.1080/00343404.2019.1652894

Langhorne, R. (2005). The diplomacy of non-state actors. *Diplomacy and Statecraft, 16*(2), 331–339. https://doi.org/10.1080/09592290590948388

Leibold, A. (2015). The extraterritorial application of the FCPA under international law. *Willamette Law Review, 51*, 225–267.

Leonard, M., Stead, C., & Smewing, C. (2002). *Public diplomacy*. Foreign Policy Centre.

Manfredi-Sánchez, J. (2025). *How disinformation ruins public diplomacy*. Routledge. https://doi.org/10.4324/9781032650524

Marcus, A. (2019). *Central bank governance and the prevention and detection of corruption*. Transparency International. Retrieved February 6, 2026, from https://knowledgehub.transparency.org/helpdesk/central-bank-governance-and-the-prevention-and-detection-of-corruption

Maronkova, B. (2018). *From crawling to walking: Progress in evaluating the effectiveness of public diplomacy*. Figueroa Press.

Martino, L. (2020). The spectrum of listening. In N. Snow & N. Cull (Eds.), *Routledge handbook of public diplomacy* (2nd ed., pp. 21–29). Routledge. https://doi.org/10.4324/9780429465543

Mccoy, J., & Heckel, H. (2001). The emergence of a global anti-corruption norm. *International Politics, 38*(1), 65–90. https://doi.org/10.1057/palgrave.ip.8892613

McDevitt, A. (2020). *Supreme audit institutions' anti-corruption strategies*. Transparency International. Retrieved February 6, 2026, from https://knowledgehub.transparencycdn.org/helpdesk/Supreme-Audit-Institutions-AC-strategies_2020_PR.pdf

Melissen, J. (2005). The new public diplomacy: Between theory and practice. In J. Melissen (Ed.), *The new public diplomacy* (pp. 3–27). Palgrave Macmillan.

Milton, N. (2010). *The lessons learned handbook*. Chandos.

Miskimmon, A., & O'Loughlin, B. (2025). Strategic narrative and public diplomacy: What artificial intelligence means for the endless problem of plural meanings of plural things. In S. Aday (Ed.), *Handbook on public diplomacy* (pp. 34–46). Elgar. https://doi.org/10.4337/9781803926568.00012

Mungiu-Pippidi, A. (2018). Seven steps to control of corruption: The road map. *Daedalus, 147*(3), 20–34. https://doi.org/10.1162/DAED_a_00500

Neff, T., & Jemielniak, D. (2024). How do transnational public spheres emerge? Comparing news and social media networks during the Madrid climate talks. *New Media & Society, 26*(4), 2066–2091. https://doi.org/10.1177/14614448221081426

Nye, J. (2004). *Soft power*. Public Affairs.

Nye, J. (2008). Public diplomacy and soft power. *The Annals of the American Academy of Political and Social Science, 616*(1), 94–109. https://doi.org/10.1177/0002716207311699

Nye, J. (2011). *The future of power*. Public Affairs.

Nye, J. (2019). Soft power and public diplomacy revisited. *The Hague Journal of Diplomacy, 14*(1–2), 7–20. https://doi.org/10.1163/1871191X-14101013

Nye, J. (2021). Soft power: The evolution of a concept. *Journal of Political Power, 14*(1), 196–208. https://doi.org/10.1080/2158379X.2021.1879572

Nye, J. (2023). *Soft power and great-power competition*. Springer. https://doi.org/10.1007/978-981-99-0714-4

Ördén, H., & Pamment, J. (2021, January). *What is so foreign about foreign influence operations?* Carnegie Endowment for International Peace. https://carnegieendowment.org/research/2021/01/what-is-so-foreign-about-foreign-influence-operations

Pamment, J. (2016). Digital diplomacy as transmedia engagement: Aligning theories of participatory culture with international advocacy campaigns. *New Media & Society, 18*(9), 2046–2062. https://doi.org/10.1177/1461444815577792

Pamment, J. (2020). Public diplomacy and development communication: Two sides of the same coin? In N. Snow & N. Cull (Eds.), *Routledge handbook of public diplomacy* (2nd ed., pp. 430–437). Routledge. https://doi.org/10.4324/9780429465543

Pamment, J., Smedberg, M., & Isaksson, E. (2025). National security and public diplomacy. In S. Aday (Ed.), *Handbook on public diplomacy* (pp. 449–461). Elgar. https://doi.org/10.4337/9781803926568.00048

Pingeot, L., & Pouliot, V. (2024). Agency is positionally distributed: Practice theory and (post)colonial structures. *International Studies Quarterly, 68*(2), 1–9. https://doi.org/10.1093/isq/sqae021

Porte, T. (2012). The impact of "intermestic" non-state actors on the conceptual framework of public diplomacy. *The Hague Journal of Diplomacy, 7*(4), 441–458. https://doi.org/10.1163/1871191X-12341241

Pouliot, V. (2025). Can IR hear? Grasping the global politics of languages. *Global Studies Quarterly, 5*(3), 1–12. https://doi.org/10.1093/isagsq/ksaf088

Riordan, S. (2005). Dialogue-based public diplomacy: A new foreign policy paradigm. In J. Melissen (Ed.), *The new public diplomacy* (pp. 180–195). Palgrave.

Rotberg, R. (2020). *Anticorruption*. MIT Press.

Rothstein, B. (2018). Fighting systemic corruption: The indirect strategy. *Daedalus, 147*(3), 35–49. https://doi.org/10.1162/DAED_a_00501

Santos, N. de A. e S. F. dos. (2021). Presidential public diplomacy 2.0: Seven lessons to prevent fire in cyberspace. *Journal of Public Diplomacy, 1*(1), 36–56. https://doi.org/10.23045/jpd.2021.1.1.036

Santos, N. de A. e. S. F. dos. (2025a). *Diplomacia pública anticorrupção: uma análise comparativa* (Doctoral thesis in International Relations). University of Lisbon.

Santos, N. de A. e S. F. dos. (2025b). City diplomacy. In S. Aday (Ed.), *Handbook on public diplomacy* (pp. 258–278). Elgar. https://doi.org/10.4337/9781803926568.00031

Scott-Smith, G. (2023). International exchanges. In E. Gilboa (Ed.), *A research agenda for public diplomacy* (pp. 251–266). Elgar. https://doi.org/10.4337/9781802207323.00025

Sevin, E. (2017). A multilayered approach to public diplomacy evaluation: Pathways of connection. *Politics & Policy, 45*(5), 879–901. https://doi.org/10.1111/polp.12227

Slaughter, A.-M. (2009). America's edge: Power in the networked society. *Foreign Affairs, 88*(1), 94–113.

Slaughter, A.-M. (2011, November 30). A new theory for the foreign-policy frontier: Collaborative power. *The Atlantic*. Retrieved February 6, 2026, from https://tinyurl.com/TheAtlantic2011

Sörensen, S., & Pamment, J. (2023). *Operationalising the framework for evaluating capability against information influence operations*. NATO.

Sparling, R. (2021). Debt, corruption, and state identity: Lessons from eighteenth-century political thought. *American Journal of Political Science, 67*(1), 89–100. https://doi.org/10.1111/ajps.12629

Treverton, G., & Jones, S. (2005). *Measuring national power*. RAND.

UN General Assembly. (2021, June 3). *Stressing no country is exempt from corruption* (Press release). Retrieved February 6, 2026, from https://press.un.org/en/2021/ga12330.doc.htm

Vukovic, S. (2020). The many faces of power in diplomatic negotiations. *SAIS Review of International Affairs, 40*(1), 45–57. https://doi.org/10.1353/sais.2020.0004

Walker, C. (2018). What is sharp power? *Journal of Democracy, 29*(3), 9–23.

Weber, M. (1978). In G. Roth & C. Wittich (Eds.), *Economy and society: An outline of interpretative sociology*. University of California Press.

Wendt, A. (1999). *Social theory of international politics*. Cambridge University Press.

White, S., Choo, Y., Zhelyazkova, D., & Brobbey, P. (2025). *Sabotaging peace: Corruption as threat to international peace and security*. Transparency International.

Wiseman, G. (2022). Expertise and politics in ministries of foreign affairs: The politician-diplomat nexus. In C. Lequesne (Ed.), *Ministries of foreign affairs in the world* (pp. 119–140). Brill. https://doi.org/10.1163/9789004505889_007

Wiseman, G. (2024). Digital diplomatic cultures. In C. Bjola & I. Manor (Eds.), *The Oxford handbook of digital diplomacy* (pp. 311–329). Oxford University Press. https://doi.org/10.1093/oxfordhb/9780192859198.013.17

Wiseman, G. (2025). The United States and fragmented multilateralism: Bookending a century of US ambivalence towards formal international organisations. *Third World Quarterly, 46*(15), 1857–1877. https://doi.org/10.1080/01436597.2025.2465519

Wu, Y. (2019). Recognizing and resisting China's evolving sharp power. *American Journal of Chinese Studies, 26*(2), 129–153. https://www.jstor.org/stable/45216268

Zaharna, R. (2013). Network purpose, network design: Dimensions of network and collaborative public diplomacy. In R. S. Zaharna, A. Fisher, & A. Arsenault (Eds.), *Relational, networked, and collaborative approaches to public diplomacy* (pp. 221–246). Routledge.

Zaharna, R. (2019). Culture, cultural diversity and humanity-centred diplomacies. In J. Melissen & J. Wang (Eds.), *Debating public diplomacy: Now and next* (pp. 117–133). Brill.

Zaharna, R. (2022). *Boundary spanners of humanity.* Oxford University Press. https://doi.org/10.1093/oso/9780190930271.001.0001

CHAPTER 3

Denmark: Projecting Integrity Through Economic Power and Global Aid Diplomacy

3.1 From Rot to Role Model: The Making of Getting to Denmark

Denmark's image as a place of political decay is immortalised in Shakespeare's oft-cited line "something is rotten in the state of Denmark" (Shakespeare, 2000, p. 58). In contemporary political and academic discourse, however, Denmark occupies a strikingly different symbolic position. The expression "getting to Denmark" (Fukuyama, 2011, p. 14) has come to signify a global benchmark of integrity, institutional quality, and social wellbeing. Popularised in debates on governance and state capacity, the phrase captures a transition from fragile and dysfunctional political orders to stable, high-trust, high-welfare societies, with Denmark frequently presented as a paradigmatic case.

This symbolic reversal is corroborated by global indices. Denmark consistently ranks among leading performers in assessments of governance quality (e.g. Chandler Good Government Index), social cohesion (e.g. Bertelsmann Stiftung Social Cohesion Radar), institutional trust (e.g. OECD Government at a Glance), rule of law (e.g. WJP Rule of Law Index), and regulatory effectiveness and innovation (e.g. WIPO Global Innovation Index). These rankings attest to the consolidation of a political and administrative system characterised by high levels of institutional trust, a robust welfare state, and consistently low levels of perceived

N. de A. e S. F. dos Santos, *Anticorruption Public Diplomacy*, Palgrave Macmillan Series in Global Public Diplomacy,
https://doi.org/10.1007/978-3-032-28668-0_3

corruption (Jensen, 2014). Taken together, they underpin Denmark's reputation as a model of functional governance and ethical statehood, often invoked as a reference point in discussions of democratic resilience.

Denmark's long-standing association with the global anticorruption norm is central to this reputation. The country ratified the OECD Anti-Bribery Convention in 2000 and the United Nations Convention against Corruption (UNCAC) in 2006. Denmark has maintained leading positions in major global anticorruption rankings over the past two decades, repeatedly topping Transparency International's Corruption Perceptions Index. It also achieved consistently high scores in the World Bank's Control of Corruption indicator, as well as in the Index of Public Integrity, developed by the European Research Centre for Anti-Corruption and State-Building.

Nevertheless, Denmark's integrity record is contested and periodically subject to scrutiny. The OECD and the Group of States against Corruption (GRECO) evaluation mechanisms have periodically highlighted weaknesses in Denmark's enforcement practices. Indicators focused on corporate and transnational corruption reveal areas of vulnerability, particularly within the private sector. The TRACE Bribery Risk Matrix shows variation over time, indicating continued exposure to corporate integrity risks. High-profile cases have challenged regulatory authorities and, more broadly, narratives of exceptionalism. Most notably, the 2018 Danske Bank money laundering scandal exposed significant regulatory and supervisory weaknesses (Bjerregaard & Kirchmaier, 2019). These episodes underscore that even highly institutionalised governance systems remain vulnerable to failure, suggesting that integrity is sustained through institutional responsiveness rather than reflecting institutional perfection.

Despite these developments, Denmark's international standing has remained quite stable, suggesting that integrity functions less as the absence of failure than as the capacity to manage scrutiny without reputational collapse. In comparative assessments of soft power and branding, the country is consistently ranked among the leading performers. Its placement in indices such as the Brand Finance Global Soft Power Index and the Good Country Index reflects the sustained appeal of its international image. Such reputational capital is particularly significant for small states, whose international influence derives less from material capabilities than from legitimacy, trust, and moral authority.

This combination of international recognition and underlying tension makes Denmark a compelling case for the study of anticorruption public diplomacy (ACPD), through which the analytical dimensions outlined in Chap. 2 can be examined empirically. Denmark is not merely a beneficiary of reputational capital; it actively communicates, supports, and diffuses anticorruption norms, thereby transforming domestic institutional credibility into diplomatic agency and normative influence. The shift from rot to role model, encapsulated in the notion of getting to Denmark, thus provides an entry point for examining how integrity became a defining feature of Denmark's international standing and how this standing is mobilised through public diplomacy.

Seen from this perspective, Denmark's integrity reputation cannot be understood in isolation from its welfare model, its collective self-understanding, and the strategic calculations of a small state operating in a competitive international environment. These interconnections form the analytical bridge to the next section, which examines the corporate and strategic foundations of Denmark's integrity reputation before turning to the historical construction of its anticorruption identity.

3.2 Welfare, Corporate and Type Identities, and Strategic Interests

Officially known as the Kingdom of Denmark (Danmarks Rige), the country is territorially and demographically small, with approximately 5.9 million inhabitants and a relatively small land area in continental Europe. Its maritime geography, alongside the territories of Greenland and the Faroe Islands, reinforces its outward-oriented strategic position. Its size belies a high degree of institutional consolidation and international embeddedness. As a constitutional monarchy under the 1953 Constitutional Act, Denmark combines parliamentary governance, legal rationality, and administrative professionalism within a predominantly civil-law framework. It has been a member of the European Union since 1973.

These institutional characteristics form part of Denmark's corporate identity, understood as the relatively stable attributes through which the state defines itself (Wendt, 1999). Central among these attributes is the welfare state (Andersen, 2008). The Danish welfare model rests on universal social protection, high taxation coupled with strong redistributive capacity, and a historically entrenched meritocratic public administration. The welfare state is not simply a policy arrangement but an organising principle of state–society relations. It fosters high levels of social trust, institutional legitimacy, and expectations of fairness in public life.

This welfare-based configuration has considerable historical depth. Denmark's institutional configuration consolidated rule-of-law governance and administrative accountability over centuries (Jensen, 2014). These developments embedded expectations of legality and accountability in Denmark's administrative culture.

The welfare state thus constitutes a foundational element of Denmark's type identity as a high-trust, rule-of-law, socially cohesive democracy. This positioning situates Denmark within a broader cluster of Nordic states characterised by equality, transparency, and institutional effectiveness (Andersen, 2008). Integrity is therefore embedded within this identity configuration, linked to meritocracy, universalism, and public-service professionalism rather than being treated as a discrete policy field.

At the same time, Denmark's self-understanding is inseparable from its condition as a small state. Small-state scholarship highlights structural constraints, including limited military capacity, dependence on trade, and vulnerability to external shocks (Keohane, 1969). Denmark's deeply globalised economy depends on stable international rules, predictable regulatory environments, and secure maritime routes. Its foreign and security policy prioritises safeguarding democracy, the market economy, and multilateral cooperation (Danish Institute for International Studies [DIIS], 2020; Rasmussen, 2023). In this context, anticorruption acquires strategic relevance. Corruption undermines precisely the conditions upon which Denmark depends: legal certainty, fair competition, and reliable governance in partner states.

For a small, trade-dependent country, promoting the rule of law abroad is not merely normative advocacy; it is also a rational strategy to protect economic interests and reduce systemic risk. Recent strategy documents make this convergence more explicit (Ministry of Foreign Affairs of Denmark [MFAD], 2026). The government emphasises the integration of foreign, security, trade, and development policy interests, underscoring that economic diplomacy and development assistance function as mutually reinforcing instruments. Within this framework, strengthening the rule of law and combating corruption are presented not only as normative commitments but also as mechanisms to secure stable markets and predictable investment environments.

As a small state with limited material capabilities, Denmark relies primarily on reputational credibility exercised through multilateral engagement, where normative authority functions as its principal currency. Alongside close collaboration with the North Atlantic Treaty Organization (NATO), Denmark maintains official development assistance (ODA) at approximately 0.7% of gross national income (GNI) (OECD, 2025), which serves both as a development instrument and as a diplomatic resource. Through development cooperation (MFAD, 2026), the country reinforces its embeddedness in institutional partnerships and rule-based networks.

The Arctic dimension, expressed through Greenland, and engagement in selected African states further illustrate the alignment between Denmark's normative self-conception and its strategic priorities. In these regions, governance stability intersects with Danish economic and security priorities, including rare minerals, maritime routes, and geopolitical competition (DIIS, 2020; MFAD, 2018, 2026; Security Policy Analysis Group, 2022). Supporting anticorruption frameworks in these contexts aligns values with interests: it reinforces Denmark's identity claims while protecting strategic assets.

Yet identity and interests do not align automatically. Denmark's exposure to corporate corruption risks, enforcement challenges identified in peer-review mechanisms of the OECD Working Group on Bribery and GRECO evaluations, and high-profile financial scandals reveal that the domestic integrity architecture is not flawless. Because Denmark's influence depends disproportionately on externally recognised legitimacy, safeguarding its international standing becomes not merely symbolic but strategically imperative. Safeguarding integrity therefore entails not the absence of shortcomings but the capacity to respond institutionally and sustain legitimacy.

Taken together, Denmark's welfare model, historical institutional development, and small-state condition converge to produce a distinctive configuration: integrity is simultaneously a moral commitment, a component of collective self-understanding, and a strategic resource. ACPD emerges at this intersection as the external articulation of Denmark's institutional self-conception and strategic calculus, translating identities into interests and interests into externally communicable objectives. These aims inform diplomatic practice while simultaneously serving material considerations related to trade, security, and geopolitical relevance. Within this configuration, Denmark's ACPD pursues three interrelated objectives: safeguarding reputational security, stabilising external economic environments, and reinforcing the rule-based international order upon which small states depend. This analytical configuration sets the stage for examining how Denmark performs and communicates this identity externally.

3.3 Constructing the Anticorruption Identity: History, Faith, and Law

This section addresses a specific question: How did integrity become a constitutive feature of Danish statehood? Promoting the global anticorruption norm is framed as a Danish priority (Udenrigsministeriet, 2019, p. 1), situated within broader security and economic interests (DIIS, 2020, pp. 10, 15). Yet Denmark's anticorruption identity is not merely a by-product of welfare state development or contemporary governance performance. It is the outcome of a long historical trajectory in which administrative reform, religious transformation, and constitutional evolution progressively entrenched anticorruption norms into the fabric of public authority.

Corruption in medieval Denmark was neither marginal nor unusual. The gradual reduction of corrupt practices unfolded over several centuries (Jensen, 2014) through evolving administrative practices and processes of socialisation (Adler-Nissen, 2023; Finnemore & Sikkink, 2001; Jensen, 2014; Wendt, 1999). Recurrent military conflicts, particularly with Sweden and Norway, and later during the Napoleonic Wars, placed sustained pressure on public finances. Expanding taxation generated demands for accountability from social and economic elites (Jensen, 2014). In responding to these pressures, Danish authorities did more than curb abuse: they helped redefine what counted as legitimate administration. Transparency and bureaucratic discipline gradually became associated with state strength rather than weakness. Integrity emerged less as an abstract moral ideal than as a governance norm embedded in processes of state consolidation.

The Protestant Reformation of 1536 played a constitutive role in this transformation of political authority. By integrating church and state authority, the Reformation reinforced moral accountability within governance structures, embedding an ethic of discipline, duty, and personal responsibility in public office (Jensen, 2014). Public office was increasingly framed as stewardship. This theological shift contributed to the moralisation of administrative conduct and to the consolidation of probity as an expectation of governance.

Seventeenth-century absolutism further strengthened rule-bound administration. Anticorruption measures, including meritocratic recruitment, sanctions for abuse of office, and protections for those reporting abuses of office, were not merely coercive tools (Jensen, 2014); they stabilised expectations. Bureaucratic discipline and corruption control became routinised practices, reinforcing the association between state authority and legal rationality.

The constitutional transition of 1849 deepened this normative evolution. Separation of powers, press freedom, and civil liberties normalised oversight and public scrutiny (Jensen, 2014). Integrity became anchored not only in administrative hierarchy but in participatory accountability. Over time, corruption ceased to be interpreted as a systemic condition and came to be treated as a deviation from an accepted norm.

This longue durée evolution illustrates how integrity became entrenched as a governing principle, embedded in Denmark's administrative routines and political expectations. By the twentieth century, anticorruption had become part of Denmark's taken-for-granted political culture, even if its practical implementation has continued to evolve over time.

Internationalisation of Identity

Denmark's engagement with the global anticorruption norm can be interpreted as an extension of this historically consolidated self-conception. Early ratification of the OECD Anti-Bribery Convention and the UNCAC, participation in GRECO, the Open Government Partnership (OGP), the Extractive Industries Transparency Initiative (EITI), and related initiatives, as well as sustained financial contributions to Transparency International, the United Nations Office on Drugs and Crime (UNODC), and related networks, signals more than compliance. They reflect behaviour coherent with Denmark's established self-conception, not only as a norm follower but also as a norm sustainer. This role, however, does not imply flawless enforcement; rather, it situates Denmark within a field of expectations against which its domestic performance is continuously assessed. It is enacted in international arenas that function as sites of recognition and validation. Financial support reinforces the institutional infrastructure of the global anticorruption norm and consolidates the networks through which it is reproduced.

Although anticorruption is framed as a foreign-policy priority aligned with broader security and economic interests (DIIS, 2020; Udenrigsministeriet, 2019), identity and interests are mutually constitutive (Wendt, 1999). Denmark's strategic engagement with anticorruption is shaped by its understanding of itself as a rule-of-law state. Acting in support of anticorruption efforts abroad reinforces that self-conception at home. International participation thus performs a dual function: it projects identity externally and stabilises it internally through recognition.

Tensions, Social Feedback, and Identity Maintenance

Yet Denmark's anticorruption identity is not without tensions. The role of norm sustainer coexists with structural vulnerabilities revealed through enforcement gaps and periodic scandals. Evaluations from the OECD Working Group on Bribery (2008, 2013, 2023) have repeatedly identified deficiencies, including weak enforcement of foreign bribery provisions, insufficient whistleblower protection (only fully implemented following the transposition of the European Whistleblower Directive in 2022), limited investigative resources for the State Prosecutor for Serious Economic and International Crime (SØIK), and the absence of a comprehensive national anticorruption strategy.

Transparency International classifies Denmark's enforcement of foreign bribery laws as "little or no enforcement" (Dell & McDevitt, 2022, p. 15). Cases such as the Maersk investigation in Brazil illustrate difficulties in domestic follow-up (OECD Working Group on Bribery, 2023). Independent assessments, including those by OGP, have raised additional concerns regarding political finance transparency, lobbying regulation, and institutional ownership (Eberholst, 2013; Hansen, 2019). Evaluations by the GRECO (2002, 2014, 2021) have pointed to the absence of revolving-door policies, the non-criminalisation of trading in influence, and weaknesses in sanction regimes. These recurring observations reveal a tension between symbolic leadership and enforcement capacity.

There are also gaps in political prioritisation of anticorruption. Several reforms appear to have been adopted primarily in response to external pressure rather than emerging from sustained domestic political initiative (Transparency International Danmark [TI Danmark], 2012, p. 38). Certain measures have fallen short of international standards, including insufficient transparency in ministerial activities (GRECO, 2021, p. 14) and delayed whistleblower protection (Heimann & Dell, 2010, p. 30).

Sanctions are frequently described as non-dissuasive (European Commission, 2014; TI Danmark, 2012), and investigative resources remain limited (OECD Working Group on Bribery, 2023). Notably, at the 18th International Anti-Corruption Conference in 2018, Transparency International Danmark (2020) raised doubts about Denmark's capacity to honour its anticorruption commitments.

High-profile scandals have further tested this identity, most notably the Danske Bank Estonian branch case. The UN Oil-for-Food case implicated at least fourteen Danish companies (Transparency International Danmark [TI Danmark], 2012). The KMD case involving a municipal chief executive and the Atea case involving officials at the MFAD (Udenrigsministeriet) and the state railways (Danske Statsbaner) exposed vulnerabilities in public procurement (TI Danmark, 2012; Breinstrup, 2019). Such cases exposed serious supervisory failures and triggered international scrutiny.

These tensions reveal a persistent gap between symbolic standing and enforcement practice, exposing the performative nature of integrity claims. Despite its top-tier performance in rule-of-law and governance rankings, Denmark's enforcement record in foreign bribery does not always match its symbolic standing. Public perception reflects this ambivalence. Although only 1–2% of citizens report direct contact with corruption, around 30% perceive an increase in corruption over time (Transparency International, 2004, 2013). Political parties, media, and the private sector are considered more vulnerable than the public administration itself.

These discrepancies function as mechanisms of social feedback (Finnemore & Sikkink, 2001). External evaluations, domestic criticism, and public perception contest the narrative of integrity and compel recalibration. Anticorruption identity is therefore not static; it is continuously reproduced, contested, and adjusted through processes of recognition and evaluation.

Identity as Ongoing Construction

Denmark's anticorruption architecture rests on multiple institutional pillars, including courts, prosecution authorities, police, parliament, ombudsman, media, civil society, and the private sector (TI Danmark, 2012). The system is widely regarded as institutionally robust in comparative perspective (TI Danmark, 2022), and the rule of law is consistently ranked among the strongest globally. Yet recurrent international recommendations highlight the need for stronger political prioritisation, improved transparency in political finance, clearer corporate liability frameworks, and enhanced investigative capacity.

Integrity in Denmark is best understood not as a static achievement, but as a historically embedded norm whose very entrenchment generates expectations of continuous institutional renewal. Its strength lies less in the absence of scandal than in the durability of institutional responses. This anticorruption identity forms the normative substratum upon which Denmark's ACPD operates. It provides the moral vocabulary, institutional credibility, and historical depth that enable Denmark to engage internationally on corruption issues with a degree of authority disproportionate to its size. In this sense, anticorruption is not merely a policy domain but a stabilised dimension of Danish political identity, structuring both domestic governance and international projection, and enabling Denmark to exercise influence beyond what its material capabilities alone would suggest.

3.4 Projecting Integrity: The External Articulation of Danish Identity

While welfare and rule-of-law governance constitute foundational pillars of Denmark's identity, public diplomacy provides the arena through which that identity is externally articulated. Denmark's international positioning is not constructed ex nihilo; it reflects the outward expression of historically embedded institutional features, selectively reframed for global audiences. As stated by Taksøe-Jensen, "Denmark's brand is a political and commercial asset to be utilised in promoting Danish interests and values abroad" (2016, p. 10). Integrity, transparency, equality, and a professional civil service are translated into narratives of reliability, fairness, and trustworthiness in international engagement.

Denmark's articulation of identity is structured around three interrelated elements: (1) reputational security; (2) relative normative coherence; and (3) multilateral activism. First, reputational security (Cull, 2024), understood as the strategic safeguarding of Denmark's credibility and international standing, operates as a strategic resource. It enhances Denmark's ability to shape perceptions and mobilise support in times of contestation. Denmark's established reputation reinforces its image as a benchmark of institutional integrity, enabling it to exercise influence disproportionate to its material capabilities. This reputational standing is not merely symbolic; it contributes to strategic resilience and strengthens Denmark's authority, enabling it to participate with recognised legitimacy in debates on governance reform, transparency, and democratic accountability.

Second, Denmark's international projection benefits from a relatively high degree of normative coherence, at the level of institutional repertoire and public narrative, rather than flawless practice or uniform effectiveness across all enforcement domains (Adler-Nissen, 2023; Finnemore & Sikkink, 2001; Wendt, 1999). Although not without domestic challenges, Denmark has successfully presented abroad a welfare-based governance model broadly aligned with its administrative traditions. Public diplomacy campaigns frequently highlight themes such as trust-based governance, integrity, transparency, green transition, social cohesion, gender equality, and sustainable development, which constitute explicit governmental priorities (MFAD, 2026). These themes resonate because they are anchored in long-standing institutional arrangements and reinforced by accumulated international recognition. The projection of integrity is therefore generally perceived as legitimate, even if it remains subject to scrutiny and ongoing adjustment.

Third, multilateral activism constitutes a significant feature of Denmark's diplomatic style and provides the operational framework through which Danish identity is enacted internationally (Keohane, 1969). Engagement through multilateral organisations enables Denmark to extend its influence beyond its relative material weight. In these arenas, Denmark consistently supports rule-of-law initiatives, anticorruption conventions, and governance standards. Multilateral engagement thus serves both as a structural necessity and as a site where Denmark performs its rule-based self-understanding.

Public diplomacy mechanisms reinforce this identity. Development cooperation, cultural diplomacy, international broadcasting, and digital communication channels disseminate narratives linking Danish welfare traditions to global governance debates. Anticorruption is framed not as a technocratic compliance issue but as a prerequisite for inclusive growth, democratic resilience, and sustainable development. By embedding anticorruption within broader themes of fairness and trust, Denmark presents integrity as a shared global good rather than a moralising prescription.

This external positioning is further sustained by Denmark's broader diplomatic resources. Economic stability, high levels of social development, strong governance indicators, digital connectivity, and technological innovation collectively reinforce the plausibility of Denmark's international messaging. Development assistance further enhances Denmark's diplomatic reach and embeds it within transnational policy networks. Cultural production, educational excellence, and advanced digital infrastructure contribute additional layers of influence. These material and immaterial assets constitute the resource base of Denmark's ACPD, enabling the conversion of institutional credibility into diplomatic influence.

Denmark's international projection of integrity is thus neither accidental nor purely rhetorical. It is rooted in institutional self-conception and operationalised through public diplomacy activities. Integrity structures both the content of Denmark's external messaging and the style of its diplomatic engagement.

At the same time, Denmark's projection strategy is calibrated rather than overtly assertive. The country rarely adopts a confrontational tone. Instead, it favours dialogue, partnership, and capacity-building approaches. This style reflects both small-state prudence and corporatist domestic traditions that privilege negotiation over coercion. In international anticorruption forums, Denmark tends to emphasise peer learning, institutional strengthening, and collaborative reform rather than naming-and-shaming.

Importantly, the projection of integrity also carries reputational risks. High expectations create vulnerability: any domestic scandal or regulatory failure may generate disproportionate international scrutiny. The external articulation of identity therefore requires continuous maintenance. Transparency in addressing financial scandals, responsiveness to OECD and GRECO evaluations, and visible corrective measures become part of reputational management. The credibility of this projection ultimately depends on visible accountability. This external positioning of integrity provides the operational background for the next section, which examines how Denmark's ACPD is enacted in practice.

3.5 Socialising Integrity: The Practice of Anticorruption Public Diplomacy

This section examines how that identity is enacted in practice through concrete diplomatic activities. These activities operate as mechanisms of international socialisation, translating normative commitments into interaction and institutional participation.

Drawing on the analytical framework introduced in Chap. 2, Denmark's ACPD can be understood as a repertoire of interrelated practices: listening, dialogical engagement, advocacy, cultural diplomacy, exchange, international broadcasting, action planning, evaluation, and institutional learning. These activities are coordinated across a wide range of agents, including ministries, enforcement authorities, diplomatic missions, and international partners. Together, they convert Denmark's institutional credibility and reputational capital into sustained normative influence.

The Danish ACPD is strongly characterised by embedded participation in rule-based governance networks. Integrity is performed through multilateral engagement, technical cooperation, and development partnerships. Activities are therefore relational rather than declaratory. They situate Denmark within dense transnational structures where norms are interpreted, contested, and reinforced. In this sense, ACPD activities are not merely diplomatic instruments; they are mechanisms of socialisation through which Denmark both reinforces and is shaped by the global anti-corruption norm.

Listening and Feedback Through Global Networks

Listening constitutes the diagnostic foundation of ACPD. In relational approaches to public diplomacy, influence presupposes attentiveness (Cull, 2019). For Denmark, listening is not episodic but institutionalised through four main methods: (1) participation in multilateral monitoring systems, (2) digital feedback mechanisms, (3) media monitoring, and (4) cooperation with transnational information networks.

One principal channel of listening operates through formal peer-review processes within organisations such as the OECD, the GRECO, and the OGP. These bodies generate periodic evaluation reports assessing Denmark's compliance with anticorruption conventions and governance standards (e.g. OECD Working Group on Bribery, 2013). The receipt and analysis of such reports involve coordination primarily by the Ministry of Justice, in collaboration with enforcement authorities, including the prosecution service and the police, as well as with the MFAD in externally facing dimensions.

Through these review mechanisms, Denmark does not merely receive criticism; it participates in a structured dialogue that has great potential to shape reform trajectories. The resources mobilised include adherence to international conventions, membership within established anticorruption networks, a legal framework enabling enforcement, and administrative infrastructure. The ideational dimension is threefold, involving the capacities to listen and to communicate (soft power), to mobilise institutional, legal, and economic resources (hard power), and to cooperate (collaborative power). These processes attribute international meaning to Denmark's openness and reinforce its image as a rule-based actor willing to subject itself to scrutiny.

Listening also occurs through digital and administrative channels. Online reporting platforms managed by Danish authorities allow individuals, including foreign stakeholders, to submit information relating to potential misconduct (e.g. Udenrigsministeriet, 2026). These mechanisms mobilise technological infrastructure, budgetary resources, and administrative expertise. They translate abstract commitments to transparency into accessible interfaces. Here, listening is both symbolic and practical: it demonstrates procedural openness while generating actionable intelligence.

Media monitoring and cooperation with international financial institutions, such as the World Bank's Integrity Vice Presidency, and integrity-monitoring bodies provide additional feedback channels. Information flows through investigative journalism, multilateral reports, and development cooperation networks (OECD Working Group on Bribery, 2023). Coordination varies depending on the issue area, but typically involves the MFAD in partnership with justice-sector authorities. These exchanges situate Denmark within a transnational ecosystem of information circulation, where standing is continuously assessed and recalibrated.

Importantly, listening in the Danish ACPD context is neither passive nor defensive. It constitutes a strategic resource. By institutionalising mechanisms for feedback and by responding—sometimes gradually, sometimes under pressure—to recommendations from international bodies, Denmark transforms potential vulnerability into evidence of accountability. The representative authority of Danish actors participating in these processes derives from multiple sources: legal competences assigned under domestic law, adherence to international conventions, contractual arrangements in development cooperation, or invitations extended within multilateral forums. Through these channels, listening becomes a mechanism of relational legitimacy.

Listening exemplifies how activities operationalise identities and interests. Denmark's self-understanding as a rule-of-law state generates a predisposition towards compliance and review. Its strategic interest in reputational security reinforces responsiveness. The outcome is a pattern of engagement in which integrity is not simply projected outward but continuously negotiated through structured feedback. Listening thus anchors the broader repertoire of ACPD activities, enabling them to unfold within an informed and reflexive framework.

Dialogue, Cooperation, and Financial Leverage

Dialogue constitutes one of the most visible and structurally significant activities of Denmark's ACPD. Rather than projecting unilateral narratives, Denmark operates through dialogical engagement embedded in international networks, forums, and financial partnerships. This engagement unfolds through five interrelated modalities: (1) responses to requests from international institutions; (2) multilateral cooperation; (3) bilateral cooperation; (4) financial support to partner-country initiatives; and (5) financial contributions to international anticorruption institutions.

A clear illustration of this responsive modality is the revision of the manual on small facilitation payments following recommendations from the OECD Working Group on Bribery (2013). Coordinated by the Ministry of Justice, this action demonstrates the conversion of normative pressure into reputational reinforcement. The resources mobilised included national anticorruption policy and the membership of the OECD Anti-Bribery Convention. These acquired international significance through soft and collaborative power capabilities, notably listening, communicative alignment, and institutional cooperation. More than technical compliance, the revision constituted a reaffirmation of Denmark's commitment to international standards.

Multilateral cooperation represents a structurally broader dimension of dialogical engagement. Denmark's participation in anti-money laundering efforts within the framework of the Financial Action Task Force (FATF) exemplifies this modality (TI Danmark, 2020). Here, anticorruption resources include anti-money laundering legislation, enforcement structures, and FATF membership. State agents such as the Ministry of Industry, Business and Financial Affairs operate alongside non state agents, including Danish banks, while interacting with international partners and foreign financial institutions operating in Denmark. Through negotiation, peer review, and cooperative compliance, Denmark transforms domestic regulatory architecture into a resource of international anticorruption credibility. Authority is exercised primarily through soft and collaborative power, via standard-setting, persuasion, coordination, and networked governance.

Regarding bilateral cooperation, a case in point is the technical assistance to China aimed at strengthening the rule of law (Udenrigsministeriet, 2017). This case demonstrates how values such as integrity and administrative accountability are translated into diplomatic instruments. Memoranda of understanding and policy dialogues functioned as formal resources, while the MFAD, the Danish International Development Agency (DANIDA), and the Ombudsman served as state representatives. On the Chinese side, the Ministry of Supervision and the national Ombudsman acted as institutional counterparts. In this configuration, soft power operates through influence, expertise, and communicative exchange, embedding Danish administrative practices within a shared reform narrative.

Dialogue, however, is not limited to verbal or institutional exchange. It frequently involves financial leverage. Two distinct situations require budgetary allocation for international anticorruption engagement: targeted assistance to partner countries and financial contributions to international norm entrepreneurs. In the first case, the financial assistance is provided to countries aligned with its development and governance priorities, including Ukraine, Afghanistan, Indonesia, and Kenya. For example, in 2019 DANIDA funded a corruption study in collaboration with Ukraine's anticorruption agency (Udenrigsministeriet, 2020). Such interventions mobilise hard power capabilities, specifically incentivising and intervening capacities, by linking financial resources to governance reforms. At the same time, they strengthen Denmark's strategic presence within reform processes.

The second case concerns Denmark's financial contributions to international anticorruption institutions and norm entrepreneurs. According to the MFAD's anticorruption programme (Udenrigsministeriet, 2019, pp. 33–36), Danish funding supports organisations such as the UNCAC Coalition, the U4 Anti-Corruption Resource Centre, the OGP, the UNODC, Transparency International, the EITI, the Maritime Anti-Corruption Network, the initiative Publish What You Pay, and the Global Anti-Corruption Consortium. These institutions produce reports, monitor treaty compliance, and shape global anticorruption benchmarks. Even modest financial support may, under certain conditions, generate relational asymmetries or expectations of reciprocity, potentially moderating overt criticism (TI Danmark, 2012, pp. 163–171). These dynamics do not necessarily imply deliberate influence or strategic manipulation; rather, they may emerge as structural effects of sustained donor–recipient relationships and networked forms of cooperation. Notably, a report commissioned by the OECD observed the alignment of Transparency International's priorities with those of its donors (Norwegian Agency for Development Cooperation [NORAD], 2010, p. 21). In such contexts, financial leverage operates at the boundary between hard and sharp power. While formally legitimate and development-oriented, funding may also activate the norms of reciprocity (Mauss, 2002), thereby creating symbolic bonds between funders and beneficiaries.

Denmark continues to rank among the least corrupt countries globally despite recurring integrity controversies and enforcement gaps, particularly in transnational corporate cases. Dialogic responsiveness, networked cooperation, and strategic funding contribute to Denmark's reputational resilience.

Regarding agency, dialogical engagement is primarily conducted by state agents, notably DANIDA and the MFAD, whose representative authority derives from their institutional position within the Danish state apparatus. However, non state actors occasionally play a role. For instance, ongoing international cooperation on asset recovery involves the Anti-Money Laundering Group of the Danish Bankers' Association and the Danish Bar Association, under coordination from the Ministry of Industry. In such cases, representative authority stems from domestic legislation and regulatory mandates. Otherwise, international counterparts derive their representative authority from formal agreements, memoranda of understanding, participation in international networks, and acceptance of financial contributions. Denmark's dialogical engagement thus operates through layered institutional legitimacy, network embeddedness, and financial interdependence.

In sum, through responsive norm adaptation, multilateral and bilateral collaboration, and strategic funding, Denmark mobilises soft, collaborative, and hard power capabilities in mutually reinforcing ways. Dialogue thus becomes a structured diplomatic practice through which norms, resources, and reputation circulate within institutionalised governance networks.

Advocacy and the Global Circulation of Best Practice

If listening anchors Denmark's ACPD in attentiveness and dialogue situates it within relational networks, advocacy constitutes its outward articulation. In this context, advocacy operates through the strategic circulation of policies, practices, research, and standards presented as transferable governance models. Denmark's ACPD features five modalities: (1) presenting national policies as best practices; (2) communicating domestic legal interpretations internationally; (3) supporting international anticorruption campaigns; (4) commissioning research and policy reports; and (5) institutionalising due diligence as a transnational compliance norm.

Recognition of national initiatives as best practices frequently occurs within international monitoring frameworks. One illustrative case is the acknowledgement by the UNODC of Denmark's National Anti-Corruption Forum, established by the Ministry of Justice to strengthen inter-institutional coordination (UNODC, 2016). Through participation in UNCAC review mechanisms, Denmark mobilised narrative resources, official statements, and institutional transparency to position this forum as an example of cooperative governance. The Ministry of Justice, acting within its legally defined mandate, coordinated the initiative, while participation extended to other state bodies, civil-society representatives, private-sector actors, and international experts invited during monitoring visits. Here, advocacy emerged not from unilateral proclamation but from negotiated recognition within multilateral structures. Collaborative power operated through negotiation and knowledge-sharing, while soft power was exercised through communication and argumentation.

An illustration of the strategic communication of domestic policy interpretations is the international dissemination of the Ministry of Justice's note clarifying that small facilitation payments should be treated as bribery (UNODC, 2016). By publicly articulating this stance, Denmark projected a restrictive interpretation aligned with international standards, thereby contributing to the interpretation and operationalisation of contested norms. The resources mobilised included legal doctrine, policy documents, and communication platforms. The capability exercised was primarily soft power, shaping expectations through persuasion and example, while the Ministry's representative authority derived from its institutional competence within the Danish legal order.

Advocacy also operates through international anticorruption campaigns, such as the Fight Against Facilitation Payments Initiative (Dell &

McDevitt, 2018). In these cases, the MFAD, often in partnership with private-sector organisations such as the Confederation of Danish Industry, mobilises economic resources to enable transnational campaigns. Financial contributions activate hard power capacities while remaining embedded in collaborative governance structures operating in the realm of collaborative power. Funding thus becomes a material and symbolic resource, signalling commitment while strengthening institutional networks.

The commissioning of research and policy reports further illustrates the interplay between advocacy and credibility. Because certain messages carry greater legitimacy when articulated by non state actors (Cull, 2019), Denmark frequently engages external expertise. For example, the Raoul Wallenberg Institute (2018), contracted by Denmark, produced a report on the relationship between corruption and human rights, seeking to advance a human rights-based approach to anticorruption globally. The MFAD provides economic resources and strategic direction, while the research institution contributes epistemic authority. Representative links are established through formal contracts and institutional mandates. The resulting publications circulate internationally, reinforcing specific interpretative frames within the global anticorruption discourse.

Finally, advocacy is embedded in the practice of due diligence. Denmark's export credit agency, EKF, applies rigorous anticorruption screening procedures to companies it finances, whether Danish firms operating abroad or foreign firms seeking access to Danish markets (OECD Working Group on Bribery, 2023). Due diligence functions not merely as internal risk management but as a mechanism for external norm diffusion. Through contractual requirements and compliance assessments, Denmark promotes anticorruption standards among private-sector actors transnationally. The principal resources mobilised are legal frameworks, technical expertise, and regulatory infrastructure. Influence operates through a combination of soft and hard power, shaping behaviour through contractual requirements, compliance assessments, and conditional engagement, while the representative authority of involved agents derives from statutory and contractual mandates.

Across these modalities, advocacy within Danish ACPD is characterised by moderation and institutional embeddedness. Rather than positioning itself as a moral adjudicator, Denmark promotes norms through example, funding, research partnerships, and regulatory practice. Advocacy thus complements listening and dialogical engagement by advancing specific interpretations of integrity within multilateral legitimacy. Through the circulation of policies, expertise, and financial resources, Denmark contributes to reinforcing and disseminating global anticorruption standards, supporting both the diffusion of best practice and the stabilisation of its own reputational authority.

Cultural and Educational Diplomacy as Ethical Performance

Cultural and educational diplomacy make integrity visible through public enactment. In this domain, anticorruption is advanced through symbolic staging, professional training, and institutional demonstration. Integrity becomes embodied practice. Danish anticorruption cultural diplomacy operates primarily through two modalities: (1) hosting international conferences and (2) organising specialised training programmes. Both function as arenas in which Denmark performs its ethical self-understanding before transnational audiences. They mobilise budgetary resources, policy expertise, institutional transparency, and network embeddedness, while generating influence primarily through soft and collaborative power, supported by organisational and financial resources. Soft power operates through narrative framing, hard power through organisational and financial capacity, and collaborative power through convening and knowledge-sharing.

A prominent example is the International Anti-Corruption Conference held in Copenhagen in 2018 (TI Danmark, 2020). Coordinated by the MFAD, the event convened state institutions, including the Digitalisation Agency, the Ministry of Health, and the Auditor General, alongside civil society, private-sector representatives, and international norm entrepreneurs such as Transparency International, the OGP, and GRECO. The conference functioned as a performative site of ethical articulation. Denmark did not merely advocate anticorruption norms; it displayed its administrative coordination, digital governance practices, and inter-institutional cooperation before a global audience. Representative authority derived from institutional mandates in the case of state agents and from formal invitation or accreditation for other participants. Domestic governance arrangements thus became internationally legible practice.

Educational diplomacy extends this logic through capacity-building. The Investment Fund for Developing Countries, IFU, for example, provides anticorruption training to Danish companies operating abroad and to their suppliers and subsidiaries (OECD Working Group on Bribery, 2013), in cooperation with institutions such as the United Nations Global

Compact. These programmes translate national compliance standards into transnational corporate routines. Resources here also include due diligence frameworks and technical expertise rooted in Danish anticorruption policy. Influence operates primarily through soft power (professional socialisation and norm internalisation), supported by financial conditionality and compliance requirements embedded in contractual arrangements (hard power). Authority stems from statutory mandates for public agencies and contractual arrangements for private-sector and international partners.

Cultural and educational diplomacy therefore differ from advocacy in tone and method. Rather than asserting normative leadership, Denmark demonstrates administrative practice. Conferences create temporary communities of governance; training programmes cultivate longer-term professional networks. Through these encounters, integrity is not proclaimed but enacted. In this sense, cultural and educational diplomacy function as ethical performance. By making institutional competence visible and collaborative commitment tangible, Denmark reinforces its normative authority through practice rather than proclamation.

Exchange, Training, and Institutional Partnerships

Exchanges consolidate networks, reinforce professional norms, and enable mutual learning within transnational governance structures. Danish anticorruption exchange unfolds through three principal modalities: (1) hosting international monitoring and assessment visits, (2) membership in anticorruption networks, and (3) participation in training programmes abroad.

In the first case, technical visits conducted within the frameworks of the OECD Anti-Bribery Convention or the UNCAC bring foreign experts and peer reviewers into direct contact with Danish institutions. A visit undertaken in June 2015 for UNCAC monitoring (UNODC, 2017) exemplifies how such exchanges operate. These encounters mobilise anticorruption legislation, national anticorruption institutions, official narratives, and administrative practice as demonstrable resources. Budgetary allocations and institutional infrastructure enable the practical organisation of the visit, while Denmark's membership in UNCAC situates the interaction within an established normative framework. The exchange is not merely procedural. It functions as reciprocal scrutiny and mutual calibration. Hard power enables participation through financial and organisational capacity; soft power operates through communication and persuasion; collaborative power emerges through engagement, negotiation, and peer review. Hosting becomes a mechanism of reputational consolidation, but also of exposure to external assessment.

An example of the second is Denmark's participation in the OGP (Digitaliseringsstyrelsen, 2019). Through this membership, Denmark mobilises values of openness, digital governance expertise, anticorruption legislation, and administrative competence. Soft power shapes perceptions through communicative framing and policy example, while collaborative power operates through negotiation, benchmarking, and shared action plans. Network participation transforms domestic policy into part of a broader transnational reform architecture.

The third modality concerns outward participation in training programmes and professional exchanges. Danish law enforcement officials' engagement in international training courses, such as those organised by the International Centre for Parliamentary Studies in London (OECD Working Group on Bribery, 2023), illustrates this dimension. Such initiatives rely on budgetary support and institutional expertise derived from national anticorruption frameworks. They facilitate professional socialisation, comparative learning, and policy diffusion. Hard power enables participation through funding, while soft power shapes influence through professional credibility and expertise.

Across these modalities, exchange operates as a form of institutional partnership rather than unilateral projection. State agents participate by virtue of their statutory mandates, while non state and international participants derive representative authority from invitations, network membership, or formal agreements. International institutions contribute to shaping expectations within these shared spaces. Such practices reinforce Denmark's embeddedness in the global anticorruption norm. They sustain communities of practice in which standards are interpreted, contested, refined, and reproduced. Denmark reinforces its position through participation, reciprocity, and institutional continuity. In doing so, it strengthens both the diffusion of anticorruption norms and the resilience of its own reputational standing.

Broadcasting Integrity Through Digital Platforms

Digital broadcasting extends the Danish anticorruption narrative beyond institutional forums. Through online publication and awareness platforms,

Denmark translates domestic standards into accessible guidance for global audiences. Two principal mechanisms structure this activity: (1) the publication of anticorruption manuals and (2) the development of digital awareness platforms.

The publication of the Prevent Corruption (Undgå korruption) manual by the Ministry of Justice (OECD Working Group on Bribery, 2013) illustrates the first mechanism. Made publicly available online, the manual codifies Danish anticorruption legislation and compliance expectations in a format directed at companies operating internationally. The resources mobilised include technical legal expertise, national anticorruption policy frameworks, and the institutional authority of justice-sector bodies. Under the coordination of the Ministry of Justice, these elements are translated into influence through communicative and persuasive capacities associated with soft power. The initiative involved multiple state institutions, including the police, courts, and local authorities, whose representative authority derives from their statutory competences. The intended audiences were Danish companies operating abroad and foreign firms conducting business in Denmark. Broadcasting here functions as preventive diplomacy: by clarifying standards and expectations, Denmark projects regulatory coherence while reducing ambiguity in transnational commercial environments.

The second mechanism is exemplified by the digital platform Corporate Social Responsibility Compass (CSR-Kompasset), developed by the Ministry of Industry, Business and Financial Affairs in cooperation with DANIDA (OECD Working Group on Bribery, 2013). Designed to support companies in identifying and mitigating corruption risks, the platform combines policy guidance, practical tools, and interactive resources. Budgetary allocations, anticorruption frameworks, and digital competences constitute the principal resources underpinning the initiative. Influence operates through a hybrid of hard and soft power. Hard power is reflected in the enabling infrastructure, including financial investment, regulatory expectation, and technical capacity. Soft power emerges through guidance, inspiration, and normative framing. Non state agents include private companies, the Confederation of Danish Industry, and the Danish Institute for Human Rights, while international engagement occurs through foreign firms interacting with the platform. Representative authority arises from institutional mandates, formal partnerships, and voluntary participation in the digital interface.

Broadcasting integrity through digital platforms renders Danish anti-corruption standards visible, intelligible, and operational to transnational agents. Denmark frames integrity as practical governance guidance. In doing so, digital broadcasting reinforces reputational credibility while embedding anticorruption norms within everyday corporate and administrative routines.

Strategising Integrity: Planning, Evaluation, and Institutional Learning

If listening, dialogue, advocacy, exchange, and broadcasting constitute the outward-facing practices of Denmark's ACPD, strategic planning and evaluation anchor these activities within an internal architecture of coordination and learning. Although situated within the domestic administrative sphere, these complementary practices are central to the coherence and sustainability of ACPD. They structure objectives, align resources, and enable reflexive adjustment over time.

A pivotal development occurred with the adoption of the Anticorruption Programme (Anti-korruptionsprogram) in 2018. Aligned with DANIDA's international assistance strategy and the 2030 Agenda, the programme focuses less on domestic corruption control and more on strengthening Denmark's anticorruption engagement through diplomatic channels. Its stated objective captures this orientation: "To enhance the effectiveness of anti-corruption efforts through strengthened cooperation, advocacy, monitoring and research in key organisations and networks at national and international level" (Udenrigsministeriet, 2019, p. 37). Importantly, the design, coordination, and evaluation of the programme remain firmly within state authority, led by the MFAD, and supported by other state agents acting within their institutional mandates. International partners implement many of the funded actions, but strategic oversight and evaluative interpretation remain domestically anchored.

The programme integrates three interrelated components: action planning, evaluation, and institutional learning. Action planning provides strategic direction, identifying priority organisations, networks, and thematic areas for engagement. It articulates five operational guidelines derived from accumulated experience: cooperation and strategic partnerships as catalysts for agency engagement; deterrence; positive incentives; mobilisation of social movements and collaborative networks; and sector-specific focus as a means of stimulating participation (Udenrigsministeriet, 2019, pp. 6–7). These guidelines translate lessons learned into structured diplomatic orientation.

Led by the MFAD, assessment mechanisms rely primarily on qualitative analysis of compliance with international standards. Indicators include implementation of UNCAC provisions, adoption of anticorruption legislation, and adherence to EITI requirements by partner states. Rather than functioning as external conditionality alone, the Danish evaluation in ACPD operates as a feedback mechanism, enabling recalibration of funding priorities and diplomatic engagement.

Institutional learning completes the cycle. Lessons drawn from monitoring reports, peer reviews, and programme assessments inform subsequent planning phases. In this sense, ACPD is institutionalised as an iterative process rather than a static policy instrument.

Through this planning architecture, Denmark's ACPD acquires durability and coherence. Strategic programming transforms dispersed activities into an integrated diplomatic posture. Evaluation and learning ensure adaptability. Integrity, in this sense, is not only projected or performed; it is systematically organised, monitored, and recalibrated. The result is a model of ACPD that combines normative commitment with administrative reflexivity, reinforcing both international influence and domestic institutional consistency.

3.6 Mapping Denmark's Anticorruption Public Diplomacy

The preceding sections have examined Denmark's ACPD through its concrete practices. This section consolidates those findings by mapping the architecture that underpins them. The aim here is analytical: to identify the actors, coordination patterns, resource base, and power configurations that structure the coherence of Denmark's ACPD.

Agents, Representational Ties, and Coordination

Denmark's ACPD involves a layered constellation of agents operating across state, non state, and international levels. State agents occupy the central coordinating role. The MFAD functions as the primary strategic hub, particularly in action planning, financial allocation, and evaluation. The Ministry of Justice, SØIK, the police, DANIDA, EKF, IFU, and relevant sectoral ministries participate according to their statutory competences. Their representational ties derive from their formal position within the Danish legal and administrative order, which grants them the mandate to act internationally on matters of governance and compliance.

Non state domestic agents include private firms, banks, business associations, consultancies, academic institutions, and civil society organisations such as Transparency International Danmark and the Danish Institute for Human Rights. Their participation is not autonomous representation of the Danish state, but mediated engagement. Representational ties are established through official invitations, cooperation agreements, legal mandates, contractual relationships, or membership in international networks. In certain cases, such as anti-money laundering compliance, participation stems directly from statutory obligations.

International agents are present across all ACPD activities. They include international organisations and norm entrepreneurs, namely the OECD, the UNODC, GRECO, Transparency International, the EITI, and the OGP, as well as partner governments, foreign regulatory authorities, and transnational corporations. Their representative authority derives from convention membership, monitoring mandates, network participation, or bilateral agreements. In monitoring visits, peer reviews, and international conferences, they act simultaneously as evaluators, interlocutors, and co-producers of norms.

Each ACPD initiative is coordinated by a Danish state authority, reinforcing the centrality of the state in defining objectives and allocating resources. Even when non state or international agents implement activities, strategic direction and oversight remain domestically anchored. This confirms that Denmark's ACPD is plural in participation but state-centred in coordination.

Activities and Governance Architecture

Denmark's ACPD did not emerge fully formed. Following its accession to the OECD and United Nations anticorruption conventions in the early 2000s, the country engaged in a range of activities that were largely reactive and dispersed across institutions. A decisive shift occurred in 2018, when the MFAD formalised these practices through the Anticorruption Programme (Udenrigsministeriet, 2019). This programme marked the transition from ad hoc participation to structured coordination, embedding ACPD within Denmark's broader foreign, development, and multilateral strategies.

The programme articulated priorities, funding mechanisms, and procedures for evaluation and institutional learning, thereby consolidating an increasingly institutionalised approach. ACPD ceased to be a collection of isolated engagements and became a programmatically anchored diplomatic field. The governance architecture that emerged integrates both core and complementary activities. Core activities, namely listening, dialogical engagement, advocacy, cultural and educational diplomacy, exchange, and digital broadcasting, constitute the outward-facing repertoire. Complementary activities, including strategic planning, evaluation, and institutional learning, provide coherence, continuity, and reflexive adjustment.

Within this architecture, financial instruments occupy a structuring role, linking activities across Denmark's ACPD architecture. The programme prioritises economically based initiatives, positioning funding and contributions to international organisations as a central modality of engagement. Contributions to entities such as the UNCAC Coalition, UNODC, EITI, OGP, and Transparency International function not merely as development assistance but as instruments of network consolidation, norm reinforcement, and diplomatic positioning (Udenrigsministeriet, 2019), supporting organisations that act as important norm entrepreneurs within the global anticorruption regime. Financial resources likewise underpin digital platforms, training initiatives, research sponsorship, advocacy campaigns, and participation in international monitoring processes.

At the same time, the governance architecture reveals persistent tensions. Despite structured planning and sustained financial engagement, several domestic reforms central to the collective anticorruption norm, such as regulations on revolving doors, lobbying transparency, whistleblower protection, and enforcement of foreign bribery, were implemented primarily in response to sustained external pressure. Transparency International's recurrent classification of Denmark as demonstrating "little or no enforcement" (Dell & McDevitt, 2022, p. 15) in foreign bribery cases underscores a gap between reputational leadership and enforcement practice.

This tension does not invalidate Denmark's ACPD; rather, it reveals the layered nature of its development. While Denmark has consolidated an internationally recognised anticorruption identity through strategic programming and multilateral engagement, domestic adaptation has at times lagged behind normative expectations, producing occasional gaps between projected identity and regulatory implementation. The governance architecture therefore reflects both institutional consolidation and uneven internalisation.

Denmark's ACPD is thus best understood as a structured but asymmetrical configuration. It combines coordinated planning, sustained financial engagement, and network participation with uneven domestic responsiveness. This duality shapes the operational logic of ACPD and conditions the ways in which Denmark's resources are translated into influence in the context of the global anticorruption norm.

The Resource Base of Danish Anticorruption Public Diplomacy

Denmark's ACPD rests on a diversified yet structured resource base. Although the country is small in territorial and demographic terms, it possesses significant economic capacity. With high GDP per capita and sustained commitments to ODA, amounting to approximately 0.7% of GNI, Denmark ranks among the leading donors within the OECD Development Assistance Committee. Denmark's financial strength provides the enabling infrastructure for ACPD, sustaining contributions to institutions, research centres, and governance networks. Economic capacity does not operate in isolation. In certain contexts, financial engagement generates relational asymmetries or expectations of reciprocity, shaping the dynamics of international interaction. These dynamics should not necessarily be interpreted as deliberate influence or strategic manipulation; rather, they may emerge as structural effects of sustained donor–recipient relationships and networked forms of cooperation. Funding may consolidate networks, reinforce partnerships, and, at times, create subtle dependencies. Economic strength thus functions not merely as material capability but as relational capital within the global anticorruption norm.

Anticorruption policies form a second and equally decisive pillar. These encompass legislation, institutional arrangements, monitoring mechanisms, adherence to international conventions, due diligence requirements, and administrative guidelines. Such policies serve both as domestic governance instruments and as transferable normative frameworks. Many of these measures were incorporated into Denmark's political identity through processes of international norm internalisation. Once mobilised through public diplomacy, they simultaneously reinforce the collective anticorruption norm, illustrating the reciprocal relationship between identity formation and norm diffusion.

A deeper normative foundation derives from anticorruption culture and values, such as openness, integrity, meritocracy, and administrative professionalism. These values underpin bilateral cooperation, advocacy initiatives, and exchange programmes, contributing to the socialisation of governance standards beyond Denmark's borders. Technology complements this normative infrastructure, particularly in listening and digital broadcasting activities, where online reporting platforms and compliance tools translate institutional commitments into accessible instruments.

Finally, network embeddedness is indispensable. Membership in UNCAC, the OECD Anti-Bribery Convention, FATF, OGP, EITI, and related initiatives provides legitimacy, channels of influence, and arenas for mutual recognition. These network nodes operate as conduits through which Denmark both internalises and projects anticorruption norms.

Although five resource categories are identifiable, namely economic strength, anticorruption policies, culture and values, technology, and network membership, two pillars are particularly decisive: economic capability and normative-policy frameworks. The former enables sustained engagement; the latter provides substantive legitimacy. Together, they transform Denmark's small-state condition into a form of normative capital, underpinning its ACPD.

Smart Power and the Politics of Influence

Denmark's ACPD operates through a calibrated combination of power styles. Smart power, in this context, refers not simply to the coexistence of soft and hard instruments, but to the strategic alignment of material and immaterial resources with ideational capacities that render them meaningful in international arenas. Resources do not automatically generate outcomes; they acquire diplomatic effect only when translated into specific modalities of influence.

Hard power is most visible in the enabling function of economic capacity. Financial assistance, infrastructure provision, and budgetary allocations support governance reforms, international conferences, digital tools, and multilateral engagement. Through these mechanisms, economic resources are endowed with anticorruption meaning and transformed into instruments of diplomatic reach.

Sharp power operates where financial relationships generate asymmetries or expectations of reciprocity. Regular contributions to international organisations and norm entrepreneurs may foster relational dependencies that subtly shape discursive environments. While formally embedded within legitimate development cooperation, such dynamics may contribute to reputational resilience and, under certain circumstances, moderate overt criticism. These dynamics do not necessarily imply deliberate influence or strategic manipulation; rather, they may emerge as structural effects of sustained donor–recipient relationships and networked forms of cooperation. Economic leverage may operate simultaneously as enablement and constraint.

Soft power underpins communicative and reputational influence. Through listening, policy dissemination, bilateral cooperation, training, and example-setting, Denmark shapes expectations and frames normative debates. Influence is exercised through persuasion, expertise, and credibility rather than coercion.

Collaborative power reflects Denmark's embeddedness within multilateral frameworks. Dialogue, peer review, negotiation, and shared action plans illustrate influence exercised through co-production. Rather than imposing standards, Denmark participates in processes that collectively interpret and refine them.

Across these modalities, the crucial mechanism is conversion. Economic strength, policy frameworks, cultural values, technological capacity, and network membership only become diplomatically consequential when combined with enabling, constraining, persuasive, or collaborative capacities. Even where domestic enforcement performance is contested, the strategic orchestration of these power styles allows Denmark to sustain a recognised position regarding the global anticorruption norm. The Danish case thus illustrates how a small state can transform institutional credibility, financial capacity, and network embeddedness into structured influence. Smart power functions as the integrative logic through which resources, identities, and strategic interests converge. ACPD becomes not merely a normative commitment but also a strategic instrument within Denmark's broader foreign policy architecture.

3.7 Integrity as Strategy: Reputational Power and National Interests

This chapter has treated Denmark not simply as a high-performing governance system, but as a case in which integrity is converted into a strategic asset with diplomatic yield. The symbolic move from Shakespeare's rotten Denmark to the contemporary metaphor of getting to Denmark captures this conversion: integrity becomes legible internationally as a stabilised national attribute and therefore as a source of diplomatic leverage. Yet the Danish case also shows that such standing is not synonymous with institutional perfection. While Denmark's record remains subject to scrutiny, its international standing depends on the capacity to sustain credibility within recognised evaluative arenas.

The core finding is that Denmark's anticorruption identity gains strategic value precisely because it is embedded at the intersection of identity and interest. Historically consolidated rule-of-law expectations and welfare state legitimacy provide the normative substrate; contemporary strategic incentives provide the impetus for outward projection. In a small, trade-dependent state, anticorruption is not merely an ethical signal but a means of securing predictability in external environments, reducing exposure to governance risk, protecting fair competition, and reinforcing the rule-based arrangements upon which Danish prosperity and security depend. This helps explain why the promotion of anticorruption is articulated as a foreign policy priority: it is aligned with democratic commitments and multilateralism, but also with the protection of national resilience in an increasingly contested international order. These objectives operate across temporal horizons: immediate reputational maintenance, medium-term economic stabilisation, and long-term reinforcement of rule-based multilateralism.

A distinctive feature of the Danish case lies in the structural weight of economic capacity in sustaining this projection. Financial strength does not function merely as background enabler of engagement; it operates as an infrastructural pillar of the global anticorruption norm itself. Through sustained contributions to international organisations, monitoring mechanisms, research centres, advocacy coalitions, and sector-specific initiatives, Denmark supports norm entrepreneurs that produce standards, benchmarks, reports, and evaluative frameworks for the global anticorruption regime. In doing so, it reinforces the institutional architecture within which anticorruption norms are interpreted and disseminated. Economic power thus helps sustain norm entrepreneurship. Rather than acting as a norm entrepreneur itself, Denmark primarily functions as a norm sustainer, reinforcing the institutional environment through which anticorruption standards are reproduced and diffused. The support provided to transnational actors does not amount to overt coercion, yet it embeds Denmark within networks of reciprocity, recognition, and agenda-setting influence. Financial commitment becomes a mechanism of norm reproduction and a stabiliser of Denmark's own reputational standing within that architecture.

Denmark's ACPD is therefore best understood as a practice of reputational statecraft grounded in material capacity. Its influence does not rely on moral proclamation, but on the capacity to keep integrity credible through continuous performance in recognised arenas and through sustained investment in the institutions that structure those arenas. The decisive mechanism is not communication alone but validation. Denmark sustains its standing by remaining embedded in institutional settings where anticorruption norms are monitored, interpreted, and reproduced, and where legitimacy is awarded through participation, responsiveness, and visible commitment. Reputational power emerges here as relational capital, produced through repeated interaction with audiences that are also evaluators. In this sense, Denmark's credibility is not self-authored; it is co-constituted through structured exposure to assessment and through the disciplined management of that exposure.

This also clarifies the political logic of the chapter's central tension. Enforcement gaps and uneven domestic responsiveness do not automatically translate into reputational collapse because Denmark's standing is buffered by the broader architecture that renders integrity believable: institutional resilience, dense network embeddedness, and sustained financial engagement. The result is a form of influence that exceeds Denmark's material scale, not because reputation replaces material resources, but because it amplifies their diplomatic conversion. Integrity functions as a multiplier: it increases the effectiveness of engagement, strengthens access to governance networks, and supports Denmark's ability to shape interpretive frames related to the global anticorruption norm.

Denmark's experience thus confirms and deepens the analytical model developed in Chap. 2. ACPD operates as a process through which identities and interests are aligned via agents, activities, resources, and smart power to produce externally communicable influence. In the Danish case, integrity becomes both normative vocabulary and strategic instrument: it underwrites Denmark's authority to participate as a trusted actor in global governance while advancing national interests tied to economic stability, security, and rule-based multilateralism. Far from symbolic ornament or moral advocacy, ACPD emerges as a structurally embedded modality of small-state statecraft, one in which economic capacity sustains norm entrepreneurship and reputational power translates into durable international influence.

References

Adler-Nissen, R. (2023). Practice. In S. Goddard, G. Lawson, & J. Sending (Eds.), *The Oxford handbook of international political sociology* (pp. 177–198). Oxford University Press.

Andersen, J. (2008). Welfare state transformations in an affluent Scandinavian state: The case of Denmark. In M. Seeleib-Kaiser (Ed.), *Welfare state transformations* (pp. 33–55). Palgrave Macmillan. https://doi.org/10.1057/9780230227392_3

Bjerregaard, E., & Kirchmaier, T. (2019, September 2). *The Danske Bank money laundering scandal*. Copenhagen Business School. https://doi.org/10.2139/ssrn.3446636

Breinstrup, T. (2019, July 12). Tre dømte i Atea-sag får længere fængselsstraf. *Berlingske*. Retrieved February 9, 2026, from https://www.berlingske.dk/virksomheder/tre-doemte-i-atea-sag-faar-laengere-faengselsstraf

Cull, N. (2019). *Public diplomacy: Foundations for global engagement in the digital age*. Polity.

Cull, N. (2024). *Reputational security*. Polity.

Danish Institute for International Studies (DIIS). (2020). *A small state addressing big problems*. DIIS. Retrieved February 9, 2026, from https://pure.diis.dk/ws/files/3297157/Perspectives_recent_Danish_foreign_and_security_strategy_DIIS_Report_2_2020.pdf

Dell, G., & McDevitt, A. (2018). *Exporting corruption*. Transparency International. Retrieved February 9, 2026, from https://files.transparencycdn.org/images/2018_Report_ExportingCorruption_English_200402_075046.pdf

Dell, G., & McDevitt, A. (2022). *Exporting corruption 2022*. Transparency International. Retrieved February 9, 2026, from https://files.transparencycdn.org/images/2022_Report-Full_Exporting-Corruption_English.pdf

Digitaliseringsstyrelsen. (2019). *Open Government Partnership: Denmark's national action plan 2019–2021*. Retrieved February 9, 2026, from https://www.opengovpartnership.org/wp-content/uploads/2020/02/Denmark_Action-Plan_2019-2021_EN.pdf

Eberholst, M. (2013). *Independent Reporting Mechanism Denmark: Progress report 2012–13*. Retrieved February 9, 2026, from https://www.opengovpartnership.org/wp-content/uploads/2019/06/Denmark_OGP_IRM_Public_Comment_Eng.pdf

European Commission. (2014, February 13). *Annex 4—Denmark to the EU anti-corruption report*. Retrieved February 9, 2026, from https://eur-lex.europa.eu/resource.html?uri=cellar:058aecf0-d9b7-11e3-8cd4-01aa75ed71a1.0012.02/DOC_4&format=DOC

Finnemore, M., & Sikkink, K. (2001). Taking stock: The constructivist research program in international relations and comparative politics. *Annual Review of Political Science, 4*, 391–416. https://doi.org/10.1146/annurev.polisci.4.1.391

Fukuyama, F. (2011). *The origins of political order*. Farrar, Straus, & Giroux.

Group of States against Corruption (GRECO). (2002, July 11). *First evaluation report*. Retrieved February 9, 2026, from https://rm.coe.int/CoERMPublicCommonSearchServices/DisplayDCTMContent?documentId=09000016806c31d3

Group of States against Corruption (GRECO). (2014, April 16). *Fourth evaluation round*. Retrieved February 9, 2026, from https://rm.coe.int/CoERMPublicCommonSearchServices/DisplayDCTMContent?documentId=09000016806c323e

Group of States against Corruption (GRECO). (2021, December 17). *Fifth evaluation round*. Retrieved February 9, 2026, from https://rm.coe.int/fifth-round-compliance-report-on-denmark-as-adopted-at-the-88th-plenar/1680a4e052

Hansen, M. O. (2019). *Independent Reporting Mechanism (IRM): Denmark's Implementation Report 2017–2019*. Retrieved February 9, 2026, from https://www.opengovpartnership.org/wp-content/uploads/2020/06/Denmark_Implementation_Report_2017-2019_EN.pdf

Heimann, F., & Dell, G. (2010). *Progress report 2010*. Transparency International. Retrieved February 9, 2026, from https://files.transparencycdn.org/images/2010_OECDProgressReport_EN.pdf

Jensen, M. (2014). *'Getting to Denmark': The process of state building, establishing rule of law and fighting corruption in Denmark 1660–1900* (QoG Working Paper Series 2014:06). The QoG Institute. Retrieved February 9, 2026, from https://pure.au.dk/ws/files/82049568/How_Denmark_got_to_be_Denmark_QoG_Workingpaper.pdf

Keohane, R. (1969). Lilliputians' dilemmas: Small states in international politics. *International Organization, 23*(2), 291–310. https://doi.org/10.1017/S002081830003160X

Mauss, M. (2002). *The gift*. Routledge.

Ministry of Foreign Affairs of Denmark (MFAD). (2018, March). *Government strategy for economic diplomacy*. Retrieved February 9, 2026, from https://thetradecouncil.dk/-/media/websites/trade-council/om-os/government-strategy-for-economic-diplomacy.ashx

Ministry of Foreign Affairs of Denmark (MFAD). (2026). *The government's priorities for Danish development cooperation*. Retrieved February 9, 2026, from https://um.dk/en/danida/strategies-and-priorities/government-priorities-danish-development-assistance

Norwegian Agency for Development Cooperation (NORAD). (2010). *Evaluation of Transparency International: Report 8/2010*. Retrieved February 9, 2026, from https://www.oecd.org/derec/norway/47447924.pdf

OECD Working Group on Bribery. (2008, July 29). *Follow-up report on the implementation of the phase 2 recommendations*. Retrieved February 9, 2026, from https://www.oecd.org/daf/anti-bribery/anti-briberyconvention/41073747.pdf

OECD Working Group on Bribery. (2013, March 15). *Phase 3 report on implementing the OECD anti-bribery convention in Denmark*. Retrieved February 9, 2026, from https://www.oecd.org/daf/anti-bribery/Denmarkphase3reportEN.pdf

OECD Working Group on Bribery. (2023). *Implementing the OECD anti-bribery convention—Phase 4 report: Denmark*. Retrieved February 9, 2026, from https://www.oecd.org/daf/anti-bribery/denmark-phase-4-report.pdf

Organisation for Economic Co-operation and Development (OECD). (2025, June 11). *Development co-operation profiles: Denmark*. Retrieved February 9, 2026, from https://www.oecd.org/en/publications/development-co-operation-profiles_04b376d7-en/denmark_49b42438-en.html

Raoul Wallenberg Institute. (2018). *The nexus between anti-corruption and human rights*. Retrieved February 9, 2026, from https://rwi.lu.se/app/uploads/2018/10/Nexus-report-online.pdf

Rasmussen, L. L. (2023, May). *Foreign and security policy strategy 2023*. Retrieved February 9, 2026, from https://um.dk/en/foreign-policy/foreign-and-security-policy-2023/

Security Policy Analysis Group. (2022, September). *Danish Security and Defence towards 2035*. The Security Policy Analysis Group. Retrieved February 9, 2026, from https://www.fmn.dk/globalassets/fmn/dokumenter/strategi/rsa/-regeringens_security-policy-report_uk_web-.pdf

Shakespeare, W. (2000). In S. Lamb (Ed.), *Hamlet*. Hungry Minds.

Taksøe-Jensen, P. (2016, May). *Danish diplomacy and defence in times of change: A review of Denmark's foreign and security policy*. MFAD. Retrieved February 9, 2026,fromhttps://um.dk/en/foreign-policy/danish-defence-and-diplomacy-in-times-of-change

Transparency International. (2004). *Transparency International global corruption barometer 2004.* Retrieved February 9, 2026, from https://images.transparencycdn.org/images/2004_GCB_EN.pdf

Transparency International. (2013). *Global corruption barometer 2013.* Retrieved February 9, 2026, from https://images.transparencycdn.org/images/2013_GlobalCorruptionBarometer_EN_200525_112757.pdf

Transparency International Danmark (TI Danmark). (2012). *Nationalt Integritetssystemstudie Danmark 2011.* Retrieved February 9, 2026, from https://transparency.dk/wp-content/uploads/2019/05/NIS-DK-20120119.pdf

Transparency International Danmark (TI Danmark). (2020). *IACC high-level segment monitoring mechanism Denmark 2018–2020.* Retrieved February 9, 2026, from https://um.dk/en/-/media/websites/umen/danida/about-danida/danida-transparency/council-for-development-policy/iacc.ashx

Transparency International Danmark (TI Danmark). (2022). *Summary of NIS.* Retrieved February 9, 2026, from https://transparency.dk/korruption/summary-of-nis/

Udenrigsministeriet. (2017). *China-Denmark joint work programme (2017–2020).* Retrieved February 9, 2026, from https://kina.um.dk/-/media/country-sites/kina-da/danmark-i-kina/chinadenmark-joint-work-program_english.ashx

Udenrigsministeriet. (2019). *Anti-corruption programme 2019–2022.* Udenrigsministeriet.

Udenrigsministeriet. (2020). *Open procedure: Corruption Survey 2019 in Ukraine for National Agency for Corruption Prevention.* Retrieved July 11, 2025, from https://um.dk/en/about-us/procurement/contracts/short/contract-opportunitie/newsdisplaypage/?newsid=5152dff1-c4d3-4129-8c63-d160c0bbacfe

Udenrigsministeriet. (2026). *Report corruption.* Retrieved February 9, 2026, from https://um.dk/en/danida/anti-corruption/report-corruption

United Nations Office on Drugs and Crime (UNODC). (2016). *Executive summary.* Retrieved February 9, 2026, from https://uncaccoalition.org/files/Cycle1-Executive-Summary-Denmark.pdf

United Nations Office on Drugs and Crime (UNODC). (2017). *Country review report of Denmark.* Retrieved February 9, 2026, from https://www.unodc.org/documents/treaties/UNCAC/CountryVisitFinalReports/2017_10_21_Denmark_Final_Country_Report.pdf

Wendt, A. (1999). *Social theory of international politics.* Cambridge University Press.

CHAPTER 4

New Zealand: High Integrity and the Diplomacy of Trust

4.1 Contextualising Integrity in the Antipodes

Few states embody the association between integrity and international reputation as consistently as New Zealand. Frequently described as a "high-integrity" society by national authorities and international organisations alike (Controller and Auditor-General, 2017, para. 2; Transparency International New Zealand [TINZ], 2018, p. 8), the country has become synonymous with clean governance and institutional reliability. Situated in the South Pacific and long framed, from a European vantage point, as part of the Antipodes (Goldie, 2010), New Zealand occupies a geographical periphery that has become a benchmark in governance terms.

Geographical isolation has shaped the country's political culture. Administrative self-reliance and rapid institutional consolidation within a settler-colonial context encouraged early bureaucratic accountability. Unlike states marked by entrenched aristocratic hierarchies or historically embedded patronage networks, New Zealand's state formation unfolded within a comparatively compressed institutional timeframe (Gregory, 2013). This facilitated the early consolidation of meritocratic public service traditions. Over time, these arrangements matured into a national narrative of clean government, social trust, and ethical public service. Gregory describes the country as shaped by a "strong egalitarian ethos" (2013, p. 27), in which justice, fairness, and equality underpin political

N. de A. e S. F. dos Santos, *Anticorruption Public Diplomacy*, Palgrave Macmillan Series in Global Public Diplomacy,
https://doi.org/10.1007/978-3-032-28668-0_4

conduct. These norms structure expectations of leadership and public administration. Even minor gratuities are socially discouraged, reflecting a deeply rooted rejection of corruption (Gregory, 2013). This normative landscape conditions domestic governance and underwrites external reputation.

This reputation is reinforced by recurring top-tier placements across global indicators. New Zealand is among the highest-performing states globally in measures of democracy (e.g. The Economist's Democracy Index), political freedom (e.g. Freedom in the World by Freedom House), policymaking and regulation (e.g. Blavatnik Index of Public Administration), and business environment (e.g. the World Bank's Ease of Doing Business). In anticorruption metrics, it has remained among the four highest-ranked countries in Transparency International's Corruption Perceptions Index since its inception in 1994 and has consistently scored in the upper 97–99 percentile range in the World Bank's Control of Corruption Indicator. It ranks fifth in the Index of Public Integrity developed by the European Research Centre for Anti-Corruption and State-Building and third in trust and integrity measures within the Blavatnik Index of Public Administration. These metrics not only describe performance but also feed back into diplomatic expectations.

Between 2014 and 2023, New Zealand held top-five positions in the TRACE Bribery Risk Matrix. In 2024, however, it fell to 16th place following a marked increase in risk in the "interactions with government" category (TRACE International, 2025). The November 2023 transition from a Labour to a National government coincided temporally with this shift, although no direct causal relationship can be established. The variation may reflect altered risk perceptions, methodological recalibration, enhanced regulatory scrutiny, policy adjustments, or other contextual dynamics not yet fully observable.

Recent domestic scrutiny introduces further nuance. A pilot report by the Serious Fraud Office (SFO) (2026) identified 446 alleged internal fraud and corruption cases within fifteen months and suggested significant under-reporting due to fragmented definitions and inconsistent reporting practices. While not indicative of systemic breakdown, these findings reveal vulnerabilities beneath the surface of high-ranking indicators. From the perspective of anticorruption public diplomacy (ACPD), such episodes are analytically significant because they expose how reputational authority depends on visible monitoring and institutional responsiveness. Put differently, integrity is sustained through contestation, defence, and recalibration. In this regard, global indices do not merely measure performance; they participate in the construction of state identity by generating expectations that shape diplomatic conduct (Finnemore & Wendt, 2024). Within ACPD, quantitative assessments are converted into symbolic authority, allowing New Zealand to speak as a state whose institutional practices have been externally validated.

This reputational capital extends beyond the field of anticorruption. Consistent placement within the top quartile of Brand Finance's Global Soft Power Index and Anholt's Good Country Index, combined with high rankings in openness (World Economic Forum, 2024, p. 35) and connectivity (Huawei, 2020, 2025), reinforces the image of a cooperative, outward-looking state. Such reputational assets operate as multipliers of influence, offsetting limited material capabilities.

Yet this image is not simply the organic outcome of institutional virtue; it is also actively curated and projected. Commitments to a rules-based international order grounded in democratic governance, human rights, and anticorruption (New Zealand Government, 2023), alongside ratification of international anticorruption conventions such as those of the OECD and the United Nations, situate New Zealand within the core architecture of the global anticorruption norm. Participation in international integrity networks such as the Egmont Group further positions the country as both a norm-taker and a norm-shaper.

The notion of the Antipodes thus acquires a second meaning. Governance models emerging from the geographical margins may attain normative centrality (Acharya, 2018). What once signified distance from imperial centres now suggests relative insulation from entrenched patronage structures. In this vein, such standing enhances diplomatic influence. At the same time, integrity in the Antipodes remains contested.

Understanding New Zealand's ACPD requires attention to this dual dynamic: a geographically distant state that transforms institutional standing into diplomatic leverage while continuously renegotiating its domestic foundations. In this sense, the Antipodes symbolise not merely geographic remoteness but a broader constructivist insight (Adler-Nissen, 2023; Finnemore & Sikkink, 2001): normative leadership emerges from sustained institutional practice, social recognition, and strategically articulated identity.

4.2 Identities and Interests: The Moral Foundations of a Small State

New Zealand's ACPD is grounded in a close alignment between identity and interest. Unlike major powers whose foreign policy is often framed through strategic competition or geopolitical projection, New Zealand presents itself through a narrative of principled state conduct. Integrity forms part of its diplomatic self-understanding (New Zealand Government, 2023), functioning as a core element of its external positioning.

Structurally, New Zealand exhibits characteristics typical of a small state. With a population of just over five million, a GDP ranking outside the top forty globally, and a mid-range diplomatic network in the Lowy Institute's Global Diplomacy Index, its material capabilities are modest. Material constraints sharpen a credibility-based strategy: integrity becomes a diplomatic asset that amplifies agency and reinforces normative influence in multilateral settings (Katzenstein, 2003). In this respect, integrity enables influence disproportionate to material capabilities in international institutions.

This identity is anchored in constitutional foundations. The common law tradition, the Constitution Act 1986, the Treaty of Waitangi, and the recognition of *Tikanga Māori* customary principles collectively shape a legal order emphasising accountability, procedural fairness, and the rule of law (TINZ, 2013). These institutional arrangements provide the domestic grounding for external legitimacy.

Two interlocking narratives sustain this positioning. First, New Zealand portrays itself as an independent voice capable of principled divergence from traditional allies (Gregory, 2013), a self-image rooted in its anti-nuclear stance of the 1980s that privileged normative commitments over alliance conformity. Second, domestic political culture emphasises fairness, transparency, and egalitarianism, reinforced consistently by high corruption-control indicators (Gregory, 2013; TINZ, 2013, 2018). Together, these narratives transform domestic norms into a source of diplomatic capital.

The convergence between identities and interests is particularly visible in the anticorruption domain. As a trade-dependent economy embedded in global markets, New Zealand relies on predictable regulatory environments and transparent governance abroad. Advocacy for anticorruption norms thereby reflects both moral commitment and self-interest (New Zealand Government, 2023), consistent with accounts of the mutual constitution of norms and interests (Wendt, 1999). Promoting integrity internationally strengthens the governance architecture that underpins its economic security and political autonomy. Normative positioning consequently operates as a strategic equaliser. By championing transparency and the rule of law in multilateral arenas, New Zealand contributes to reinforcing a rules-based order. Participation in Pacific initiatives and transnational enforcement networks exemplifies this norm-oriented engagement (United Nations Office on Drugs and Crime [UNODC], 2017). As a result, integrity functions as a core diplomatic asset.

Yet the contestation of this moral posture generates tensions that complicate any portrayal of seamless ethical coherence (TINZ, 2013, 2018) and underscore the contingent character of integrity. The credibility of New Zealand's ACPD therefore depends less on claims of perfection than on sustained institutional reflexivity and responsiveness. In this respect, ACPD reflects the mutual constitution of identity and interest, internalised domestically and externalised diplomatically (Wendt, 1999; Finnemore & Sikkink, 2001). As a consequence, ACPD functions not merely as a policy instrument but as a foundational pillar of New Zealand's international engagement.

4.3 National Integrity as Political Culture: The Historical Formation of an Anticorruption Identity

Any account of New Zealand's anticorruption identity must begin not with contemporary compliance regimes but with deeper normative foundations that predate colonial statehood. Before the transplantation of Westminster institutions, Māori governance traditions regulated authority through relational and moral frameworks. *Tikanga Māori* encompasses moral principles and social expectations linking leadership to responsibility (Williams, 2013). Authority required continual validation within the community, and reputation functioned as a mechanism of social discipline. Although these normative structures did not resemble modern anticorruption law, they cultivated enduring expectations that power be exercised visibly, responsibly, and justly.

The signing of the Treaty of Waitangi in 1840 created a constitutional interface between Māori authority and British sovereignty. Although its implementation was historically uneven and frequently contested, the

Treaty has progressively evolved into a central reference point for legitimacy and accountability (Gregory, 2013; TINZ, 2013). Contemporary constitutional interpretation increasingly reinforces expectations of partnership, consultation, and procedural fairness (Gregory, 2013). European influences included a strong Protestant culture, largely of Scottish origin, and the British public-service tradition, characterised by meritocracy, ethical principles, and competitive remuneration (Gregory, 2013). Consequently, New Zealand's integrity culture reflects layered institutional development combining indigenous and British colonial traditions.

Similarly, twentieth-century reforms were decisive in consolidating bureaucratic probity. Early professionalisation efforts, consolidated through successive reforms and later reviewed by the Hunt Commission, strengthened transparency and merit-based recruitment (Gregory, 2013). The period often described as the "age of mandarins" (1940–1951) further entrenched meritocracy within the higher civil service, reinforcing a professional administrative ethos centred on competence and ethical restraint (Gregory, 2013, p. 30). As state intervention expanded, particularly through the welfare architecture (e.g. Social Security Act 1938), public trust became structurally indispensable, pulling integrity from cultural expectation into institutional necessity (Gregory, 2013). Transparency was no longer peripheral; it became foundational to sustaining an egalitarian political order.

Institutional innovation further consolidated oversight mechanisms. The adoption of the Ombudsman model in 1962 embedded independent administrative review within political governance (TINZ, 2013). The Crimes Act 1961 codified offences of public and political corruption, with subsequent amendments extending criminal liability to trading in influence, misuse of official information, and the bribery of foreign public officials (OECD, 2002). Over time, integrity evolved from a predominantly cultural expectation into a legal obligation, embedded within an increasingly complex institutional-normative framework.

New Zealand's international commitments further consolidated this trajectory. The country acceded to the OECD Anti-Bribery Convention in 1997 and ratified it in 2001 (OECD, 2002). It signed the United Nations Convention against Corruption (UNCAC) in 2003 and ratified it in 2015 (UNODC, 2017). Participation in initiatives such as the Open Government Partnership (OGP) and networks including the Egmont Group, the Asia–Pacific Economic Cooperation (APEC) and Financial Action Task Force (FATF) further embedded transparency within multilateral governance frameworks (UNODC, 2017). Structured engagement with civil society, particularly through collaboration with Transparency International New Zealand and OGP, has reinforced this reflexive dynamic, creating channels through which societal agents participate in shaping integrity standards and monitoring institutional performance.

By the early twenty-first century, these cumulative reforms had converged into a measurable governance profile. Petty corruption levels have consistently remained exceptionally low compared with global averages (Transparency International, 2013). External assessments and indices corroborate institutional analysis, reflecting a political culture in which corruption appears structurally anomalous.

Yet this reputation sits alongside more complex enforcement dynamics. OECD monitoring has repeatedly noted limited prosecutorial outcomes in foreign-bribery cases despite multiple investigations over extended periods (OECD, 2013). Enforcement has tended to prioritise legislative refinement and policy recalibration over high-volume prosecution, reflecting an emphasis on regulatory strengthening rather than punitive visibility. Revelations concerning prominent cases involving foreign trusts and shell companies, particularly in the wake of the Panama and Pandora Papers, exposed vulnerabilities in corporate registration and beneficial ownership transparency (Dell & McDevitt, 2018, 2022). Subsequent reforms, including enhanced trust disclosure requirements and the development of a public beneficial ownership register, illustrate a pattern of legislative adaptation triggered by reputational pressures. Nevertheless, this trajectory exposes a recurring tension between institutional design and enforcement visibility, an issue that later conditions role credibility in ACPD.

The institutional architecture sustaining integrity encompasses Parliament, the executive, the judiciary, oversight institutions such as the Ombudsman and Auditor-General, enforcement bodies including the SFO, regulatory agencies, media, civil society, and the private sector (TINZ, 2013, 2018). Political will has generally manifested in legislative responsiveness, ministerial accountability in cases attracting substantial public scrutiny, and sustained cooperation with oversight institutions (Heimann et al., 2014). New Zealand's influence in global anticorruption governance has derived primarily from active participation rather than from financial leverage or large-scale sponsorship of anticorruption initiatives.

The cumulative effect of these historical layers is a political culture in which corruption appears structurally anomalous yet institutionally monitored. Integrity is reinforced through institutional practice and multilateral embedding. This reflects the internalisation of norms that structure both behaviour and expectation simultaneously (Wendt, 1999). This institutional configuration rests not on claims of perfection, but on the durability and reflexivity of the structures through which integrity is continually renegotiated and reaffirmed.

4.4 Role and Collective Identities in Public Diplomacy

If political culture explains the domestic foundations of integrity, role performance explains how that integrity is enacted externally. In the international arena, New Zealand does not merely possess an anticorruption identity; it enacts it through structured diplomatic roles that shape expectations, guide behaviour, and sustain recognition. Integrity thereby operates as a patterned mode of external conduct.

States act according to internalised conceptions of appropriate behaviour and role expectations, shaped simultaneously by self-perception, institutional frameworks, and external recognition (Breuning, 2024; Holsti, 1970; Wendt, 1999). New Zealand's ACPD is enacted through recognisable roles, namely the principled small state, the honest broker, and the responsible Pacific partner, each translating domestic integrity into patterned external conduct.

The role of the principled state is foundational. New Zealand frames its international engagement in terms of rule adherence (New Zealand Government, 2023), with limited reliance on coercive leverage. In such settings, integrity enhances New Zealand's capacity to exercise influence in multilateral settings where persuasion often matters more than material power.

Closely linked is the role of honest broker. In trade negotiations, regional diplomacy, and multilateral deliberation, New Zealand cultivates procedural fairness and legal reliability (Gregory, 2013). Anticorruption principles underpin this posture. Transparency, impartiality, and adherence to international legal standards reinforce perceptions that New Zealand operates without hidden agendas. For a state whose leverage derives from trust and eschews coercion, such perceptions are diplomatically decisive. Cultural attributes, including egalitarian social norms and comparatively high levels of interpersonal trust (Gregory, 2013), further reinforce this image of transparency and non-threatening engagement, enhancing credibility in consensus-based forums.

Regionally, New Zealand performs the role of responsible Pacific partner. Governance capacity-building, financial accountability initiatives, and institutional strengthening feature prominently in its Pacific engagement (UNODC, 2017).

Within this regional frame, anticorruption measures are framed as collaborative efforts to enhance institutional resilience, avoiding the logic of externally imposed conditionality. Collective identity operates here as shared regional responsibility: New Zealand positions itself as part of a Pacific community committed to accountable governance in contexts vulnerable to institutional fragility.

At the systemic level, New Zealand consistently enacts the role of defender of the rules-based international order (TINZ, 2013). Participation in multilateral anticorruption frameworks reflects role-consistent behaviour. Advocacy for transparency and peer-review processes aligns with normative commitments and structural self-interest alike. Accordingly, ACPD functions simultaneously as an ethical commitment and a strategic equaliser.

Beyond role performance, New Zealand's international embeddedness facilitates participation in transnational governance networks and the diffusion of integrity narratives across diplomatic, regulatory, and civil-society channels. In this way, network centrality operates as an enabling condition for ACPD: integrity claims travel more effectively when embedded in dense institutional and informational circuits.

External recognition consolidates role expectations that reinforce identity (Wendt, 1999; Finnemore & Sikkink, 2001). Sustained high performance generates anticipatory legitimacy: international partners expect New Zealand to champion transparency and compliance in multilateral settings. Quantitative evaluation, however, also introduces asymmetry. While domestic corruption-control indicators remain exceptionally strong, international monitoring of foreign-bribery enforcement has been more reserved. This enforcement visibility gap also conditions the credibility of New Zealand's international role performance. This dissonance does not negate the identity claim; it tightens scrutiny and raises the diplomatic costs of even limited enforcement gaps. Even marginal enforcement weaknesses become symbolically amplified in light of sustained top-tier rankings. ACPD unfolds within a measurable environment in which performance indicators both enable and constrain diplomatic identity. Reputation thus functions simultaneously as asset and constraint.

Collective identity further extends beyond formal state agents. Independent oversight institutions, including the Ombudsman and the SFO (TINZ, 2013), investigative journalism, regulatory authorities, and civil-society organisations contribute to the external perception of transparency and accountability. Public diplomacy in this regard transcends ministerial rhetoric. It encompasses the broader institutional ecosystem through which integrity is communicated, contested, and validated. Ultimately, New Zealand's ACPD operates through the convergence of identity, role, and network embeddedness, enacted through principled diplomacy and multilateral engagement. Moral credibility is sustained through consistency between domestic practice, international commitments, and enforcement coherence, ensuring that integrity remains not merely a claim of identity but a continuously enacted diplomatic practice.

4.5 The Operational Repertoire of Anticorruption Public Diplomacy

New Zealand's ACPD is enacted through a structured repertoire of practices that translate domestic institutional performance into sustained international engagement. The country projects integrity through concrete procedures, partnerships, and professional exchanges embedded in regional and multilateral settings. Through smart power capabilities, state agents mobilise legal authority, technical expertise, and budgetary resources alongside immaterial assets such as transparency, accountability, and commitment to rules-based cooperation. Integrity becomes operational: it is enacted through action.

This repertoire unfolds across six interconnected activity clusters: listening and mutual accountability; dialogical engagement; advocacy; cultural diplomacy; exchange; as well as broadcasting and digital engagement. Together, these dimensions form an integrated architecture through which credibility is converted into diplomatic capital. The following subsections examine each activity in turn.

Listening and Mutual Accountability

Listening constitutes the diagnostic foundation of New Zealand's ACPD. It reflects a governing principle in which integrity is sustained through institutionalised feedback mechanisms that allow scrutiny, correction, and adaptation. Listening is both inward-facing and outward-facing: it strengthens domestic accountability while reinforcing international credibility.

New Zealand employs two principal modalities of listening. The first involves structured research initiatives with target publics designed to assess the effectiveness of integrity frameworks. One illustrative example was the survey conducted by the State Services Commission in 2007 on whistleblower protection within the public service, undertaken in collaboration with the Ethics Resource Center of the American non-governmental organisation (NGO) Business & Human Rights Resource Centre (OECD, 2009, p. 9). This initiative mobilised material resources, including budgetary allocation and survey instruments, alongside immaterial resources rooted in openness and self-assessment. By involving an international non state agent, the process enhanced external credibility and signalled willingness to subject domestic practices to independent scrutiny. Listening in this instance served as reputational reinforcement: the act of evaluation itself became a diplomatic signal.

The second modality consists of digital reporting platforms that enable confidential and anonymous disclosure of misconduct. An example of this approach is the online reporting mechanism, created pursuant to the statutory competences of the Financial Markets Authority (2025). This platform integrates legal safeguards, technological infrastructure, and investigative capacity, allowing individuals to report concerns without fear of retaliation. Although primarily domestic in function, such mechanisms contribute to New Zealand's international reputation for transparency by demonstrating the practical accessibility of accountability processes. In doing so, it converts the value of openness into procedural accessibility.

Across both modalities, listening operates at the intersection of soft power capabilities (communicating, engaging, listening) and hard power capabilities (financing, regulating, enabling). Receiving and responding to feedback enhances trust and relational legitimacy, while the legal authority to investigate and sanction wrongdoing ensures that listening is not merely symbolic. Mutual accountability thus becomes performative: integrity is not presented as moral superiority but as institutional reliability subject to continuous verification.

Building Integrity Through Dialogical Engagement

Dialogical engagement constitutes a central dimension of New Zealand's ACPD by operationalising reciprocity. Integrity is projected, negotiated, and co-constructed through sustained interaction with international partners. In practice, this dialogical engagement unfolds through four principal mechanisms: (1) multilateral cooperation, (2) bilateral cooperation, (3) responses to international commitments and demands, and (4) long-term relationship management within global governance networks. Notably, beyond specific interactions, long-term relationship management sustains dialogue over time.

The first mechanism is multilateral cooperation, exemplified by New Zealand's participation in the Egmont Group (UNODC, 2017). Coordinated domestically by the SFO, engagement within this network mobilises technical competences, investigative expertise, direct professional contacts, and established anticorruption laws and policies. These resources, grounded in domestic institutional capacity and embedded in transnational networks, are translated into international influence through the capacities to communicate, negotiate, influence, share intelligence, and cooperate. The effectiveness of this mechanism derives primarily from collaborative and soft power. Influence is exercised within a network through credibility and professional trust. The participation of international agents is institutionalised through membership in the Egmont Group, reinforcing mutual accountability among financial intelligence units.

The second mechanism, bilateral cooperation, illustrates how dialogue operates within economic diplomacy. The trade agreement between New Zealand and China, which contains provisions relating to anticorruption, provides a representative example (New Zealand Foreign Affairs and Trade [NZFAT], 2021). This initiative mobilises anticorruption legislation, procurement standards, trade policy instruments, and the binding force of the international agreement itself. Through negotiation and policy alignment, these material and normative resources are translated into international commitments under coordination of the NZFAT. The capacities activated here, namely communication, persuasion, and negotiation, are characteristic of soft power operating within formal diplomatic channels. The representational link of international agents is embedded in the agreement, which formalises reciprocal obligations and embeds integrity norms within economic exchange.

The third mechanism consists of responses to international commitments and demands. New Zealand's endorsement of the Santiago Commitment under the APEC framework exemplifies this dynamic (OECD, 2006). In this context, ACPD is shaped by responsiveness to regional expectations. Coordinated by the New Zealand government, this engagement draws upon domestic anticorruption policies, technical expertise, and established relationships within APEC. These resources are converted into diplomatic outcomes through the capacities to communicate standards (soft power) and share best practices (collaborative power), thereby signalling alignment with regional norms. Representation occurs through formal adherence to the commitment itself, which publicly situates New Zealand within a community of practice committed to integrity.

Finally, relationship management sustains dialogue over time. This mechanism involves maintaining continuous engagement with global institutions and networks, including the United Nations, OECD, FATF, and the Egmont Group (UNODC, 2017). Coordinated primarily by the Ministry of Justice, this activity mobilises domestic legal frameworks, institutional performance, official narratives, and positions within international governance structures. It frequently involves non state agents, particularly private-sector organisations, alongside foreign agencies and international bodies. Representation is formalised through network membership, official invitations, and participation in joint initiatives. Here, soft and collaborative power operate to attribute meaning to domestic integrity performance, transforming institutional reliability into reputational capital.

Across these four mechanisms, dialogical engagement shows that New Zealand's ACPD is relational rather than declaratory. Integrity is constructed through interaction, sustained through reciprocity, and stabilised through networks of cooperation. In this way, dialogue functions simultaneously as a diplomatic method, a reputational strategy, and a mechanism through which anticorruption norms acquire international legitimacy.

Advocacy and Norm Diffusion

Advocacy is one of the most visible and normatively charged dimensions of New Zealand's ACPD. It operates in the terrain of norm projection, shaping expectations, behaviours, and institutional standards beyond national borders. It reflects the externalisation of an internalised integrity identity. Five interrelated mechanisms structure this process: (1) strategic control of investigations and prosecutions; (2) projection of national policies as international best practice; (3) dissuasive contractual measures; (4) international communication campaigns; and (5) official speeches in multilateral fora. Together, they illustrate advocacy as identity-based norm diffusion.

The first mechanism concerns the strategic control of investigations and prosecutions. Coordinated primarily by the Ministry of Justice, it reflects calibrated handling of corruption cases with potential international repercussions. Safeguarding New Zealand's reputation as a fair and corruption-free market constitutes a national interest aligned with its "high-integrity" identity (Controller and Auditor-General, 2017, para. 2; New Zealand Government, 2023). It involves discretionary case management and visibility calibration under legal mandates, aimed at minimising reputational spillovers and drawing on sharp-power capacities, particularly information and visibility control within lawful discretion. This reflects awareness of the global implications of high-profile cases. Unlike coercive external interference, this form of sharp power remains inward-facing yet externally consequential. By coupling vigilance with reputational stewardship, New Zealand avoids reputational damage while reinforcing its position as a reliable and clean jurisdiction. Advocacy works indirectly in such a case: more than proclaimed, integrity is enacted through disciplined institutional conduct observed and internalised by foreign partners and multilateral bodies.

A second mechanism projects domestic anticorruption frameworks as exportable best practice. UNODC's recognition of New Zealand as a provider of technical assistance in the Pacific illustrates this dynamic (UNODC, 2017). Coordinated by the SFO with participation from NZFAT, the initiative mobilises institutional expertise, assistance policies, technical competences, and infrastructure to host international visits and training. Soft power (communication), collaborative power (knowledge-sharing), and hard power (material enabling) converge. New Zealand positions itself as a regional partner facilitating reform, distinguishing its approach from the imposition of standards. Norm diffusion occurs through emulation and capacity transfer, reinforcing its collective identity as a responsible Pacific partner and aligning normative commitment with regional strategic interests.

A third mechanism involves dissuasion embedded in anticorruption clauses included in contracts issued by the New Zealand Export Credit Office (ECO) (OECD, 2006). These provisions condition access to state-backed internationalisation on compliance with anticorruption standards. Though contractual, their implications are transnational. Companies operating abroad under ECO guarantees carry a normative framework linked to New Zealand's integrity identity. This mechanism reflects soft power (norm communication) combined with hard power (material incentive). Norm diffusion operates through conditionality and example, as firms become vectors of normative transmission by integrating anticorruption compliance into international commercial practice.

A fourth mechanism materialises through awareness campaigns, such as the one following ratification of the OECD Convention (OECD, 2009). Coordinated by the Ministry of Justice with NZFAT support, this initiative targeted private-sector stakeholders to publicise the criminalisation of foreign bribery. Mobilising legal reforms, communication tools, and budgetary resources, the campaign combines soft power persuasion with the enabling hard power force of legislative enforcement. These campaigns are not solely inward-looking; by demonstrating proactive implementation, New Zealand reinforced its image as a norm-consistent actor within OECD frameworks. Treaty ratification thus became performative action, embedding commitments domestically while signalling compliance externally. Norm diffusion operated both horizontally (among firms) and vertically (within global governance structures).

Finally, advocacy unfolds through official speeches delivered in multilateral settings. Statements by NZFAT at United Nations sessions emphasising good governance and anticorruption in contexts such as Afghanistan (NZFAT, 2016) illustrate this discursive dimension in which domestic policies are translated into international narratives. Through communication, persuasion, and inspiration, soft power reinforces collective expectations. Symbolic articulation is central to norm diffusion: by repeatedly framing anticorruption as integral to development and stability, New Zealand contributes to shaping the moral vocabulary of global governance.

State agents, including the SFO, the Ministry of Justice, the NZFAT, and the ECO, form the institutional backbone of this process. Non state agents, such as companies, academia, civil society organisations and chambers of commerce, participate through representational ties grounded in legal mandates, partnerships, monitoring processes and international networks. International agents, including foreign firms, export-credit agencies, and monitoring bodies, enter through formalised mechanisms of cooperation and evaluation.

Across these mechanisms, advocacy in New Zealand's ACPD reveals a consistent pattern: the outward multi-level performance of a domestically consolidated integrity identity. It is therefore not unidirectional but entails feedback, recognition, and social validation. Through international socialisation, New Zealand promotes anticorruption norms while reinforcing its identity as a principled small state; norm diffusion and identity consolidation occur in parallel. Accordingly, advocacy emerges not as an isolated instrument but as a structural component of an integrity-based foreign policy posture. It strengthens both the global anticorruption norm and New Zealand's credibility as a high-integrity society, bridging domestic institutional practice and international normative projection.

Cultural and Educational Diplomacy

Cultural and educational diplomacy constitute an important dimension of New Zealand's ACPD, consistently coordinated by the SFO. Here, anticorruption circulates through professional exchange, training, and epistemic engagement, reflecting a broader understanding of cultural diplomacy centred on the transmission of professional norms and practices. Two modalities predominate: (1) specialised training and (2) participation in international conferences.

The first focuses on strengthening prosecutorial and institutional capacities abroad. An illustrative example is the training delivered to the Pacific Prosecutors' Association in Tonga (UNODC, 2017). Comparable initiatives include training for prosecutors from Samoa and the Cook Islands to enhance international cooperation (UNODC, 2017). These activities mobilise technical expertise, legal frameworks, and financial resources allocated to international programmes. Soft power derives from professional credibility, while hard power enables action through material support. New Zealand does not prescribe reform; it supports capacity-building, positioning itself as a cooperative partner in regional integrity governance. Representational links are established through technical cooperation agreements, embedding international agents within professional networks. Norms diffuse through shared practice, procedural alignment, and the gradual internalisation of standards within prosecutorial communities.

The second involves participation in international conferences and symposia. Coordinated by SFO, New Zealand has contributed to events such as the Hong Kong Symposium on Corruption, the Cambridge International Symposium on Economic Crime, and the Australian Public Sector Anti-Corruption Conference (UNODC, 2017). In these settings, anticorruption laws, expertise, and institutional narratives are articulated through soft power capacities of communication and influence. Conferences operate as epistemic arenas in which meanings are constructed and reproduced. Through dialogue and the presentation of domestic practices, New Zealand translates its internal integrity framework into internationally recognisable standards. This form of public diplomacy shapes expectations within specialised communities and consolidates transnational professional anticorruption networks. Outcomes extend beyond information exchange to the co-production of norms and shared interpretative frameworks.

Across both modalities, cultural and educational diplomacy reinforce New Zealand's identity as a principled and technically competent small state. Normative commitment aligns with regional cooperation, particularly within Asia–Pacific contexts. Cultural diplomacy thus operates as professional socialisation: anticorruption standards circulate through learning, emulation, and peer recognition, consolidating both the global anticorruption norm and New Zealand's recognition as a high-integrity jurisdiction.

Exchange, Collaborative Diplomacy, and Regional Leadership

International exchange is also a central mechanism of New Zealand's ACPD, grounded in relational engagement with regional partners. Three modalities stand out: (1) visits and technical missions involving normative entrepreneurs, (2) participation in international meetings, and (3) membership in transnational anticorruption networks. Together, these initiatives position New Zealand as a collaborative leader in regional integrity governance.

An illustrative example of the first is the UNODC monitoring visit to Wellington in February 2017 (UNODC, 2017). The visit mobilised anticorruption institutions, legal frameworks, official narratives, hosting infrastructure, and network capital derived from UNCAC membership. Outcomes resulted from the interplay of soft power (communication and influence), hard power (institutional and logistical enabling), and collaborative power (inclusion and co-engagement). Coordinated by the SFO, the initiative involved NZFAT, the Financial Intelligence Unit, other ministries, and state agencies under their statutory mandates. Non state agents, including private firms, academia, and civil society, participated through formal invitations, while experts from Turkey and Cameroon engaged via representational ties grounded in UNCAC membership. Such visits function as reciprocal evaluation mechanisms, reinforcing compliance, transparency, and professional trust. Norm diffusion occurs through structured interaction and peer review.

The second involves participation in regional meetings, notably within the Asia–Pacific Group (UNODC, 2017). Coordinated by NZFAT, with the participation of SFO, these activities mobilise legal frameworks, technical expertise, institutional narratives, and accumulated credibility. Soft power (communication) and collaborative power (knowledge-sharing and joint deliberation) predominate. New Zealand contributes to collective agenda-setting and regional interpretative alignment, avoiding the unilateral export of norms and reinforcing its identity as a cooperative, high-integrity, and technically competent small state.

The third concerns membership in transnational anticorruption networks, exemplified by New Zealand's participation in the OGP (2026). It mobilises capacities to communicate, influence, negotiate and connect, derived from soft and collaborative power, alongside substantive resources, including openness as a public value, anticorruption policies and institutions, expertise, and network membership. Network engagement translates domestic commitments into internationally benchmarked standards, facilitating peer learning, policy diffusion and reputational reinforcement. Norm diffusion thereby occurs through connectivity and iterative review within multilateral frameworks.

Across these modalities, exchange constitutes collaborative diplomacy. New Zealand does not project anticorruption norms unilaterally but co-produces them through sustained interaction with states, experts, and civil society. Leadership is exercised through participation, technical credibility, and normative consistency. International exchange, consequently, strengthens both the global anticorruption norm and New Zealand's regional standing through processes of mutual socialisation in which influence and recognition remain reciprocal.

Broadcasting Trust: Narrative and Digital Engagement

Broadcasting anticorruption commitments institutionalises transparency and reinforces trust among global audiences. New Zealand operationalises this dimension through three mechanisms: (1) online training platforms, (2) digital manuals, and (3) electronic policy briefings.

The first is exemplified by the online anticorruption training module available on the SFO website, including risk-analysis tools (UNODC, 2017). This initiative mobilises technical competences, financial resources for platform maintenance, and legal, regulatory and enforcement frameworks. Soft power operates through communication and influence, as the platform disseminates standards to domestic and international users, while hard power enables delivery of institutional and financial capacity. By providing open access to compliance tools, New Zealand signals procedural transparency and institutional reliability. Digital training thus functions as preventive diplomacy, shaping behaviour by equipping stakeholders with practical compliance instruments and reinforcing a rules-based governance framework.

The second and third mechanisms involve electronic publications. The manual Saying No to Bribery and Corruption, designed for businesses operating overseas (Ministry of Justice, 2015) and the electronic leaflet clarifying extraterritorial jurisdiction in corruption cases (OECD, 2006, p. 47) illustrate this approach. In these initiatives, anticorruption policies are operationalised primarily through soft power capacities (communication, persuasion, inspiration, and influence). These documents translate complex legal frameworks into accessible guidance, aligning normative expectations with practical implementation. As a result, digital materials clarify legal standards while constructing a narrative of responsibility. By articulating extraterritorial reach and compliance expectations, New Zealand reinforces enforcement credibility and projects regulatory transparency.

Across these mechanisms, digital engagement broadcasts trust. Online tools and publications generate reputational capital by framing anticorruption as integral to national governance and international engagement. Recurrent association of transparency, accountability, and rule compliance with institutional practice consolidates New Zealand's image as a high-integrity jurisdiction. Digital dissemination therefore advances norm diffusion while sustaining the credibility that underpins New Zealand's regional and global influence.

Embedded Integrity and the Absence of Strategic Formalisation

The absence of formal action plans, systematic evaluation frameworks, or structured lessons-learned processes suggests an embedded rather than programmatic ACPD. Integrity is enacted through governance, although greater formalisation could strengthen coherence and long-term accountability. Coherence is generated through routinised practice, not through a dedicated strategy document. The country operates as a "high integrity society" (TINZ, 2013, p. 8), characterised by a "natural" approach to integrity and anticorruption (Gregory, 2013, p. 27). Integrity is not strategically manufactured; it is culturally embedded. The norm permeates both state institutions and societal expectations, reducing the need for deliberate image management. New Zealand enacts integrity as an intrinsic element of national identity, integrating anticorruption into routine governance without reliance on formal planning or evaluation cycles. This organic configuration reflects deep institutional trust and normative internalisation. ACPD thus functions as an extension of established institutional practices and normative expectations rather than as a separately engineered policy domain. Yet the absence of formalisation also leaves scope for refinement. Although outcomes remain consistently positive, structured action plans, systematic evaluation, and formal feedback mechanisms could enhance coherence, accountability, and the long-term strategic visibility of New Zealand's ACPD.

4.6 Mapping New Zealand's Anticorruption Public Diplomacy

Mapping New Zealand's ACPD requires moving beyond isolated initiatives to identify the patterned architecture through which domestic integrity is translated into outward-facing practice: who acts, how they act, with what resources, and with which power logics. This section analyses ACPD through four interrelated dimensions: agents and their representational ties; the range and strategic orientation of activities; the material and institutional resource base that sustains external engagement; and, finally, the configuration of smart power through which these elements acquire international meaning. These dimensions reveal how domestic integrity is translated into outward-facing diplomatic action.

The analysis interprets ACPD as a patterned and normalised process embedded within New Zealand's governance system. By examining who acts, how they act, with what resources, and through which interpretative capacities, this mapping clarifies how anticorruption becomes both a national interest and a relational diplomatic practice situated within evolving international normative structures.

Agents, Representational Ties, and Coordination

New Zealand does not assign a formal whole-of-government coordinating mandate to a single authority. In practice, however, the SFO functions as a nodal coordinator across many ACPD-related initiatives within a dispersed governance structure. ACPD unfolds as a structured process of international socialisation involving state, non state, and international agents. These agents are not merely operational units but carriers of identity, interests, and normative commitments (Finnemore & Sikkink, 2001). The New Zealand case illustrates how legitimate representational ties are institutionally constructed to sustain the projection of integrity beyond national borders.

State agents form the backbone of this representational architecture. Core institutions include the SFO, the NZFAT, the Ministry of Justice, the Financial Intelligence Unit, the Financial Markets Authority, the ECO, the Ombudsman, the Inland Revenue, the Police, and the State Services Commission (TINZ, 2013, 2018), all operating within statutory mandates. Their authority derives from legal delegation and administrative design, not from personal influence, ensuring that external engagement reflects recognised state competences. The representational link authorising these agents stems from the legal organisation of the state and may take the form of statutory delegation, hierarchical appointment, or formal selection procedures, conferring a representative mandate. Hence, representation is juridically grounded; it is not merely symbolic.

Non state agents also play a substantive role. Private-sector organisations, both domestic and internationally active, academics, civil-society representatives, and business associations such as Business New Zealand (OECD, 2002, 2009, 2013; TINZ, 2013, 2018) contribute to the diffusion and internalisation of anticorruption norms. ACPD is thus not monopolised by the state apparatus but operates through a multi-layered network in which authority and expertise circulate across institutional boundaries.

International agents complete this constellation. These include export-credit agencies, such as the Swedish Export Credit Agency, foreign ministries, particularly within the Asia–Pacific region, foreign citizens and companies, as well as UNCAC peer reviewers (UNODC, 2017). Multilateral bodies including UNODC, OECD, FATF, the Asia–Pacific Group, APEC, INTERPOL, and the Egmont Group (OECD, 2009, 2013; UNODC, 2017) function as arenas in which anticorruption standards are negotiated, monitored, and reinforced. Membership in the Egmont Group exemplifies how participation in transnational networks generates sustained representational commitments (UNODC, 2017, p. 293). Such membership signals adherence to shared standards and reinforces collective expectations regarding integrity. In constructivist terms (Finnemore & Sikkink, 2001), repeated interaction within these forums contributes to the internalisation of anticorruption as a constitutive norm.

Representational ties of non state agents are constructed through concrete institutional mechanisms, including international contracts, cooperation agreements, and official invitations, as well as through more flexible forms of engagement such as participation in training programmes and digital interaction. The agreement between the State Services Commission and the Ethics Resource Centre to conduct listening-stage surveys illustrates contractual delegation (OECD, 2009, p. 9). Regarding cooperation agreements, a case in point is the inter-institutional partnership with the Pacific Prosecutors' Association (UNODC, 2017, p. 292). Official invitations extended by the SFO to companies, academics, and civil-society representatives during the UNODC monitoring visit to Wellington further demonstrate inclusion within international review processes (UNODC, 2017). In relation to more flexible forms of engagement, participation in ECO export-credit programmes embeds companies within anticorruption compliance frameworks (OECD, 2009, p. 14), while engagement in online anticorruption training provided by the SFO (UNODC, 2017, p. 7) extends representational participation through digital channels.

Taken together, these agents and representational ties indicate that New Zealand's ACPD is neither informal nor episodic. It is a legally grounded, institutionally coordinated, and normatively structured process of multi-level engagement. Through statutory authority, contractual arrangements, cooperation agreements, network membership, programme participation, and official invitations, representation links domestic institutional authority to international action.

Coordination relies less on hierarchical centralisation than on institutional coherence and shared normative orientation. The resulting model combines procedural legitimacy, administrative continuity, and dense multilateral embeddedness, features consistent with a high-integrity governance system.

Activities and Strategic Orientation

Although ACPD lacks a single consolidated programme document, its activities align consistently with broader economic and security priorities, especially in the Pacific, thereby producing coherence through repetition rather than central design. Anticorruption is explicitly framed as a national interest (New Zealand Government, 2023). Because foreign policy action reflects the interplay between identity and interest (Wendt, 1999), strategic orientation need not depend exclusively on formal planning structures. The absence of a consolidated ACPD strategy therefore does not diminish its strategic character.

Although all activity types are present, dialogical engagement, advocacy, and educational-cultural diplomacy assume particular prominence. Anchored in domestic anticorruption policies and administrative capacities, these domains illustrate continuity between internal governance and external engagement. The sustained Pacific focus provides a stabilising axis across multilateral, bilateral, and technical cooperation initiatives. Capacity-building programmes, participation in regional fora, and active positioning in anticorruption debates form a patterned mode of engagement, far removed from episodic interventions.

This coherence is best understood as emerging from institutionalised practice, without reliance on a comprehensive grand strategy. Diplomatic action often emerges through routinised competences and everyday institutional performance (Adler-Nissen, 2023). In the New Zealand case, existing capacities are activated through recurring operational steps: engaging regional partners, delivering technical training, participating in peer-review mechanisms, and reaffirming anticorruption commitments in multilateral settings. Through repetition, these practices generate strategic consistency without requiring a centralised blueprint.

Importantly, these activities extend beyond the mere transmission of domestic policy. They situate New Zealand within ongoing processes of international socialisation and norm evolution in the global anticorruption landscape. Norm development proceeds through interaction, persuasion, and socialisation rather than through unilateral imposition (Finnemore & Sikkink, 2001). By participating in multilateral fora, providing technical assistance, and engaging in review mechanisms, New

Zealand contributes to the reproduction and incremental refinement of anticorruption standards. Activities do not simply reflect pre-existing national interests; they also reproduce and stabilise the country's identity as a cooperative and high-integrity agent within international society (Wendt, 1999). Dialogical and capacity-building practices reinforce shared expectations of transparency and accountability, embedding anticorruption within a relational framework of regional cooperation.

On the whole, New Zealand's ACPD activities reveal a governance architecture characterised by decentralised coordination, policy continuity, and sustained alignment between domestic commitments and external engagement. The prominence of dialogical engagement, advocacy, and culturally oriented training, particularly in the Asia–Pacific region, shows that strategic orientation is generated through institutionalised practice and norm interaction; formal centralisation is not its primary source. In this configuration, coherence emerges from patterned engagement through which national interests, institutional practices, and international normative expectations are continuously aligned and mutually reinforced.

The Resource Base of New Zealand's Anticorruption Public Diplomacy

New Zealand's international standing derives less from military projection or economic magnitude than from the perceived quality of its governance architecture. Although New Zealand maintains professional defence capabilities and participates in international operations (New Zealand Ministry of Defence, 2026), it does not constitute a military power (Global Firepower, 2026), nor does it rank among the world's major economic actors. Its prominence rests instead on the credibility of its public policies and institutional performance (Good Country, 2023). This structural profile extends to ACPD, whose resource base is anchored primarily in domestic governance capacities, with limited reliance on material coercion.

The core resources mobilised in ACPD derive from anticorruption policies and legal frameworks. National anticorruption institutions, whistleblower protection legislation, criminalisation regimes, procurement safeguards, export regulations, civic participation mechanisms, development assistance instruments, and public information policies constitute the institutional foundation from which external engagement proceeds. These frameworks provide more than regulatory content; they supply organisational stability and procedural legitimacy to outward-facing initiatives. In this sense, domestic governance structures function as structural resources for international action.

Cultural and value-based factors reinforce this institutional base. The value of openness, deeply embedded in New Zealand's integrity-oriented political culture, underpins listening practices (Financial Markets Authority, 2025) and facilitates dialogical engagement. Transparency norms, administrative accountability, and expectations of fairness form part of the normative environment that sustains ACPD activities. These cultural and value-based resources are not peripheral but integral to the domestic governance system that supports external projection.

Another major component of the resource base lies in network embeddedness. Membership in global and regional frameworks, including UNCAC, the Egmont Group, APEC, FATF, and the Asia–Pacific Group, integrates New Zealand within established anticorruption architectures. These nodes provide structured channels for ACPD activities, ensuring that national policies operate within recognised multilateral frameworks, thereby avoiding institutional isolation. Network participation functions as a structural resource, positioning domestic standards within transnational normative orders and reinforcing their legitimacy through collective oversight and interaction.

Technological and economic capacities further enable ACPD engagement. Digital infrastructure expands the reach and accessibility of norm dissemination, while online training modules, communication platforms, and electronic tools facilitate cross-border interaction. Economic resources, particularly budget allocations and administrative infrastructure, finance research on target audiences, advocacy campaigns (OECD, 2009), training programmes, surveys, digital platforms, and the hosting of international partners (UNODC, 2017). Although modest relative to larger powers, these financial and infrastructural capacities are sufficient to sustain consistent engagement, especially in the Pacific.

Overall, this resource configuration reflects and reproduces New Zealand's broader national identity. The same governance qualities that underpin domestic integrity, namely, legal robustness, administrative competence, cultural commitment to transparency, and multilateral embeddedness, also constitute the material and institutional foundation of ACPD. New Zealand's ACPD is structurally grounded in institutional credibility, administrative capacity, financial sufficiency, and dense participation in international networks.

Smart Power Configuration and Ideational Capacities

New Zealand's smart power configuration is structured around a calibrated articulation of soft, hard, and collaborative power, while sharp power plays only a residual, non-systemic role. In the present framework, sharp power is understood in a broader sense as the strategic management of visibility and information within lawful institutional discretion. In contrast to major powers whose smart power frequently combines coercive leverage with attraction, New Zealand's configuration reflects the strategic logic of a small state whose influence derives primarily from normative credibility and institutional embeddedness.

Soft power constitutes the dominant modality. Consistent with Nye's (2004) conception, attraction in the New Zealand case does not rest on cultural spectacle or geopolitical projection, but on reputational authority grounded in institutional performance. Through listening, communication, persuasion, and example-setting, domestic anticorruption resources are translated into internationally legible standards. Anticorruption clauses embedded in Export Credit Office (ECO) contracts, for instance, transform national compliance frameworks into transnational governance expectations. In the circumstances, soft power operates ideationally: it attributes shared meaning to domestic regulatory practices and converts internal policy coherence into external normative influence.

Hard power appears as enabling capacity (Nye, 2011). Budget allocations for whistleblower assessments, funding for compliance mechanisms, and the hosting of UNODC and OECD monitoring missions attach material weight to normative commitments. In this scenario, hard power functions infrastructurally: it sustains the institutional conditions under which soft power can operate credibly. Together, economic resources, legislative reforms, and administrative investments provide the material foundations for normative projection. Hard power in New Zealand's ACPD is therefore supportive; its purpose is not to impose outcomes but to stabilise credibility.

Collaborative power introduces a further dimension: the capacity to generate influence through relational embeddedness. Participation in the OECD Anti-Bribery Convention and UNCAC, alongside engagement in networks such as FATF and the Egmont Group, transforms formal membership into reputational and diplomatic capital. Influence is exercised not through unilateral assertion but through the co-production of standards, peer review, and shared monitoring processes. This aligns with Zaharna's

(2013, 2022) conception of network-based influence, where power derives from relational positioning rather than hierarchical dominance. Network centrality consequently becomes a multiplier of normative authority. New Zealand's role within Asia–Pacific anticorruption networks illustrates how small states convert institutional participation into agenda-shaping capacity.

Sharp power, by contrast, appears only marginally and remains structurally constrained. It may surface in the strategic calibration of prosecutorial priorities or in reputational management during high-profile investigations. Where discretion is exercised, it concerns lawful prioritisation and communications discipline, constraints that follow from an integrity-based reputational logic. Yet these instances do not amount to a systematic strategy of narrative manipulation or coercive interference. They reflect the tension inherent in any integrity-based diplomacy: reputational capital must be protected, but overt manipulation would undermine the very legitimacy upon which influence depends. Where present, sharp power remains intertwined with soft or collaborative modalities and is circumscribed by institutional transparency and democratic accountability.

Analytically, the key point lies in the articulation between resources and ideational capacities. Domestic institutional strength, legislative architecture, and budgetary allocations do not automatically generate international influence. Material and institutional resources acquire diplomatic significance only when embedded in shared normative understandings (Finnemore & Sikkink, 2001) and activated through interpretative framing, communicative translation, and relational engagement. Smart power in the New Zealand case thus operates as a meaning-making process: it converts domestic integrity into externally recognised authority through discursive, relational, and institutional channels.

The case demonstrates that even a high-integrity society must continuously perform and narrate its compliance in order to sustain normative leadership. As a result, ACPD emerges not as the projection of static virtue but as a dynamic configuration in which attraction, enablement, and collaboration interact. Norm diffusion depends less on material scale than on the coherence between domestic practice, institutional investment, and ideational articulation. For a small state, the strategic sophistication of this articulation determines whether integrity remains a domestic asset or becomes a source of international leverage.

4.7 Enacting Integrity Through Relational Transparency

New Zealand's ACPD is best understood not as a discrete policy instrument but as a mode of enacting state identity through relational transparency. Throughout this chapter, integrity appears as domestic political culture and as external diplomatic currency. It is rooted in administrative traditions, constitutional expectations, and oversight institutions, yet is continually converted into international authority through recognition, benchmarking, and repeated role practice (Breuning, 2024; Adler-Nissen, 2023; Finnemore & Wendt, 2024). The Antipodes metaphor therefore does more than mark geographic distance. It also captures a constructivist dynamic: normative centrality can emerge from the margins when institutional practice becomes internationally legible, socially validated, and strategically narrated (Acharya, 2018; Adler-Nissen, 2023). New Zealand's influence is a function of credibility sustained by the ways partners, indexers, and multilateral peers read it as a reliable integrity performer.

That credibility, however, is neither automatic nor secure. High rankings in global governance and integrity metrics generate reputational capital, but they also raise expectations and intensify scrutiny (Finnemore & Wendt, 2024). Recent slippage in the TRACE Bribery Risk Matrix, alongside the SFO's pilot findings on internal fraud and corruption reporting, shows how integrity is negotiated under conditions of expectation management. Where a state is widely positioned as "high integrity," even limited vulnerabilities become diplomatically consequential. Not because they negate the identity claim, but because they test the coherence between identity, enforcement visibility, and institutional reflexivity. New Zealand's ACPD depends less on projecting perfection than on sustaining a visible capacity for self-correction. Integrity therefore depends on visible monitoring and self-correction, an ongoing defence of credibility rather than a settled attribute.

In practice, this identity is enacted through a repertoire that privileges dialogue, professional exchange, advocacy, and digitally mediated transparency, with a consistent Asia–Pacific orientation informed by regional stability concerns and governance-capacity imperatives. Coordination remains decentralised, yet coherent. The SFO functions as a practical nodal point within a dispersed governance architecture, while NZFAT and the Ministry of Justice translate domestic integrity resources into multilateral participation, peer review, technical assistance, and norm-consistent discourse.

The strategic distinctiveness lies in embedded coherence: continuity emerges from routinised competences and dense network participation that stabilise behaviour and expectations through repetition (Adler-Nissen, 2023). In smart power terms, soft power predominates through attraction-by-governance; hard power remains enabling and infrastructural; and collaborative power multiplies influence via networked co-production of standards. Sharp power, by contrast, is residual and constrained by the reputational logic of integrity itself.

The New Zealand case supports a core claim of this book: ACPD is a process of international socialisation in which identity and interest are mutually constituted, and influence depends on translating domestic institutional performance into internationally recognised authority. New Zealand enacts integrity through relational transparency, using listening practices, cooperative scrutiny, capacity-building, compliance signalling, and the public legibility of oversight ecosystems. In doing so, it reinforces the collective anticorruption norm while sustaining a small-state strategy of credibility-based agency.

This conclusion also prepares the comparative move that follows: if New Zealand exemplifies integrity as an embedded and largely non-strategised performance sustained by trust, the next case examines how a major power enacts anticorruption through different logics of interest, visibility, and leverage.

References

Acharya, A. (2018). *The end of American world order* (2nd ed.). Polity.

Adler-Nissen, R. (2023). Practice. In S. Goddard, G. Lawson, & J. Sending (Eds.), *The Oxford handbook of international political sociology* (pp. 177–198). Oxford University Press.

Breuning, M. (2024). National roles and foreign policy. In J. Kaarbo & C. Thies (Eds.), *The Oxford handbook of foreign policy analysis* (pp. 211–228). Oxford University Press.

Controller and Auditor-General. (2017). *Back at number one and it's personal.* Retrieved February 9, 2026, from https://oag.parliament.nz/blog/2017/back-at-number-one

Dell, G., & McDevitt, A. (2018). *Exporting corruption.* Transparency International. Retrieved February 9, 2026, from https://files.transparencycdn.org/images/2018_Report_ExportingCorruption_English_200402_075046.pdf

Dell, G., & McDevitt, A. (2022). *Exporting corruption 2022*. Transparency International. Retrieved February 9, 2026, from https://files.transparencycdn.org/images/2022_Report-Full_Exporting-Corruption_English.pdf

Financial Markets Authority. (2025). *Make a protected disclosure (whistleblowing)*. Retrieved February 9, 2026, from https://www.fma.govt.nz/contact/make-a-protected-disclosure-whistleblowing/

Finnemore, M., & Sikkink, K. (2001). Taking stock: The constructivist research program in international relations and comparative politics. *Annual Review of Political Science, 4*, 391–416. https://doi.org/10.1146/annurev.polisci.4.1.391

Finnemore, M., & Wendt, A. (2024). When "old" constructivism was new: Reflections on classical constructivism. *Perspectives on Politics, 22*(4), 1248–1268. https://doi.org/10.1017/S1537592724001464

Global Firepower. (2026). *2026 Military Strength Ranking*. Retrieved February 9, 2026, from https://www.globalfirepower.com/countries-listing.php

Goldie, M. (2010). *The idea of the antipodes: Place, people, and voices*. Routledge.

Good Country. (2023). *The Good Country Index*. Retrieved February 9, 2026, from https://index.goodcountry.org

Gregory, R. (2013). *Assessing 'good governance' and corruption in New Zealand* (University of Wellington, Working paper 13/03). Wellington: Institute for Governance and Policy Studies. Retrieved February 9, 2026, from https://ndhadeliver.natlib.govt.nz/delivery/DeliveryManagerServlet?dps_pid=IE20611511

Heimann, F., Földes, Á., & Báthory, G. (2014). *Exporting corruption*. Transparency International. Retrieved February 9, 2026, from https://images.transparencycdn.org/images/2014_ExportingCorruption_OECDProgressReport_EN.pdf

Holsti, K. (1970). National role conceptions in the study of foreign policy. *International Studies Quarterly, 14*(3), 233–309. https://doi.org/10.2307/3013584

Huawei. (2020). GCI global connectivity index. Retrieved February 9, 2026, from https://www.huawei.com/minisite/gci/en/

Huawei. (2025). *Global Digitalization and Intelligence Index 2025*. Huawei Technologies. Retrieved February 9, 2026, from https://www.huawei.com/minisite/gci/en/

Katzenstein, P. (2003). Small states and small states revisited. *New Political Economy, 8*(1), 9–30. https://doi.org/10.1080/1356346032000078705

Ministry of Justice. (2015). *Saying no to bribery and corruption: A guide for New Zealand businesses*. Retrieved February 9, 2026, from https://www.justice.govt.nz/assets/Ministry-of-Justice-Anti-Corruption-Guide.pdf

New Zealand Foreign Affairs and Trade (NZFAT). (2016, September 14). *UN Security Council quarterly debate on Afghanistan, statement delivered by H.E Murray McCully, Minister of Foreign Affairs of New Zealand*. Retrieved February 9, 2026, from https://www.mfat.govt.nz/en/media-and-resources/un-security-council-quarterly-debate-on-afghanistan

New Zealand Foreign Affairs and Trade (NZFAT). (2021, January). *Protocol to upgrade the New Zealand-China free trade agreement.* Retrieved February 9, 2026, from https://www.mfat.govt.nz/assets/Trade-agreements/China-NZ-FTA-Upgrade/China-FTA-Upgrade-NIA.pdf

New Zealand Government. (2023). *National Security Intelligence Priorities 2023.* Retrieved February 9, 2026, from https://www.dpmc.govt.nz/sites/default/files/2023-08/2023%20NSIPs.pdf

New Zealand Ministry of Defence. (2026). *Defence deployments.* Retrieved February 9, 2026, from https://www.defence.govt.nz/what-we-do/diplomacy-and-deployments/deployment-map/

Nye, J. (2004). *Soft power.* Public Affairs.

Nye, J. (2011). *The future of power.* Public Affairs.

Open Government Partnership (OGP). (2026). *New Zealand.* Retrieved February 9, 2026, from https://www.opengovpartnership.org/members/new-zealand/

Organisation for Economic Co-operation and Development (OECD). (2002, May). *Review of implementation of the convention and 1997 recommendation phase 1 report: New Zealand.* Retrieved February 9, 2026, from https://www.oecd.org/daf/anti-bribery/anti-briberyconvention/2088257.pdf

Organisation for Economic Co-operation and Development (OECD). (2006, October 27). *Report on the application of the Convention on Combating Bribery of Foreign Public Officials in International Business Transactions and the 1997 Recommendation on Combating Bribery in International Business Transactions - Phase 2 report: New Zealand.* Retrieved February 9, 2026, from https://www.oecd.org/daf/anti-bribery/anti-briberyconvention/37658136.pdf

Organisation for Economic Co-operation and Development (OECD). (2009, March 13). *Follow-Up report on the implementation of the phase 2 recommendations: New Zealand.* Retrieved February 9, 2026, from https://www.oecd.org/en/publications/follow-up-report-on-the-implementation-of-the-phase-2-recommendations-new-zealand_14440fc5-en.html

Organisation for Economic Co-operation and Development (OECD). (2013, October). *Phase 3 report on implementing the OECD anti-bribery convention in New Zealand.* Retrieved February 9, 2026, from https://www.oecd.org/en/publications/implementing-the-oecd-anti-bribery-convention-phase-3-report-new-zealand_6072f0d5-en.html

Serious Fraud Office (SFO). (2026). *Pilot report of the Anti-Corruption Taskforce: Assessing fraud and corruption risks in the New Zealand public sector.* Serious Fraud Office. Retrieved February 9, 2026, from https://www.sfo.govt.nz/assets/Uploads/Anti-Corruption-Taskforce-Assessing-fraud-and-corruption-risks-FINAL-Feb2026.pdf

TRACE International. (2025). *TRACE Bribery Risk Matrix.* Retrieved February 9, 2026, from https://www.traceinternational.org/trace-matrix

Transparency International (TI). (2013). *Global corruption barometer 2013*. Transparency International. Retrieved February 9, 2026, from https://images.transparencycdn.org/images/2013_GlobalCorruptionBarometer_EN_200525_112757.pdf

Transparency International New Zealand (TINZ). (2013). *Integrity plus 2013: New Zealand National Integrity System Assessment*. TINZ. Retrieved February 9, 2026, from https://images.transparencycdn.org/images/2013_NewZealandNIS_EN.pdf

Transparency International New Zealand (TINZ). (2018). *New Zealand National Integrity System Assessment*. TINZ. Retrieved February 9, 2026, from https://files.transparencycdn.org/images/National-Integrity-System-Assessment-2018-update-summary.pdf

United Nations Office on Drugs and Crime (UNODC). (2017). *Country review report of New Zealand*. Retrieved February 9, 2026, from https://www.unodc.org/documents/treaties/UNCAC/CountryVisitFinalReports/2020_10_21_New_Zealand_Final_Country_Review_Report.pdf

Wendt, A. (1999). *Social theory of international politics*. Cambridge University Press.

Williams, J. (2013). Lex Aotearoa: An heroic attempt to map the Māori dimension in modern New Zealand law. *Waikato Law Review, 21*(2), 1–34.

World Economic Forum. (2024). *Travel & Tourism Development Index 2024*. World Economic Forum. Retrieved February 9, 2026, from https://www3.weforum.org/docs/WEF_Travel_and_Tourism_Development_Index_2024.pdf

Zaharna, R. (2013). Network purpose, network design: Dimensions of network and collaborative public diplomacy. In R. S. Zaharna, A. Fisher, & A. Arsenault (Eds.), *Relational, networked, and collaborative approaches to public diplomacy* (pp. 221–246). Routledge.

Zaharna, R. (2022). *Boundary spanners of humanity*. Oxford University Press. https://doi.org/10.1093/oso/9780190930271.001.0001

CHAPTER 5

The United States: From Denying Safe Haven to Shaping Global Norms

5.1 Contextualising the Case: From the American Dream to Denying Safe Haven

Few political texts have shaped the global political imagination as enduringly as the United States Declaration of Independence. By proclaiming that "all men are created equal" and endowed with unalienable rights to "Life, Liberty and the pursuit of Happiness" (United States, 1776), it did more than justify separation from the British Crown. It laid the normative foundations of what would later crystallise as the American Dream (Adams, 2012, p. 416). These ideas of opportunity, merit, and upward mobility formed a powerful national narrative. The American Dream fused personal initiative with an expectation of fairness. It projected an image of an egalitarian society in which talent, not lineage, determined success; ambition was virtuous; and prosperity could be earned. Over time, this ideal became inseparable from the country's national self-understanding and its international projection as a land of opportunity and freedom, shaping expectations of its external role.

Yet this narrative carries an enduring tension. The competitive drive has also legitimised aggressive ambition that may blur into illegality. The cultural valorisation of entrepreneurial risk-taking coexists with illicit financial practices and transnational corruption (Johnston, 2005, p. 1). The openness and economic dynamism that attract global investment to the United

N. de A. e S. F. dos Santos, *Anticorruption Public Diplomacy*,
Palgrave Macmillan Series in Global Public Diplomacy,
https://doi.org/10.1007/978-3-032-28668-0_5

States also render it vulnerable to illicit capital inflows (Johnston, 2012, p. 330). Consequently, entrepreneurial dynamism and vulnerability are co-constitutive features of American identity, revealing a structural ambivalence in which openness simultaneously generates normative authority and governance risk.

It is within this tension that the United States' anticorruption identity has taken shape. In the long run, the expression *Denying Safe Haven* evolved into a central organising doctrine of anticorruption policy. It appears in presidential rhetoric across Democratic and Republican administrations (Biden, 2021; Bush, 2004; Clinton White House, 1997; Obama, 2009; Trump, 2017), as well as in statements by law enforcement and diplomatic authorities (Blinken, 2023; Department of Justice [DoJ], 2022; Luna, 2005). The doctrine institutionalises a particular understanding of sovereign responsibility in which jurisdictional reach becomes a normative mechanism of defence. It makes clear that the American financial and legal system, considered pillars of global capitalism (Helleiner, 2014), must not function as a haven for corrupt actors or illicit assets. In doing so, it marks a shift from declaratory integrity to enforcement-oriented regulatory assertiveness.

The Foreign Corrupt Practices Act (FCPA) became the cornerstone of this enforcement-oriented approach. It reshaped domestic compliance culture while contributing to the emergence of a global anticorruption norm (Mccoy & Heckel, 2001). This normative influence unfolded despite sustained critique regarding the limits of sovereign reach (Ashe, 2005). By extending prosecutorial prerogatives to situations in which foreign corrupt acts intersect with the United States' territory, financial circuits, or digital infrastructure, the FCPA institutionalised an assertive extraterritorial anticorruption posture. Even attenuated connections, including communications routed through servers located in the United States, may suffice to establish jurisdiction.

Policymakers soon recognised that unilateral enforcement risked placing national firms at a competitive disadvantage. In response, American efforts shifted towards multilateralisation (Pieth, 2012). The country played a decisive role in advancing anticorruption conventions within the OECD, the United Nations, and the Organization of American States (OAS). Legislative developments abroad, including France's Loi Sapin II and the United Kingdom's Bribery Act 2010, reflect this process of regulatory convergence (Pieth, 2012; Stephenson, 2017). The FCPA thus evolved into an international regulatory reference point, anchoring a model of enforcement-led norm diffusion in which legal practice precedes and shapes multilateral standard-setting.

In this context, the language of Denying Safe Haven migrated from Washington into multilateral discourse (Asian Development Bank & OECD, 2006; BRICS, 2022; G8, 2003; World Bank & United Nations Office on Drugs and Crime [UNODC], 2010). What began as an American enforcement doctrine became embedded in the global anticorruption framework. This diffusion illustrates how national enforcement practices were translated into multilateral norms.

As the originator of this doctrine, the United States is a founding signatory of key international anticorruption conventions and stands out for its enforcement performance (Dell & McDevitt, 2022). Although it does not rank alongside Scandinavian countries in anticorruption indices, it consistently remains within the first quartile in assessments such as those of Transparency International, the European Research Centre for Anti-Corruption and State-Building, and TRACE International. These positions reinforce its reputation for comparatively strong institutional integrity among advanced democracies.

A further milestone in the American trajectory is the 2021 National Strategy on Countering Corruption, which explicitly recognises the role of public diplomacy in addressing corruption (White House, 2021, p. 14). This alignment is unsurprising in a country that inspired the concept of soft power (Nye, 2004), has frequently ranked among the leading countries in Brand Finance's Global Soft Power Index, and maintains the world's second-largest diplomatic network (Lowy Institute, 2024). Yet fluctuations in reputational indicators, including declines in measures such as Anholt's Good Country Index, suggest that credibility remains contested rather than structurally secured.

Against this backdrop of consolidated yet contested authority, recent developments introduce a new layer of uncertainty. Since January 2025, FCPA enforcement has entered a phase of renewed domestic contestation. The system analysed in this chapter therefore reflects primarily the pattern of American anticorruption public diplomacy (ACPD) as it consolidated over previous decades, up to December 2024. Developments emerging from 2025 are considered in the sections that follow, particularly where they affect enforcement priorities and external projection. While it is difficult to predict with precision which trajectory will ultimately consolidate, the ACPD framework developed in this book enables a prospective assessment of possible pathways.

5.2 Identities and Interests: Power, Pluralism, and the American Creed

Officially named the United States of America, the country spans a continental scale and is the third-largest country in the world. Bordered by two vast oceans, with access to the Arctic, and sharing land frontiers with Canada and Mexico, it combines territorial breadth with strategic maritime access. This structure has long shaped its outward orientation and its identity as a northern colossus exercising structural preponderance over the Caribbean basin and adjacent regions, particularly Mexico (Spykman, 1942). In this sense, geography has provided security buffers while facilitating global projection.

The United States is a federal constitutional republic composed of fifty states and the District of Columbia. Its 1789 Constitution is widely regarded as a foundational charter of modern democracy (Group of States against Corruption [GRECO], 2004, p. 4). The legal order follows the common law tradition, rooted in British origins, and enriched by Spanish, French, and indigenous legal influences (Cohen, 1989). These institutional arrangements have sustained a type identity anchored in constitutionalism, separation of powers, judicial independence, and the rule of law.

Material capabilities add another layer to American identity. The country remains the world's foremost military power (Global Firepower [GFP], 2026) and the largest economy with a GDP exceeding US$28 trillion (World Bank, 2024a), accounting for roughly 8–9% of global exports (Dell & McDevitt, 2022). It possesses significant strategic resources, including the world's largest coal reserves (CIA, 2025). This military-economic centrality reinforces its structural position within global governance hierarchies (Helleiner, 2014; Nye, 2004). In the American case, power is not peripheral to identity; it is constitutive, shaping both self-understanding and external recognition of legitimacy.

Importantly, the national creed grounded in liberty, democracy, and opportunity provides the interpretative lens through which material capabilities are mobilised. Foreign policy strategies have consistently framed national interests in terms of protecting the American people, expanding prosperity, and defending democratic values (White House, 2022, p. 7). The 2025 strategy narrows core national interests to security and sovereignty (including border control), economic strength and industrial resilience, and the preservation of the American way of life and fundamental rights (White House, 2025a, pp. 3–6). Despite this tightening, American external action continues to rest on a triad of security, economic power, and normative projection. This suggests that the national creed continues to be projected outward, albeit within a strategic logic more explicitly filtered through sovereignty and national self-preservation.

From an interpretivist standpoint, these interests are not only objective responses to material conditions; they are also socially constructed through narratives that link power to principle (Finnemore, 1996). This process transforms material capabilities into intelligible instruments of action. For instance, security becomes more than territorial defence; it signifies the protection of the American way of life. Economic expansion becomes a symbol of moral purpose and national self-affirmation. Democratic values remain reference points, yet are more explicitly grounded in national identity rather than universalist missionary undertones.

This intertwining of power and principle generates a distinctive role identity within the global integrity landscape structured by shared expectations (Wendt, 1999). The United States continues to frame its global engagement within a rule-based order. Because identities and interests are mutually constitutive (Finnemore & Sikkink, 2001), this role conception produces expectations of normative consistency. Within a dense anticorruption regime formed by multilateral conventions and peer-review tools (Hough, 2013; Mccoy & Heckel, 2001), credibility becomes a relational asset. Anticorruption thus becomes intelligible as a question of legitimacy: role performance in a rule-based order implies alignment between declared values and conduct (Adler, 2013). A state that claims to champion democracy and the rule of law must address corruption both as a regulatory challenge and as a condition of international legitimacy and recognised authority.

The relationship between identities and interests is therefore recursive: material assets enable global projection, while ideational commitments support its meaning and direction. In the United States case, they jointly form a foreign policy logic in which anticorruption intersects with national security and economic competitiveness. The country's structural scale, traditions, and global status create expectations and pressures. ACPD operates within this identity model, where power and principle are continuously negotiated and where legitimacy relies heavily on sustained coherence between identity claims and institutional performance. This context sets the credibility stakes for such an archetype of anticorruption statecraft, examined in the following section.

5.3 Denying Safe Haven: Security, Law, and the American Anticorruption Identity

The United States' anticorruption identity evolved through the interaction of constitutional design, legislative innovation, and shifting conceptions of national security. What began as a concern with republican virtue gradually acquired strategic significance. Corruption came to be framed as a structural vulnerability capable of distorting markets, weakening democracy, and enabling undue influence. This reflects a process of securitisation, whereby an issue is constructed as an existential threat requiring exceptional measures and coordination (Buzan et al., 1998). The 2021 strategy consolidated this shift by integrating anticorruption into the national security framework (White House, 2021), embedding it within the strategic domain and elevating enforcement to a security instrument.

The strategy embodies a legalistic and interventionist profile. It is structured around five interrelated pillars, including intelligence integration; law enforcement coordination; illicit-finance legislation; the promotion of accountability abroad through international cooperation and foreign assistance; and diplomacy, explicitly encompassing public diplomacy (White House, 2021). External assessments, however, reveal asymmetries. GRECO (2023) notes emphasis on transnational corruption alongside comparatively limited attention to corruption risks within the Executive Branch. This imbalance reflects a model that privileges external enforcement.

Concerns regarding corruption and foreign undue influence date back to the founding republic. Anxieties over foreign gifts, illustrated by the 1785 gift offered by Louis XVI to Benjamin Franklin, led to the adoption of the *Foreign Emoluments Clause* (Teachout, 2014). This constitutional recognition established corruption as grounds for presidential impeachment. In 1853, bribery of federal officials was criminalised (Noonan, 1987). Subsequent reforms, including the Pendleton Civil Service Reform Act of 1883, the Tillman Act of 1907, and New Deal-era administrative restructuring, further institutionalised merit-based recruitment and regulatory oversight (Cuèllar & Stephenson, 2022; Teachout, 2014). Collectively, these developments indicate that anticorruption has not been an episodic response but is constitutive of the American constitutional system.

Currently, the national integrity system covers a dense institutional network ranging from the Department of State (DoS), the DoJ, the

Department of Defense (DoD) and the Treasury to intelligence agencies, United States Agency for International Development (USAID), Congress, the Federal Election Commission, and civil society actors (White House, 2021; GRECO, 2011). This arrangement, involving bodies in charge of foreign policy, reinforces the extraterritorial orientation of the American anticorruption identity.

From a legal perspective, this outward tendency strengthened in 1977 with the adoption of the FCPA following the Watergate scandal. Initially prohibiting bribery of foreign officials by American companies, the statute was expanded in 1998 to cover corrupt acts committed by foreigners abroad, provided the conduct had a jurisdictional nexus to the country, including, for instance, communication routed through servers located in the United States (Bixby, 2010). Following the attacks of 11 September 2001, enforcement became intertwined with counterterrorism financing (Hough, 2013). Anticorruption was increasingly integrated within intelligence cooperation and geopolitical risk management (Krishnakumar, 2023). The FCPA thus evolved into a strategic vector gathering legal legitimacy, financial concerns, and security policy, with enforcement becoming a geopolitical signal.

The FCPA enforcement prototype became a vehicle of norm entrepreneurship and played a decisive role in advancing multilateral anticorruption conventions (Mccoy & Heckel, 2001; Pieth, 2012). It has informed the participation of the United States in global initiatives such as the United Nations Global Compact, the Open Government Partnership (OGP), GRECO, and the Extractive Industries Transparency Initiative. Despite structural blind spots in areas including beneficial ownership and revolving-door regulation (GRECO, 2023; OECD Working Group on Bribery, 2020; UNODC, 2023b), the country remains recognised as one of the most active enforcers of the OECD Anti-Bribery Convention (Dell & McDevitt, 2022), which reflects FCPA principles.

Since early 2025, this trajectory has undergone a recalibrated phase marked by a temporary pause in FCPA enforcement (White House, 2025b). Prosecutorial priorities were subsequently redirected towards organised crime and cartels engaged in human, narcotics, and firearms trafficking, as well as cases involving national security or substantial economic harm (Deputy Attorney General, 2025), mirroring the National Security Strategy (White House, 2025a). This guidance narrowed enforcement priorities while signalling restraint in corporate cases. The 2025 White-Collar Memorandum (Galeotti, 2025), though not confined to the

FCPA, further consolidated this shift by softening certain corporate obligations and making prosecutorial selectivity more explicit. The reorientation was reflected in enforcement output: while 2024 recorded nine corporate resolutions, 2025 registered only two (DoJ, 2026a, 2026b), indicating a marked contraction in case volume.

These developments reproduce a structural tension: regulatory activism coexists with reputational vulnerability. On one side, the country shows robust extraterritorial enforcement capacity, regulatory leadership, and sustained political will, alongside thousands of convictions of public officials for bribery-related offences (UNODC, 2018). On the other, integrity narratives are undermined by recurring corruption scandals involving Congresspeople, senior federal officials, presidents, and major corporations (Dell & McDevitt, 2022; Heimann & Dell, 2010; House of Representatives, 2024). Although petty corruption remains comparatively limited (Transparency International, 2013), such high-profile cases shape corruption perception indices. While consistently ranking within the upper quartiles, the United States has not occupied the top positions.

Recent political developments have provided particularly visible illustrations of these broader tensions between regulatory leadership and reputational credibility. These tensions became particularly visible during the Trump era, which generated extensive academic and policy debates concerning conflicts of interest, nepotism, and the relationship between public office and private economic interests. Scholarship on public integrity emphasises that corruption-related concerns do not necessarily depend upon findings of criminal wrongdoing but may also arise when public values, ethical standards, and institutional safeguards are perceived to be at risk (Bozeman, 2025, pp. 1585–1588; Ceva & Ferretti, 2021, pp. 1–4). In this context, issues ranging from the continued relationship between the presidency and private business interests to the prominent advisory roles assumed by family members have been socially and academically scrutinised (Goldstein & Drybread, 2023). These debates were particularly salient given that nepotism is commonly understood as the preferential treatment of relatives in institutional settings and has long been associated with concerns regarding fairness, trust, and good governance (Jones, 2012, p. 253; Vveinhardt & Bendaraviciene, 2022). Similarly, conflict-of-interest scholarship highlights that democratic governance may be compromised whenever there is a substantial risk that public judgement becomes unduly influenced by private interests, irrespective of whether legal violations are ultimately established (Fung & Thompson, 2025, pp. 2–3). While interpretations of these controversies remain politically contested, their prominence illustrates how debates concerning institutional integrity, ethical standards, and accountability increasingly intersect with questions of international legitimacy and normative authority.

This paradox cannot be explained solely by institutional design or prosecutorial output. Anticorruption leadership is mediated through domestic political structures that shape external credibility. Under heightened polarisation and politicisation, externally projected regulatory ascendancy becomes entangled with internal contestation over institutional legitimacy (Wiseman & Scott, 2026), complicating the sustainability of reputational security (Cull, 2024; Pamment et al., 2025). ACPD thus reflects not only enforcement capacity but also the resilience of domestic recognition structures, rendering international authority structurally contingent upon internal political cohesion and institutional trust.

From a perspective grounded in role identity (Breuning, 2024; Holsti, 1970; Wendt, 1999), the American anticorruption identity can best be conceptualised as that of a regulatory guardian state within the global integrity landscape. Rather than projecting reputational purity, it enacts leadership through legal enforcement, agenda-setting, and strategic norm entrepreneurship. In this configuration, security framing and legalism are constitutive rather than ancillary: corruption is constructed as a threat to sovereignty and democratic integrity, and law functions as the primary instrument of response. ACPD therefore reflects an enforcement-centred performance of authority in which national interest and normative ambition are mutually constituted. The doctrine of Denying Safe Haven encapsulates this orientation, translating role identity into jurisdictional practice.

5.4 Performing Anticorruption: American Public Diplomacy Potential

Public diplomacy is identified in the 2021 anticorruption strategy as a key instrument for engaging foreign audiences. Engagement with such publics is not an add-on but a constitutive aspect of modern statecraft; it is the public dimension of diplomacy (Gregory, 2024). It mediates the translation of anticorruption identity claims into internationally recognised authority. Such legitimacy is generated through routinised institutional conduct and socially situated leadership performances (Adler-Nissen, 2023), stabilising expectations of reliability through processes of validation, contestation, and social embedding of projected identity (Adler, 2013; Finnemore & Wendt, 2024). The perceived alignment between identity claims and institutional conduct generates normative authority (Nye, 2004; Wendt, 1999), underpinning reputational security and enhancing strategic resilience (Cull, 2024; Pamment et al., 2025). The accumulated repertoire of institutional practice may thus strengthen the plausibility of these normative claims.

The United States possesses considerable symbolic capital that enhances the plausibility of its anticorruption normative claims, despite structural inequalities, concerns over press freedom, and incomplete ratification of certain human rights treaties (Reports Without Borders, 2025; United Nations, 2024; World Bank, 2024b). This capital is rooted in narratives of pluralism, civic engagement, opportunity, and cultural influence shaping global imaginaries (Nye, 2004). However, such prominence does not automatically secure recognition of its anticorruption identity; rather, it fosters receptive environments in which integrity ideals diffuse beyond diplomacy and public diplomacy arenas.

Public diplomacy operates through the articulation of smart power (Nye, 2011) within a broader ecology of resources, including policies, values, material capabilities (military and economic), technological and informational infrastructures, and participation in international anticorruption networks. Among these policies and values, anticorruption laws stand out alongside values such as openness, meritocracy, and transparency, and policies reflected in administrative capacity, regulatory sophistication, legal robustness, consistently high levels of human development, and strong rule of law indicators (United Nations Development Programme, 2023; World Intellectual Property Organization [WIPO], 2024; World Justice Project, 2025). In the American ACPD, policies and values assume particular prominence, as expected in a state whose international legitimacy is deeply anchored in normative self-representation.

Material resources amplify this potential. First, the centrality of the United States in global financial markets provides leverage for promoting compliance-based regulatory standards institutionalised in its policies (Drezner, 2007). When articulated by smart power (Nye, 2011) and nested in shared normative frameworks that define proficiency (Wendt, 1999), these resources acquire diplomatic meaning. Beyond its status as a leading military and economic actor (GFP, 2026; World Bank, 2024a), the United States benefits from the structural weight of its industrial base, export profile, and provision of official development assistance (ODA). In this regard, although it remains the largest ODA provider in absolute terms, this amounts to roughly 0.22% of gross national income (OECD, 2025), well below the United Nations' 0.7% benchmark. This constellation of material resources underpins American ACPD, translating structural centrality into recognised anticorruption leadership through aid conditionality, regulatory leadership, and market-based leverage.

Technological and informational infrastructures deepen this reach. The enormous American capacity in this domain is reflected in sustained investment in research and development, global leadership in scientific production, expansive higher education networks, and advanced digital connectivity (WIPO, 2024). These resources enable transnational norm circulation and socialisation.

Network density further consolidates this position. In addition to one of the world's most extensive diplomatic and organisational presences (Lowy Institute, 2024), the United States participates in numerous multilateral institutions and regulatory regimes (DoS, 2026a). High connectivity in financial, digital, logistical, and organisational domains is pivotal to its norm-entrepreneurial and agenda-setting role. Central actors within networks possess enhanced capacity to shape interpretive frames and diffuse regulatory expectations (Adler-Nissen, 2014). As norms travel through communities of practice that embed shared understandings within professional routines (Adler, 2005; Adler-Nissen, 2023), these networked resources place American ACPD in a structurally advantaged position for normative socialisation. Compliance networks and epistemic communities function as public diplomacy arenas in which governance standards are debated and internalised.

Within American ACPD, the security dimension remains central. Securitising frames may generate endorsement or scepticism depending on audience reception (Buzan et al., 1998). Robust enforcement can signal commitment to a rule-based order but may also be perceived as unilateralism or selective jurisdictional activism. The balance among resources and smart power must therefore account for this dynamic. Credibility is relational and continuously negotiated, particularly where domestic political fragmentation shapes external perceptions. When domestic practice diverges from external perceptions, credibility gaps emerge.

Debates surrounding conflicts of interest, nepotism, and the use of public office for private gain in the United States have received extensive international media coverage in recent years and circulated widely across diplomatic, political, and civil society networks (Jacobs, 2025; Petry,

2025). Such controversies became part of broader international discussions regarding the consistency between the United States' external promotion of transparency, accountability, and integrity and developments within its domestic political sphere. As legitimacy and normative authority are socially recognised rather than unilaterally asserted (Adler, 2013; Wendt, 1999), perceptions of inconsistency may weaken the persuasive force of anticorruption narratives among foreign audiences. Recent survey data suggest a deterioration in international perceptions of American leadership, including among long-standing allies. Favourability ratings declined across several European countries, while global approval of U.S. leadership fell from 39% in 2024 to 31% in 2025, accompanied by record levels of disapproval (Ray et al., 2026; Wike et al., 2025). Although such trends cannot be attributed solely to corruption-related controversies, they illustrate how domestic political developments may shape external evaluations of American credibility. Because public diplomacy relies on recognition by external audiences, and ACPD depends upon the credibility of governance-related narratives, sustained perceptions of divergence between proclaimed anticorruption commitments and domestic political practice may complicate efforts to project normative authority internationally. In this sense, the doctrine of Denying Safe Haven gains persuasive force only when situated within recognised institutional consistency. The following section examines how this coherence is operationalised in practice.

5.5 Practising Anticorruption Public Diplomacy

The United States' ACPD is most clearly observed at the level of institutional routines. Across the subsections that follow, practice is structured around a coherent sequence of activities. They include listening mechanisms that generate actionable knowledge; dialogical engagement channels that operationalise cooperation through enforcement; advocacy initiatives; cultural and educational diplomacy; and exchange programmes that socialise anticorruption standards. They also include digital narratives that mediate these themes through digital broadcasting infrastructures. This set of activities demonstrates how American ACPD is enacted as a structured system of international influence.

Listening Through Enforcement: Feedback Loops in the FCPA Ecosystem

The United States' listening practices in ACPD prioritise detection, verification, and institutional learning. Listening is anchored in a law-centred feedback design linking multilateral monitoring, whistleblowing channels, corporate compliance incentives, financial intelligence, field reporting, and media scrutiny. Rather than privileging a single audience, this structure captures corruption signals across multiple sites and converts them into actionable regulatory and diplomatic knowledge.

Eight methods structure this repertoire. First, the United States incorporates feedback from international institutions through monitoring and peer review. The UNODC country visit in 2015 (United States, 2015) illustrates how international standards are listened to, internalised, and used to adjust national practice. Second, through hotlines, USAID embeds listening within development assistance, enabling reporting of corruption linked to foreign assistance (UNODC, 2018). Third, digital reporting platforms, including the FCPA anticorruption report website (UNODC, 2018), expand access to disclosure. Fourth, corporate self-reporting under the FCPA transforms compliance obligations into information infrastructures (OECD Working Group on Bribery, 2022), encouraging firms to convert internal controls into disclosure flows that would otherwise remain concealed.

Fifth, listening is increasingly mediated through artificial intelligence. The Financial Crimes Enforcement Network (FinCEN) employs AI to generate automated reports on suspected cases, converting financial flows into prioritised risk patterns (OECD Working Group on Bribery, 2020). Sixth, diplomatic missions and FBI legal attachés provide field-based inputs for enforcement and risk assessment, extending detection beyond domestic visibility (OECD Working Group on Bribery, 2020; McMann, 2017). Seventh, foreign media monitoring accounts for approximately 15% of FCPA cases (OECD Working Group on Bribery, 2022), integrating investigative journalism into enforcement triggers. Eighth, DoJ FCPA roundtables (United States, 2015) institutionalise structured dialogue, allowing stakeholder feedback to refine enforcement communication and interpretation.

Collectively, these methods draw on resources rooted in anticorruption policies (notably the FCPA), transparency and openness values, legal authority, institutional expertise, budgetary and technological capacity, financial intelligence infrastructures, diplomatic networks, media ecosystems, and the country's nodal position within multilateral anticorruption networks. They generate international effects through the combined mobilisation of soft, hard, and collaborative power. Soft power operates through listening and communicating to convert resources such as openness and reputational signalling into administratively intelligible listening practices. Hard power functions through the coercive and enabling capacities anchored in the FCPA and related statutes, as well as in the allocation of budgetary resources, transforming detected misconduct into prosecutorial action, sanctions, and deterrence effects that extend beyond territorial jurisdiction. Through cooperation and coordination, collaborative power structures peer review, multilateral monitoring, and corporate partnerships into feedback mechanisms.

The DoS and the DoJ generally coordinate these arrangements, involving states and non state agents, including foreign experts and norm entrepreneurs such as the UNODC and the OECD Working Group on Bribery, thereby enhancing the international legibility of American integrity performances. State agencies act under legal mandate, while non state and international agents participate through treaty adherence, official invitation, or public knowledge production (in the journalists' case). Listening remains enforcement-anchored. It does not merely gather information; it converts dispersed signals into regulatory action and diplomatic credibility. In the American model, to listen is to detect, interpret, and recalibrate, an ongoing practice of safeguarding legitimacy in a contested integrity environment. Listening thus becomes an instrument of entitlement maintenance, sustaining the credibility of the United States' anticorruption identity through continuous feedback, adjustment, and externally visible enforcement outcomes.

Engaging Through Jurisdiction: Enforcement and Transnational Authority

Dialogical engagement is central to American ACPD and unfolds primarily through law, enforcement, and institutional cooperation. It relies on sustained cross-border interactions with foreign publics and authorities, as well as multilateral networks. The United States engages counterparts by coordinating investigations, initiating proceedings, sharing intelligence, tracing assets, and shaping the interpretation of anticorruption norms.

At least nine action types structure this collection. First, the extraterritorial application of anticorruption laws signals the distinctly legal profile of American ACPD and its regulatory reach in global markets. This is illustrated by high-level FCPA prosecutions led by the DoJ against political elites (UNODC, 2012) and major corporations (Bixby, 2010; Dell, 2020). This orientation anchors an interventionist enforcement framework extending beyond the FCPA to include the Racketeer Influenced and Corrupt Organizations Act (RICO), the Magnitsky Act, and the International Emergency Economic Powers Act (IEEPA). Between 2005 and 2024, related actions averaged 32 cases annually (Dell & McDevitt, 2022; Heimann & Dell, 2010), producing diplomatic effects beyond courtrooms. Such dialogical enforcement is norm-generative: American legislation has influenced multilateral anticorruption conventions (Pieth, 2012) and informed subsequent foreign laws (Stephenson, 2017). In this constellation, law operates simultaneously as instrument and message.

Second, American courts accept actions brought by foreign plaintiffs, creating procedural avenues for redress within American institutions. One example involves a Russian citizen bringing a civil action under RICO (Gomez-Moreno, 2024). Third, the United States assists foreign governments in tracing and recovering overseas assets, notably through the Kleptocracy Asset Recovery Initiative established in 2010 (UNODC, 2023b). Fourth, the strategic deployment of legal attachés supports partner governments through specialised expertise, legislative drafting assistance, consultancy, and training (UNODC, 2012). These actions perform largely under DoJ coordination.

Fifth, engagement extends to military investigations into fraud abroad. Investigations into contractual misconduct involving American companies in Afghanistan and Iraq (UNODC, 2012), coordinated by the DoD, exemplify this dimension.

Types six to eight illustrate the networked character of jurisdictional engagement. Sixth, the United States maintains more than 80 bilateral mutual legal assistance treaties (UNODC, 2018). Seventh, it participates in multilateral anticorruption structures, including the Financial Action Task Force (FATF), the Caribbean Financial Action Task Force, the Camden Asset Recovery Interagency Network, and GRECO (UNODC, 2018, 2023b). Often coordinated by the DoJ, these practices routinise engagement through institutionalised interaction, bringing together judicial, police, and regulatory authorities.

Collectively, these first eight types of actions mobilise resources derived from anticorruption legal frameworks, anticorruption and foreign assistance policies, administrative capacity, institutional expertise, technical knowledge, international agreements, economic strength, and nodal positions within anticorruption networks. These resources are activated through the combined exercise of soft, hard, and collaborative power: soft power through communication and reputational influence; hard power through enabling, sanctioning, and incentivising capabilities; and collaborative power through negotiated cooperation and institutional coordination.

Finally, the ninth type of action involves financial support provided by DoS to selected norm entrepreneurs. Although American ACPD relies primarily on legal and administrative instruments, it allocates limited and targeted funding (e.g. Transparency International, 2023). Alongside the financial strength of hard power, and the influence of anticorruption policies, such actions may entail sharp power dynamics. Even modest contributions may generate relational asymmetries under norms of reciprocity (Mauss, 2002), blurring the boundary between assistance and influence.

Across these nine types, representational authority derives from institutional mandate. State agents act by virtue of legal competence, while non state and international agents participate through agreements, network membership, involvement in legal proceedings, or acceptance of funding. Dialogical engagement, in this sense, is not episodic but patterned: a system of jurisdictional interaction that renders anticorruption cooperation operational and internationally legible.

Advocacy, Commitment, and Enforcement Partnerships

Advocacy also carries substantial weight in American ACPD. It frames commitments, signals priorities, disseminates standards, and leverages enforcement visibility to shape expectations. In the United States pattern, it operates through fifteen modalities anchored in legal instruments, economic agreements, sanctions regimes, and enforcement practices, transforming anticorruption into a narrative of legitimacy and strategy.

First, securitisation is the most consequential modality (Buzan et al., 1998). By framing corruption as a threat to prosperity, democratic values, and national security, the United States elevates it from a regulatory concern to a strategic imperative (White House, 2021). Coordinated by the

DoS and endorsed at presidential level, this framing mobilises soft power and signals political centrality to domestic and international audiences.

Second, anticorruption commitments are reaffirmed in presidential and executive speeches, embedding integrity within broader foreign policy discourse (Biden, 2021; Bush, 2004; Clinton White House, 1997; Obama, 2009; Trump, 2017). Video statements by the Secretary of State broadcast during peer review missions reiterate integrity commitments in multilateral settings (OECD Working Group on Bribery, 2010). These initiatives are generally coordinated by the DoS.

Subsequent modalities institutionalise advocacy communicatively. Third, the DoJ and the Securities and Exchange Commission (SEC) actively participate in international anticorruption forums, reinforcing compliance expectations by advocating reporting mechanisms and transforming technical procedures into public standards (OECD Working Group on Bribery, 2020). Fourth, press releases, such as those concerning investigations, settlements, and sanctions (DoJ, 2023), amplify the external visibility of enforcement and regulatory resolve. A similar logic underpins the fifth modality: the international dissemination of reports and indicators. For instance, those issued by USAID establish benchmarks (OECD Working Group on Bribery, 2020) that shape evaluative expectations abroad. Sixth, international campaigns, including corporate compliance initiatives led by the Department of Commerce (OECD Working Group on Bribery, 2020), rely on persuasion within the shadow of enforcement.

Modalities seven to nine consolidate credibility. The seventh modality encompasses presentations during institutional visits and peer review processes, exemplified by information about the International Corruption Unit shared during the UNODC visit in 2011 (UNODC, 2012). The eighth modality concerns the international recognition of national practices as good practices, which illustrates peer validation, reinforcing credibility in multilateral arenas. An example is the DoJ's coordinated efforts resulting in OECD recognition of the United States enforcement system (OECD Working Group on Bribery, 2020). Ninth, advocacy may also be undertaken by third parties, including the defence of FCPA principles by the Swiss criminal law scholar Mark Pieth (Pieth, 2012), who chaired the OECD Working Group on Bribery during the convention's negotiation. It illustrates how epistemic leadership diffuses American preferences beyond formal diplomacy.

Tenth, specialised task forces reinforce the advocacy–enforcement nexus. Established to hold foreign oligarchs accountable through enforcement, the KleptoCapture Task Force (DoJ, 2022) illustrates the projection of regulatory resolve beyond national borders.

Modalities eleven to thirteen consolidate integrity within economic statecraft. Eleventh, anticorruption clauses in international agreements, such as trade and procurement contracts, institutionalise this normative stance within economic cooperation frameworks (OECD Working Group on Bribery, 2020). Twelfth, it involves due diligence requirements linked to export credit arrangements (OECD Working Group on Bribery, 2020), while thirteenth refers to deterrent measures such as SEC disgorgement orders. An example is the US$933 million returned in the Brazilian oil company case (OECD Working Group on Bribery, 2020), converting penalisation into communicative force. Enforcement capacity and strategic signalling thus operate in tandem.

These advocacy initiatives mobilise capabilities to communicate, influence, and inspire (soft power); to penalise and enable financial and compliance-dependent structures (hard power); and to cooperate within anticorruption networks (collaborative power). Democratic values and culture, anticorruption policy and legislation, enforcement expertise, international agreements, economic strength, technology, and network positions are converted into ACPD outcomes through this smart power arrangement.

The final two modalities sharpen this posture under DoJ coordination. Visa sanctions against foreign officials (White House, 2013) merge anticorruption policy with coercive functions inherent to sharp power. Likewise, strategic control of indictments and judicial timing (OECD Working Group on Bribery, 2010) turns prosecutorial discretion into a diplomatic signal by means of sharp power.

American ACPD advocacy involves state and non state agents. State agents derive their authority from institutional mandate; non state and international agents, including norm entrepreneurs such as the UNODC, participate through trade agreements, partnerships, official invitations, membership in networks, or nomination in institutional processes.

Collectively, these modalities show the inseparability of advocacy and enforcement in American ACPD. Advocacy frames corruption as threat, disseminates normative commitments through networks, and deploys enforcement outcomes as communicative instruments. Regulatory action thus becomes diplomatic influence.

Cultural and Educational Diplomacy for Institutional Integrity

Cultural and educational diplomacy fosters long-term normative alignment (Cull, 2019). In this domain, influence unfolds through training, institutional modelling, and the socialisation of foreign officials, students, and practitioners into anticorruption standards associated with the American system, which features four principal tools.

First, hosting international anticorruption conferences translates technical gatherings into normative diffusion. The 1994 Summit of the Americas provides a prominent illustration (Feinberg, 1997). Beyond symbolic visibility, it contributed to tangible outcomes, notably the adoption of the OAS anticorruption convention, which incorporated FCPA principles. Coordinated by the DoS, the summit convened state representatives, civil society actors, including Transparency International US, and Latin American delegations.

Second, American ACPD includes training programmes aimed at foreign capacity-building, such as FBI-led programmes for domestic and foreign companies (OECD Working Group on Bribery, 2002). Third, it involves establishing anticorruption academies abroad. Implemented across Europe, Africa, Asia, and Latin America through bilateral agreements coordinated by the DoJ (UNODC, 2012), these institutions formalise long-term capacity-building partnerships. The fourth tool involves anticorruption education for foreign students in contexts where the United States maintains military operations. Coordinated by the DoD (McMann, 2017), these initiatives insert integrity training into broader security and stabilisation structures. These initiatives present anticorruption norms as components of institutional resilience and governance reform.

Budgetary allocations, anticorruption legislation, foreign assistance schemes, and specialised legal expertise constitute the main material and normative resources that make cultural and educational diplomacy operational. Such resources are translated into ACPD results through the action of collaborative, soft, and hard power. The first operates through structured cooperation within multilateral systems and international events. Soft power functions communicatively, transmitting and inspiring regulatory standards, professional norms, and institutional schemes that foster alignment and legitimacy. Hard power underpins these initiatives by enabling the financial, infrastructural, and institutional resources necessary to sustain long-term capacity-building.

As in other activities of American ACPD, representational ties derive from institutional mandate. State agents act within their organisational competences under legal mandates, while non state and international actors participate through formal agreements, bilateral arrangements, or official invitation. Engagement is thus structured and reciprocal: foreign partners enter these programmes through institutional channels, reinforcing the rule-based and cooperative character of cultural and educational diplomacy.

Within the broader architecture of American ACPD, cultural and educational diplomacy performs a stabilising function. It complements the enforcement-centred pattern by cultivating shared understandings, professional expertise, and institutional trust. Through conferences, training programmes, academies, and educational initiatives, the United States embeds its anticorruption approach within transnational professional communities. Influence therefore extends beyond jurisdiction and strategic framing, operating through the gradual socialisation of partners into a recognisable model of institutional integrity.

Exchange on Integrity and Governance

Exchange functions as a structured arena of mutual exposure and institutional learning (Scott-Smith, 2023) through which the United States situates itself within transnational circuits of anticorruption dialogue that reinforce accountability and influence. Three modalities are particularly salient. First, hosting visits from international organisations, such as the 2011 UNODC monitoring visit (UNODC, 2012). Grounded in adherence to the UNCAC and supported by national laws, policies, institutions, and logistical capacity, this activity acquired international meaning through the convergence of hard power (enabling capacity), soft power (communicating and influencing), and collaborative power (engagement). The monitoring visit thus functioned as a performative display of institutional credibility.

Second, the United States hosts international delegations seeking to learn anticorruption benchmarks. In 2018 alone, nineteen foreign delegations were received under the Outreach and Assistance Programme (UNODC, 2018). These exchanges mobilised budgetary resources, institutional infrastructure, anticorruption and international assistance schemes, and technical expertise. Through enabling, communicative, and inspiring capacities associated with hard and soft power, such elements were translated into internationally legible governance systems. The United States thereby acted as a demonstrator of institutional design and enforcement practice.

Third, participation in international anticorruption networks, such as GRECO, reinforces this exchange logic. Network affiliation generates outcomes primarily through soft and collaborative power, operating via peer review, transparency mechanisms, and policy alignment with multilateral standards. Through such participation, the United States positions itself within an institutionalised community of practice, reinforcing its dual role as both contributor to and subject of international evaluation.

Across these mechanisms, state, non state, and international agents interact within structured representational systems. State agents derive their representational status from institutional mandate, while other agents engage through invitation, treaty adherence, or network membership. Exchange therefore performs as institutionalised encounter, reinforcing accountability through scrutiny while projecting regulatory competence through demonstration and participation.

Digital Narratives and the Mediation of Integrity

International broadcasting increasingly unfolds in networked digital environments (Cull, 2019), extending regulatory narratives across borders in real time. The first salient mechanism is the use of social media as an instrument of soft power. The Office of Government Ethics uses X (formerly Twitter) to disseminate information on public ethics to global audiences (UNODC, 2018). Values such as openness, alongside integrity policies and ethics legislation, are translated into accessible digital messages. Through communicative and inspirational capacities, these resources acquire diplomatic meaning, projecting institutional transparency beyond territorial boundaries.

A second prominent mechanism concerns online compliance tools. The FCPA Resource Guide created by the DoJ (2024) illustrates how digital tools enable regulatory diffusion. Designed to support corporate compliance, the guide mobilises technical expertise, legal structures, and budgetary resources. These elements gain international significance through the combined enabling and communicative capacities of hard and soft power.

Across both mechanisms, digital narratives mediate integrity by converting legal frameworks and institutional practice into globally accessible content. The online sphere thus expands the reach of ACPD, allowing norms to circulate internationally and reinforcing the United States' regulatory presence in digital space.

Ancillary Activities: Action Plans, Evaluation, and Lessons Learned

Beyond operational tools, the country structures its ACPD through strategic planning, evaluation, and institutional learning. These mechanisms align procedural with reflexive adaptation. The 2021 anticorruption strategy formalised this direction, aiming to "accelerate and amplify ... efforts to prevent and combat corruption at home and abroad; bring transparency to the United States' and international financial systems; and make it increasingly difficult for corrupt actors to shield their activities" (White House, 2021, p. 4). The subsequent implementation plan organised measures into five priorities: (1) diplomatic engagement and foreign assistance; (2) protection of whistleblowers and the media; (3) innovation; (4) enhanced risk analysis in foreign assistance; and (5) risk analysis into military and national security plans (DoS, 2023, pp. 35–40). These instruments embed anticorruption across diplomatic, security, and development agendas.

Evaluation mechanisms reinforce accountability. Several legislative acts and programmes require reporting to Congress. For example, the 2001 DoS report on the International Anti-Corruption and Good Governance Act (DoS, 2001) assessed the effectiveness of diplomatic action, assistance, and intergovernmental cooperation. Such reporting subjects ACPD to oversight and performance review, strengthening transparency and internal consistency. Lessons learned are incorporated into programme design: following the UNCAC implementation review, the DoS integrated findings into subsequent initiatives (United States, 2015). Likewise, the DoJ drew on lessons from corporate resolutions to develop its 2019 compliance training programme (OECD Working Group on Bribery, 2022). These practices illustrate adaptive management, whereby enforcement outcomes and peer review findings inform policy refinement and capacity-building.

Together, strategic planning, evaluation, and institutional learning underscore the reflexive character of American ACPD. The projection of integrity is not static but integrated into iterative processes of adjustment and recalibration.

5.6 Mapping the United States' Anticorruption Public Diplomacy

Having examined the operational dimensions of American ACPD, this section synthesises the case through an analytical mapping of its structural components. Drawing on accounts of norm diffusion and role performance (Breuning, 2024; Finnemore & Sikkink, 2001; Wendt, 1999), as well as networks and smart power schemes (Nye, 2011; Zaharna, 2022), this section shows American ACPD as a coordinated yet distributed system of influence. It produces international socialisation effects at the intersection of public diplomacy and anticorruption enforcement. The subsections that follow reveal four analytical layers: agents and coordination; activities and governance design; resource ecology; and the politics of influence generated through smart power.

Agents, Representational Ties, and Coordination

American ACPD operates through a stratified configuration in which representational ties are produced through the interaction of legal mandate, performative enactment, and network situatedness. The model resembles a coordinated enforcement–diplomacy ecosystem structured across three analytically distinct layers: state core, mediated non state actors, and institutionalised international partners.

The State Core: Legal Mandate as Representational Authority

At its centre, ACPD is state-anchored. Representational ties derive from formal competences situated in the federal structure. The DoS functions as the principal coordinator at the strategic level, aligning anticorruption objectives with foreign policy priorities. The DoJ, alongside enforcement bodies such as the FBI, SEC, FinCEN, and federal prosecutors, operationalises this legitimacy through jurisdictional reach. USAID and DoD extend the system into assistance and security domains.

In theoretical terms, this layer exemplifies role performance (Breuning, 2024; Holsti, 1970). Authority is not inherent but enacted through practice. Extraterritorial prosecutions, peer-review participation, treaty implementation, and diplomatic engagement translate domestic legal competences into internationally recognisable roles. Through repetition and institutionalisation, these practices consolidate the United States' role identity as a regulatory architect within the global anticorruption regime

(Wendt, 1999). Coordination remains formally state-centred, but normative leadership becomes internationally meaningful only when validated through interaction within multilateral regimes (Finnemore & Sikkink, 2001). Legal mandate provides the foundation; repeated participation generates recognition.

Mediated Non State Agents: Relational Amplifiers
A second layer consists of corporations, law firms, consultancies, compliance professionals, civil society organisations (e.g. Transparency International), investigative journalists, and legal practitioners. These agents do not possess sovereignty but enter the ACPD arena through mediated representational ties: governmental invitation, contractual engagement, enforcement exposure, public–private partnerships, or media authorship.

Though contingent and relational, their authority may expand globally through the persuasive force of their narratives (Adler, 2005). Investigative journalism triggering FCPA cases, corporate self-reporting under compliance incentives, and civil society participation in peer review illustrate how non state agents shape regulatory agendas without exercising formal state power. This dynamic aligns with transnational advocacy network theory (Keck & Sikkink, 1998), but in the American case it remains structurally situated within a state-coordinated design strategically articulated by the DoS. Non state agents therefore compound a community of practice (Adler, 2005), where they function less as autonomous norm entrepreneurs and more as amplifiers and transmitters within a governance platform grounded on legal structures.

International Agents: Embedded Reciprocity and Socialisation
A third layer comprises international organisations, such as OECD, UNODC, APEC, and GRECO, foreign governments, courts, regulatory bodies, financial-intelligence units, foreign companies, and corporate executives. Their participation derives from treaty adherence, peer-review mechanisms, network membership, and, in some cases, exposure to American extraterritorial jurisdiction. In this context, norm diffusion becomes reciprocal rather than unilateral (Finnemore & Sikkink, 2001). The United States contributes to standard-setting while simultaneously being evaluated and socialised through monitoring mechanisms (Acharya, 2018). Participation in the UNCAC review mechanism or OECD peer evaluations illustrates this dual position: governing and governed. This

layer demonstrates relational legitimacy production (Wendt, 1999). Recognition within institutionalised communities of practice (Adler, 2005) transforms enforcement capacity into legitimate influence. Authority is thus co-produced through structured interaction rather than imposed hierarchically.

Activities and Governance Architecture

The United States' ACPD has evolved from a strategic effort to multilateralise domestic legal innovation, particularly the FCPA principles (Mccoy & Heckel, 2001; Pieth, 2012). What began as national regulatory reform transformed into a process of norm entrepreneurship projected into multilateral arenas and progressively institutionalised (Finnemore & Sikkink, 2001; Mccoy & Heckel, 2001). Over time, ad hoc initiatives were absorbed into structured planning and evaluative tools, embedding anticorruption across diplomatic, legal, security, and development domains. Anticorruption thus ceased to function as a discrete policy tool and became integrated within a broader institutional framework.

Within this institutional design, activity density is most pronounced in dialogical engagement and advocacy. Dialogical engagement unfolds primarily through legal and procedural instruments rooted in domestic enforcement capacity but converted into international leadership through extraterritorial reach and institutional cooperation. Jurisdictional extension, whether through financial systems, territorial nexus, or digital infrastructure, illustrates how enforcement transcends compliance control to become a mode of legitimacy projection within global governance (Zürn, 2018). Although extraterritoriality has attracted critique (Ashe, 2005), its progressive multilateralisation and replication indicate processes of diffusion, contestation, and consolidation characteristic of norm cascade dynamics (Finnemore & Sikkink, 2001). Enforcement thus becomes institutionalised as a structuring principle of global anticorruption order.

Advocacy complements this legal landscape through sustained reputational reinforcement. Enforcement outcomes, fiscal oversight mechanisms, and compliance regimes are repeatedly referenced in peer review processes and multilateral evaluations, contributing to symbolic continuity across administrations (OECD Working Group on Bribery, 2010; UNODC, 2012, 2018, 2023b). Through discursive repetition (Biden, 2021; Bush, 2004; Clinton White House, 1997; Obama, 2009; Trump, 2017) and sustained institutional participation, role performance stabilises expectations of regulatory seriousness (Breuning, 2024; Holsti, 1970; Wendt, 1999). In this sense, advocacy does not merely communicate policy; it consolidates recognition within international regimes.

Importantly, structural influence does not correlate mechanically with ranking dominance. Although typically within the top quartile, the United States does not consistently occupy the highest positions in integrity perception indices; it nevertheless exerts disproportionate structural influence over regulatory design, enforcement standards, and multilateral norm development. This distinction reflects the difference between reputational capital and institutional power (Barnett & Duvall, 2005). American ACPD operates less through symbolic exemplariness than through the capacity to structure compliance environments and normative expectations across jurisdictions. The resulting structure combines vertical coordination, through state-centred strategic planning, with horizontal diffusion across multilateral and transgovernmental networks (Slaughter, 2004; Zaharna, 2022). Enforcement, advocacy, monitoring, and cooperation are not isolated instruments but interlocking components of a structured governance field.

In this context, domestic legal innovation, once multilateralised, enters transgovernmental networks and informs peer review structures. Norm entrepreneurship evolves into structural positioning (Barnett & Duvall, 2005; Finnemore & Sikkink, 2001). Authority is no longer derived from unilateral enforcement alone but from the capacity to organise the institutional field within which anticorruption expectations are defined and reproduced (Slaughter, 2004; Zürn, 2018). In this context, the United States performs not merely as an enforcer but as a regulatory architect within the global anticorruption regime.

The Resource Base of United States Anticorruption Public Diplomacy

The resource base of the United States' ACPD is best understood as a structured ecology in which material and immaterial assets are converted into outcomes through practice (Adler, 2005; Zürn, 2018). These resources do not act in isolation; their significance emerges when they are mobilised within international institutional contexts (Nye, 2004). Power, therefore, is not derived merely from possession of resources but from their successful translation into recognised influence within global anticorruption regimes.

At the core of this ecology stand legal and regulatory instruments. Anticorruption policies, most prominently the FCPA, function simultaneously as domestic regulatory mechanism and diplomatic assets. Once projected beyond national borders, they become convertible resources capable of shaping expectations and structuring compliance environments. In this sense, policy is performative: it regulates behaviour internally while projecting institutional influence externally. Through processes of social recognition (Finnemore & Wendt, 2024; Wendt, 1999) within multilateral regimes, these instruments acquire normative weight beyond their territorial origin. Such legal structures embody institutional and productive forms of power (Barnett & Duvall, 2005), defining permissible conduct, shaping opportunity structures, and stabilising expectations of transparency and accountability. Enforcement thus works not only as compulsory sanction but as a mechanism of normative reproduction, reinforcing the institutional design within which anticorruption standards are interpreted and applied.

Cultural and ideational dimensions reinforce this legal foundation. Values associated with transparency, rule-based order, legalism, and institutional accountability enhance the plausibility of enforcement claims and contribute to reputational security. Identity and practice remain co-constitutive (Finnemore & Sikkink, 2001; Wendt, 1999): American anticorruption identity both contributed to and was reinforced by the consolidation of the global anticorruption norm. ACPD therefore reflects not merely resource mobilisation but the reproduction of identity through performance.

Technological capacity and strategic discretion introduce another layer of influence. Digital infrastructures, financial intelligence systems, and prosecutorial selectivity transform jurisdiction into a flexible instrument of governance. In such cases, law functions simultaneously as normative frame and strategic lever, illustrating how institutional authority can generate different effects across contexts (Zürn, 2018). Enforcement decisions, particularly in extraterritorial settings, show how legal capacity becomes an instrument of structured influence rather than merely reactive prosecution.

Economic strength provides enabling capacity but does not constitute the primary source of legitimacy. Budgetary allocations sustain investigative infrastructure, peer-review participation, and international engagement, yet material leverage remains subordinated to legal framing and normative positioning. This reinforces the character of American ACPD as law-centred practice rather than materially coercive diplomacy.

Finally, nodal positioning within international anticorruption networks significantly enhances this resource ecology. Participation in multilateral conventions, peer-review bodies, and transgovernmental networks situates the United States within dense circuits of regulatory interaction. Through these relationships, it is simultaneously governed and governing. Recognition emerges through sustained participation in overlapping institutional arenas rather than through hierarchical command alone (Slaughter, 2004; Zaharna, 2022). In this institutional order, authority is co-produced (Finnemore & Sikkink, 2001) through institutional and normative situatedness.

Taken together, legal legitimacy, symbolic capital, technological capacity, economic enablement, and network embeddedness form a platform for authority performance. In this context, the United States does not merely enforce anticorruption norms but helps organise the institutional field within which those norms acquire operational meaning. Identity and norm remain mutually reinforcing within this feedback loop (Finnemore & Sikkink, 2001), positioning the United States simultaneously as architect and embedded actor within the contemporary anticorruption regime.

Smart Power and the Politics of Influence

The United States' ACPD performs through a structured smart power arrangement that integrates four differentiated modalities of power, namely soft, hard, sharp, and collaborative, to convert material and immaterial resources into recognised international influence. Smart power, in this context, does not denote strategic eclecticism but a patterned alignment between resources, capabilities, and governance objectives (Nye, 2011). Legal instruments, institutional capacity, economic resources, normative commitments, and network positioning acquire diplomatic meaning only when activated through specific modalities of power that generate international effects.

Soft power contributes ideational factors through capabilities such as listening, communicating, engaging, negotiating, attracting, influencing, inspiring, and persuading. These capabilities operate upon resources rooted in anticorruption policies, political culture, and normative commitments to openness and transparency. For example, the budget allocated to USAID's whistleblower hotline, combined with the cultural value of openness (UNODC, 2018), produces international effects through the capacities of listening and dialogue. This style of power provides interpretive framing. Through communicative, persuasive, and agenda-setting capacities, anticorruption policies and political values are translated into normative expectations. Listening mechanisms, transparency practices, and public justification strategies reinforce the plausibility of enforcement claims. The explicit framing of corruption as a national security interest in the 2021 anticorruption strategy (White House, 2021) exemplifies communicative capability as a vehicle for agenda-setting. In this modality, authority emerges through attraction and recognition rather than coercion, stabilising the United States' anticorruption identity within international discourse.

Hard power functions through enabling and penalising capacities situated in legal and institutional frameworks. Enforcement actions, financial sanctions, compliance regimes, and investigative infrastructures convert economic and legal resources into compulsory power (Barnett & Duvall, 2005). However, such coercive elements are embedded within rule-based structures that frame sanction as institutional enforcement rather than unilateral imposition. For instance, economic resources applied to enforcement become instruments of signalling and deterrence while budget allocations for FBI compliance training programmes contribute to norm diffusion (OECD Working Group on Bribery, 2020). Hard power thus reinforces regulatory credibility and enforceable commitment.

Sharp power introduces calibrated control over jurisdictional and informational space. Through prosecutorial discretion, extraterritorial reach, and selective enforcement prioritisation, legal authority becomes an instrument of structured influence (Biersteker, 2020). In the United States' ACPD, rather than overt coercion, sharp power shapes opportunity conditions and constrains alternatives, illustrating how jurisdiction functions as governance (Zürn, 2018). For instance, visa sanctions against foreign officials combine communicative and exclusionary functions, transforming anticorruption enforcement into reputational pressure (White House, 2013). This modality reveals the strategic dimension of enforcement-centred diplomacy.

Collaborative power situates the American ACPD within multilateral and transgovernmental networks. Participation in peer-review mechanisms, treaty arrangements, and regulatory communities situates the United States within shared transnational networks and institutional procedures where legitimacy is simultaneously exercised and constrained

(Slaughter, 2004; Zaharna, 2022). An illustration of such socialisation processes within norm communities (Finnemore & Sikkink, 2001) is the country's engagement in UNCAC review mechanisms (United States, 2015), transforming external evaluation into structured listening and reciprocal learning. Through cooperation and reciprocal evaluation, enforcement capacity is legitimised within communities of practice, mitigating perceptions of unilateral dominance.

The interaction of these modalities reveals the political logic of American ACPD. Soft power shapes normative interpretation; hard power secures and enables compliance; sharp power structures jurisdictional space; collaborative power stabilises legitimacy. Leadership, therefore, does not derive from any single modality but from their coordinated articulation within a governance pattern. In this configuration, smart power operates as the integrative mechanism through which regulatory capacity is transformed into sustained structural influence. By aligning these modalities of power with legal influence, institutional practice, and network embeddedness, the United States converts enforcement into a durable form of authority production within the global anticorruption regime.

5.7 Recalibrating Norm Entrepreneurship: The FCPA After 2025

As emphasised throughout this book, the FCPA contributed to the emergence of the global anticorruption norm (Mccoy & Heckel, 2001) and the broader anticorruption movement that expanded from the late twentieth century onwards (Hough, 2013). The statute not only structured domestic compliance cultures but also contributed to consolidating the United States' international standing as a technically capable pioneer of enforcement (Spalding, 2012). The FCPA has functioned simultaneously as a regulatory tool, diplomatic signal, and norm-generating device, while also reflecting the gradual securitisation of corruption within American strategic thinking. It created a regulatory-driven model that was gradually internalised within multilateral regimes and emulated across jurisdictions.

Against this background, domestic contestation and the pause in FCPA enforcement that began in early 2025 (White House, 2025b) generated immediate global concern (Bonucci et al., 2025). The reaction was proportionate to the statute's situatedness within the architecture of international anticorruption governance. The issue was not merely legislative adjustment at the domestic level but the potential recalibration of a norm entrepreneur whose authority had long rested on enforcement credibility.

Following the 180-day pause, enforcement priorities were redefined (Deputy Attorney General, 2025), with corporate bribery relatively deprioritised and greater emphasis placed on corruption linked to transnational criminal organisations, particularly narco-terrorist groups and cartels framed as national security threats (Deputy Attorney General, 2025; White House, 2025b). The DoS (2026b) maintains an updated list of foreign terrorist organisations designated with congressional concurrence, signalling that such entities are likely to occupy a central position within the revised enforcement agenda.

From the perspective developed in this chapter, and in light of the United States' role as a norm entrepreneur, this shift represents not merely an operational adjustment but a discursive reorientation. It consolidates a security-centred framing of corruption enforcement. Whether this reframing broadens global coordination or instead narrows anticorruption into a subset of security performance remains analytically indeterminate.

Estimates suggest that these organisations generate illicit financial flows valued between US$1.6 and US$2.2 trillion annually (Global Financial Integrity, 2026). Unlike many corporate bribery schemes, which often leave trails susceptible to reporting and compliance mechanisms (Spalding, 2012), such flows are frequently opaque and structurally resistant to traceability. Combating crimes perpetrated by these organisations is exceptionally difficult due to their substantial financial resources, institutional infiltration, and adaptive capacity vis-à-vis enforcement strategies (UNODC, 2026). They combine bribery, coercion, institutional capture, and targeted violence, including assassinations, thereby complicating both accountability and international cooperation. Evidence indicates that transnational criminal groups have contracted killings to silence activists and witnesses in parts of Africa (Thomas, 2021) and even in Europe (Luyten, 2025). The UNODC (2023a, p. 31) further reports that the post-2020 surge in cocaine production, together with the expansion of these organisations, has contributed to rising levels of lethal violence, with nearly 40% of global homicides linked to organised crime.

Redirecting anticorruption enforcement towards organised crime thus reflects a strategic choice within a broader global landscape. In this context, the United States operates within an extensive institutional infrastructure. Since the adoption of the FCPA, it has strengthened not only its intelligence capabilities but also its anticorruption enforcement capabilities. The broader statutory framework remains in operation with a strong and active enforcement structure (Dell & McDevitt, 2022). High-impact prosecutions remain viable in cases involving national security, organised crime financing, or substantial economic harm (Deputy Attorney General, 2025). International coordination mechanisms also remain active, signalling continuity in multilateral engagement. This continuum suggests adjustment in emphasis rather than immediate institutional dismantlement, though longer-term implications remain uncertain. However, sustained selectivity in corporate enforcement may gradually reshape perceptions regarding the United States' enforcement commitment. The effectiveness, proportionality, and legitimacy of such recalibrated FCPA enforcement remain subject to international scrutiny and normative debate.

Within the ACPD paradigm, this recalibration has manifested in concrete initiatives. The Mexican military operation conducted in Tapalpa in February 2026, which reportedly resulted in the death of a senior leader of a Mexican drug cartel, was officially described as the product of intelligence collaboration with the United States (Secretaría de la Defensa Nacional, 2026). Likewise, the transfer of thirty-seven members of Mexican criminal organisations to United States prisons in January 2026 (Corona & Dina, 2026) demonstrated operational reach in addressing corruption-financed criminal networks. Such actions combine communicative signalling with coercive capacity, illustrating the coordinated articulation of soft and hard power within ACPD practice.

A similar dynamic was reflected in debates surrounding the reported 2026 capture in Caracas of the Venezuelan political leader and his spouse by United States forces, based on a longstanding indictment for corruption and drug trafficking pending before a New York court, according to publicly available records (United States of America v. Nicolás Maduro Moros et al., 2011). Although the operation provoked indignation among some political leaders due to concerns regarding potential violations of international law (Keenan, 2026), public opinion data indicated support among significant segments of Venezuelan and Latin American respondents (Stott & Stabe, 2026; Bubola, 2026). From an ACPD perspective, the episode illustrates a structure in which soft, hard, and sharp power elements intersect. While involving direct intervention within another state's sovereign space, it simultaneously generated positive recognition among parts of the affected publics, highlighting the complex reputational effects of enforcement-centred diplomacy.

Moreover, FCPA principles remain embedded within multilateral anti-corruption conventions, including those of the OAS, the OECD, and the United Nations, while comparable enforcement models have been adopted across other jurisdictions (Pieth, 2012; Stephenson, 2017). Reflecting processes of norm diffusion, consolidation, and internalisation (Finnemore & Sikkink, 2001; Wendt, 1999), what began as an expansive national enforcement pattern became institutionalised within international governance schemes. Consequently, even in scenarios of domestic retreat, the crystallisation of FCPA-derived principles in multilateral conventions sustains the possibility of enforcement by foreign regulators and international bodies.

Although this may alter the symbolic register through which enforcement is externally perceived, it does not automatically amount to systemic withdrawal. At the same time, it reflects the permeability of enforcement priorities to domestic political pressures, as security-oriented narratives resonate more readily within a polarised public sphere than abstract commitments to regulatory universalism (Wiseman & Scott, 2026). In this strategic landscape, cartels and transnational organised crime operate as strategic filters guiding resource allocation within an otherwise stable legal system. Even in a scenario of more pronounced American retrenchment, continuity would likely persist, reflecting the resilience of practitioner communities whose patterned modes of operation tend to outlast episodic political adjustments (Gregory, 2024). Whether this phase represents consolidation or durable transformation will depend on longitudinal enforcement patterns, judicial interpretation, institutional continuity, and international reception.

5.8 Enforcement, Authority, and the Contingency of Norm Leadership

The United States case illustrates that ACPD can function not primarily through reputational purity but through regulatory structuring power. The American approach rests on an enforcement-led model. Integrity is projected less as moral exemplariness and more as jurisdictional assertiveness.

From the constitutional anxieties of the founding era to the securitised framing of corruption in the 2021 strategy and the 2025 FCPA enforcement pause, anticorruption has evolved from a domestic virtue concern into a strategic instrument of governance. The doctrine of *Denying Safe Haven* crystallised this transformation by converting sovereign jurisdiction into a tool of normative defence. The FCPA became the operational core of this scheme, placing legal legitimacy within diplomatic practice and catalysing multilateral diffusion. Through extraterritorial enforcement and multilateralisation, the United States contributed decisively to the emergence of a collective anticorruption norm institutionalised in the OAS, OECD, and United Nations conventions.

Yet the American case also reveals a persistent tension of norm leadership. While the United States continues to occupy a central position within the global anticorruption architecture, its leadership can no longer be assumed to be uncontested. Recent declines in international confidence, growing scrutiny of domestic governance practices, and the increasing institutionalisation of anticorruption norms beyond the American jurisdiction suggest a more complex landscape in which authority is increasingly negotiated rather than taken for granted. Notably, the country's authority derives from institutional power, network centrality, and enforcement capacity rather than from ranking supremacy. While not consistently occupying the top positions in global perception indices, the United States exerts disproportionate influence over enforcement standards, compliance expectations, and institutional architectures. This distinction between reputational capital and institutional power clarifies how anticorruption leadership may work through agenda-setting and structural organisation rather than symbolic purity.

The recalibration initiated in 2025 introduces a further layer of contingency. The temporary pause in FCPA enforcement and the reprioritisation towards organised crime reflect the permeability of anticorruption enforcement to domestic political and security narratives. Whether this phase consolidates a securitised sub-field of anticorruption governance or narrows the normative scope of the global regime remains an open question. What appears less contingent, however, is the embeddedness of FCPA-derived principles within multilateral conventions and transgovernmental enforcement communities. Through repetition and institutionalisation, these practices consolidate the United States' role identity as a regulatory architect within the global anticorruption regime.

This institutionalisation also suggests that contemporary anticorruption governance is becoming less dependent upon the leadership of any single state. While states such as Denmark and its Scandinavian neighbours are frequently recognised for strong integrity performance, institutional trust, and high standards of public governance, their influence operates through mechanisms different from those historically associated with the United States. They provide important normative examples, but do not necessarily possess the same agenda-setting capacity, enforcement reach, or structural leverage historically linked to the FCPA and the centrality of the United States within global financial and regulatory networks. At the same time, recent developments in European Union anticorruption legislation, including Directive (EU) 2026/1021, illustrate how regulatory innovation and anticorruption norm development are increasingly emerging from institutional frameworks beyond the United States. In this sense, a less US-centred anticorruption order is unlikely to be organised around a single replacement leader. Rather, it is more plausibly emerging as a multipolar governance field in which international organisations, regional organisations, coalitions of states, transgovernmental enforcement networks, civil society actors, and communities of practice collectively shape, diffuse, and contest anticorruption norms.

The governance controversies discussed throughout this chapter also highlight a broader challenge inherent in ACPD. The effectiveness of norm promotion depends not only on enforcement capacity, regulatory sophistication, or diplomatic activism, but also on the perceived consistency between the principles promoted internationally and the practices observed domestically. The United States has long advocated transparency, accountability, integrity, conflict-of-interest regulation, and the rule of law through multilateral frameworks, development assistance programmes, and diplomatic engagement. Consequently, controversies affecting these same principles within the domestic sphere may generate credibility costs that extend beyond national borders. This does not negate the country's substantial contribution to the global anticorruption regime or its continued capacity for norm entrepreneurship. Rather, it illustrates the contingent nature of normative authority and the extent to which leadership is shaped by the alignment between external advocacy and domestic governance practices. In this sense, anticorruption public diplomacy is ultimately sustained not only through projection but also through recognition, requiring a degree of coherence between what states promote abroad and what they are perceived to uphold at home.

The United States thus emerges as a regulatory guardian state within the anticorruption field: not the most symbolically pristine actor, but a central organiser of enforcement structures and norm interpretation. Its ACPD demonstrates how smart power can convert legal instruments, economic capacity, technological infrastructure, and network endurance into authority performance within global governance. Soft, hard, sharp, and collaborative modalities operate in coordinated fashion, transforming domestic regulatory practice into internationally recognised influence.

Ultimately, the American case underscores a core theoretical insight of this book: ACPD is not reducible to communication or moral signalling. It is a structured performance of leadership through which states negotiate identity, interest, and legitimacy within international society. In the United States, identity and norm remain co-constitutive. The country shaped the contemporary anticorruption regime; yet it is also constrained and socialised by it. Its future dominance will depend less on rhetorical reaffirmation than on sustained coherence between enforcement practice, domestic institutional integrity, and the evolving expectations of the global anticorruption community. In this sense, the United States continues to shape global anticorruption norms, but increasingly within an environment it no longer singularly controls.

References

Acharya, A. (2018). *The end of American world order* (2nd ed.). Polity.

Adams, J. (2012). *The epic of America*. Transaction Publishers.

Adler-Nissen, R. (2014). *Opting out of the European Union*. Cambridge University Press.

Adler-Nissen, R. (2023). Practice. In S. Goddard, G. Lawson, & J. Sending (Eds.), *The Oxford handbook of international political sociology* (pp. 177–198). Oxford University Press.

Adler, E. (2005). *Communitarian international relations*. Routledge.

Adler, E. (2013). Constructivism in international relations: Sources, contributions, and debates. In W. Carlsnaes, T. Risse, & B. Simmons (Eds.), *Handbook of international relations* (2nd ed., pp. 112–144). Sage. https://doi.org/10.4135/9781446247587

Ashe, D. (2005). The lengthening anti-bribery lasso of the United States: The recent extraterritorial application of the U.S. foreign corrupt practices act. *Fordham Law Review, 73*(6), 2897–2945.

Asian Development Bank & OECD. (2006). *Denying safe haven to the corrupt and the proceeds of corruption*. ADB. Retrieved February 9, 2026, from https://www.oecd.org/content/dam/oecd/en/publications/reports/2006/11/denying-safe-haven-to-the-corrupt-and-the-proceeds-of-corruption_g1gh8a9f/9789264041370-en.pdf

Barnett, M., & Duvall, R. (2005). Power in international politics. *International Organization, 59*(1), 39–75. https://doi.org/10.1017/S0020818305050010

Biden, J. (2021, June 3). *Memorandum on establishing the fight against corruption as a core United States national security interest.* Retrieved February 9, 2026, from https://www.presidency.ucsb.edu/documents/memorandum-establishing-the-fight-against-corruption-core-united-states-national-security

Biersteker, T. (2020). The potential of Europe's sharp and soft power. *Global Policy, 11*(3), 384–387. https://doi.org/10.1111/1758-5899.12815

Bixby, M. (2010). The lion awakens: The foreign corrupt practices act—1977 to 2010. *San Diego International Law Journal, 12*(1), 89–146.

Blinken, A. (2023, December 11). *Promoting accountability for corruption globally.* Retrieved February 9, 2026, from https://2021-2025.state.gov/promoting-accountability-for-corruption-globally/

Bonucci, N., Schricke, C., Small, D., Goudriaan, D., Kos, D., & Pieth, M. (2025, February 13). *Letter to Pamela Bondi.* Retrieved February 9, 2026, from https://globalanticorruptionblog.com/wp-content/uploads/2025/03/oecd-lawyers-letter.pdf

Bozeman, B. (2025). Impervious corruption: President Trump and the deformation of democracy. *Public Administration Review, 85*(6), 1582–1597. https://doi.org/10.1111/puar.70027

Breuning, M. (2024). National roles and foreign policy. In J. Kaarbo & C. Thies (Eds.), *The Oxford handbook of foreign policy analysis* (pp. 211–228). Oxford University Press.

BRICS. (2022, June). *BRICS initiative on denial of safe haven to corruption.* Retrieved February 9, 2026, from http://brics2022.mfa.gov.cn/eng/dtxw/202206/P020220608765769502751.pdf

Bubola, E. (2026). *Majority of Latin Americans endorsed Trump's raid in Venezuela. New York Times.* Retrieved February 9, 2026, from https://www.nytimes.com/2026/01/21/world/americas/latin-america-venezuela-us-raid-maduro-polls.html

Bush, G. (2004, November 1). *Fact Sheet: Fighting corruption, ensuring transparency.* Retrieved February 9, 2026, from https://www.presidency.ucsb.edu/documents/fact-sheet-fighting-corruption-ensuring-transparency

Buzan, B., Wæver, O., & Wilde, J. (1998). *Security.* Lynne Rienner.

Ceva, E., & Ferretti, M. P. (2021). *Political corruption: The internal enemy of public institutions.* Oxford University Press. https://doi.org/10.1093/oso/9780197567869.001.0001

CIA. (2025). *The World Factbook.* Retrieved July 11, 2025, from https://www.cia.gov/the-world-factbook/countries/united-states/

Clinton White House. (1997). *International Crime Control Strategy.* Retrieved February 9, 2026, from https://clintonwhitehouse4.archives.gov/WH/EOP/NSC/html/documents/iccs-frm.html

Cohen, M. (1989). The common law in the American legal system. *Law Library Journal, 81*, 13–32.
Corona, S., & Dina, E. (2026, January 21). Sheinbaum dice que entrega de 37 capos a EU fue una "decisión soberana". *El Universal.* Retrieved February 9, 2026, from https://www.eluniversal.com.mx/nacion/sheinbaum-dice-que-entrega-de-37-capos-a-eu-fue-una-decision-soberana-descarta-que-este-relacionada-con-llamada-de-trump/
Cuèllar, M.-F., & Stephenson, M. (2022). Taming systemic corruption: The American experience and its implications for contemporary debates. *World Development, 155*, 105755. https://doi.org/10.1016/j.worlddev.2021.105755
Cull, N. (2019). *Public diplomacy: Foundations for global engagement in the digital age*. Polity.
Cull, N. (2024). *Reputational security.* Polity.
Dell, G. (2020). *Exporting corruption.* Transparency International. Retrieved February 9, 2026, from https://images.transparencycdn.org/images/2020_Report-Full_Exporting-Corruption_EN.pdf
Dell, G., & McDevitt, A. (2022). *Exporting corruption 2022.* Transparency International. Retrieved February 9, 2026, from https://files.transparencycdn.org/images/2022_Report-Full_Exporting-Corruption_English.pdf
Department of Justice (DoJ). (2022, March 2). *Attorney General Merrick B. Garland Announces Launch of Task Force KleptoCapture.* (Press release). Retrieved February 9, 2026, from https://www.justice.gov/archives/opa/pr/attorney-general-merrick-b-garland-announces-launch-task-force-kleptocapture
Department of Justice (DoJ). (2023, March 2). Press releases. Retrieved February 9, 2026, from https://www.justice.gov/news/press-releases
Department of Justice (DoJ). (2024, December 16). *FCPA resource guide.* Retrieved February 9, 2026, from https://www.justice.gov/criminal/criminal-fraud/fcpa-resource-guide
Department of Justice (DoJ). (2026a). *Related enforcement actions: 2024.* Retrieved February 9, 2026, from https://www.justice.gov/criminal/criminal-fraud/case/related-enforcement-actions/2024
Department of Justice (DoJ). (2026b). *Related enforcement actions: 2025.* Retrieved February 9, 2026, from https://www.justice.gov/criminal/criminal-fraud/case/related-enforcement-actions/2025
Department of State (DoS). (2001). *Report to Congress pursuant to the International Anticorruption and Good Governance Act (Public Law 106–309).* Retrieved February 9, 2026, from https://2009-2017.state.gov/j/inl/rls/rpt/c6698.htm
Department of State (DoS). (2023, September 6). *U.S. strategy on countering corruption implementation plan.* Retrieved February 9, 2026, from https://www.

state.gov/wp-content/uploads/2023/10/U.S.-Strategy-on-Countering-Corruption-Implementation-Plan-Updated-09.21.2023.pdf

Department of State (DoS). (2026a). *Multilateral relations and cooperation.* Retrieved February 9, 2026, from https://www.state.gov/policy-issues/multilateral-relations-and-cooperation

Department of State (DoS). (2026b). *Foreign Terrorist Organizations.* Retrieved February 9, 2026, from https://www.state.gov/foreign-terrorist-organizations/

Deputy Attorney General. (2025, June 9). *Guidelines for Investigations and Enforcement of the Foreign Corrupt Practices Act (FCPA).* Retrieved February 9, 2026, from https://www.justice.gov/dag/media/1403031/dl

Drezner, D. (2007). *All politics is global.* Princeton University Press.

Feinberg, R. (1997). *Summitry in the Americas.* IIE.

Finnemore, M. (1996). *National interests in international society.* Cornell University Press.

Finnemore, M., & Sikkink, K. (2001). Taking stock: The constructivist research program in international relations and comparative politics. *Annual Review of Political Science, 4*, 391–416. https://doi.org/10.1146/annurev.polisci.4.1.391

Finnemore, M., & Wendt, A. (2024). When "old" constructivism was new: Reflections on classical constructivism. *Perspectives on Politics, 22*(4), 1248–1268. https://doi.org/10.1017/S1537592724001464

Fung, A., & Thompson, D. (2025). Conflict of interest in government: Avoiding ethical and conceptual mistakes. *Governance, 38*(1), 1–13. https://doi.org/10.1111/gove.12870

G8. (2003, June 2). *Fighting corruption and improving transparency.* Retrieved February 9, 2026, from http://www.g7.utoronto.ca/summit/2003evian/corruption_en.html

Galeotti, M. (2025, May 12). *Focus, fairness, and efficiency in the fight against white-collar crime.* Retrieved February 9, 2026, from https://www.justice.gov/criminal/media/1400046/dl

Global Financial Integrity. (2026). *Transnational crime.* Retrieved February 9, 2026, from https://gfintegrity.org/issue/transnational-crime/

Global Firepower (GFP). (2026). *2026 Military Strength Ranking.* Retrieved February 9, 2026, from https://www.globalfirepower.com/countries-listing.php

Goldstein, D. M., & Drybread, K. (2023). Editor's introduction: Anthropology meditations: Illiberal politics and corruption in the Trump era. In D. M. Goldstein & K. Drybread (Eds.), *Corruption and illiberal politics in the Trump era* (pp. 3–18). Routledge. https://doi.org/10.4324/9781003152729

Gomez-Moreno, J. (2024). Yegiazaryan v. Smagin (U.S. Sup. Ct.). *International Legal Materials, 63*(2), 301–311. https://doi.org/10.1017/ilm.2023.58

Gregory, B. (2024). *American diplomacy's public dimension*. Palgrave Macmillan.

Group of States against Corruption (GRECO). (2004, March 25). *First evaluation round*. Retrieved February 9, 2026, from https://rm.coe.int/CoERMPublicCommonSearchServices/DisplayDCTMContent?documentId=09000016806ca512

Group of States against Corruption (GRECO). (2011, December 9). *Third evaluation round*. Retrieved February 9, 2026, from https://rm.coe.int/CoERMPublicCommonSearchServices/DisplayDCTMContent?documentId=09000016806ca558

Group of States against Corruption (GRECO). (2023, December 12). *Fifth evaluation round*. Retrieved February 9, 2026, from https://rm.coe.int/fifth-evaluation-round-preventing-corruption-and-promoting-integrity-i/1680adc93d

Heimann, F., & Dell, G. (2010). *Progress report 2010*. Transparency International. Retrieved February 9, 2026, from https://files.transparencycdn.org/images/2010_OECDProgressReport_EN.pdf

Helleiner, E. (2014). *Global financial governance after the 2008 meltdown*. Oxford University Press. Retrieved February 9, 2026, from https://doi.org/10.1093/acprof:oso/9780199973637.001.0001

Holsti, K. (1970). National role conceptions in the study of foreign policy. *International Studies Quarterly, 14*(3), 233–309. https://doi.org/10.2307/3013584

Hough, D. (2013). *Political corruption & governance*. Palgrave Macmillan. https://doi.org/10.1057/9781137268716

House of Representatives. (2024, January 4). *White House for sale*. Retrieved February 9, 2026, from https://oversightdemocrats.house.gov/imo/media/doc/2024-01-04.COA%20DEMS%20-%20Mazars%20Report.pdf

Jacobs, R. (2025, February 3). *CREW is tracking Trump's unprecedented corruption (again)*. Retrieved June 13, 2026, from https://www.citizensforethics.org/reports-investigations/crew-investigations/crew-is-tracking-trumps-unprecedented-corruption-again/

Johnston, M. (2005). *Syndromes of corruption: Wealth, power and democracy*. Cambridge University Press.

Johnston, M. (2012). Corruption control in the United States: Law, values, and the political foundations of reform. *International Review of Administrative Sciences, 78*(2), 329–345. https://doi.org/10.1177/0020852312438782

Jones, R. G. (2012). Defining a psychology of nepotism. In R. G. Jones (Ed.), *Nepotism in organizations* (pp. 253–267). Routledge.

Keck, M., & Sikkink, K. (1998). *Activists beyond borders*. Cornell University Press.

Keenan, C. (2026, January 4). 'Deeply shocked': World leaders react to US attack on Venezuela. *BBC*. Retrieved February 9, 2026, from https://www.bbc.com/news/articles/czx1rpxzyx9o

Krishnakumar, T. (2023). The security-shaped hole in global anti-corruption: Closing the loop on the FCPA. *Hastings Business Law Journal, 19*(1), 3–30.
Lowy Institute. (2024). *Global Diplomacy Index 2024*. Retrieved February 9, 2026, from https://globaldiplomacyindex.lowyinstitute.org
Luna, D. (2005, December 9). *Prosecuting kleptocrats: denying safe haven to corrupt officials and their illicitly-acquired assets*. Retrieved February 9, 2026, from https://2001-2009.state.gov/p/inl/rls/rm/58041.htm
Luyten, K. (2025). *Violence and organised crime in the EU*. European Parliament. Retrieved February 9, 2026, from https://www.europarl.europa.eu/RegData/etudes/BRIE/2025/769498/EPRS_BRI(2025)769498_EN.pdf
Mauss, M. (2002). *The gift*. Routledge.
Mccoy, J., & Heckel, H. (2001). The emergence of a global anti-corruption norm. *International Politics, 38*(1), 65–90. https://doi.org/10.1057/palgrave.ip.8892613
McMann, J. (2017). *Independent Reporting Mechanism*. Retrieved July 11, 2025, from https://www.opengovpartnership.org/wp-content/uploads/2001/01/United-States_End-of-Term_IRM-Report_2015-2017.pdf
Noonan, J. (1987). Bribery. *Notre Dame Journal of Law, Ethics & Public Policy, 2*, 747–751.
Nye, J. (2004). *Soft power*. Public Affairs.
Nye, J. (2011). *The future of power*. Public Affairs.
Obama, B. (2009, December 1). *Remarks by the president in address to the nation on the way forward in Afghanistan and Pakistan*. Retrieved February 9, 2026, from https://obamawhitehouse.archives.gov/the-press-office/remarks-president-address-nation-way-forward-afghanistan-and-pakistan
OECD Working Group on Bribery. (2002, October). *Report on the application of the Convention on Combating Bribery of Foreign Public Officials in International Business Transactions and the 1997 Recommendation*. Retrieved February 9, 2026, from https://www.oecd.org/daf/anti-bribery/anti-briberyconvention/1962084.pdf
OECD Working Group on Bribery. (2010, October). *Phase 3 report on implementing the OECD Anti-Bribery Convention in the United States*. Retrieved February 9, 2026, from https://www.oecd.org/content/dam/oecd/en/publications/reports/2010/12/implementing-the-oecd-anti-bribery-convention-phase-3-report-united-states_f2fd5956/78851371-en.pdf
OECD Working Group on Bribery. (2020, October 16). *Implementing the OECD Anti-Bribery Convention Phase 4 Report*. Retrieved February 9, 2026, from https://www.oecd.org/content/dam/oecd/en/publications/reports/2020/09/implementing-the-oecd-anti-bribery-convention-phase-4-report-united-states_501faf3a/0cd34e9f-en.pdf
OECD Working Group on Bribery. (2022, October 20). *Implementing the OECD anti-bribery convention*. Retrieved February 9, 2026, from https://www.oecd.

org/en/publications/implementing-the-oecd-anti-bribery-convention-phase-4-follow-up-report-united-states_d994f92a-en.html

Organisation for Economic Co-operation and Development (OECD). (2025, June 11). *Development co-operation profiles: United States*. Retrieved February 9, 2026, from https://www.oecd.org/en/publications/development-co-operation-profiles_04b376d7-en/united-states_884f742e-en.html

Pamment, J., Smedberg, M., & Isaksson, E. (2025). National security and public diplomacy. In S. Aday (Ed.), *Handbook on public diplomacy* (pp. 449–461). Elgar. https://doi.org/10.4337/9781803926568.00048

Petry, E. (2025, February 21). *Uncovering conflicts of interest and self-dealing in the executive branch*. Retrieved June 13, 2026, from https://www.brennancenter.org/our-work/research-reports/uncovering-conflicts-interest-and-self-dealing-executive-branch

Pieth, M. (2012). *Collective action and corruption* (International Centre for Collective Action, Working Paper Series 13). Basel Institute on Governance.

Ray, J., Vigers, B., & Ritter, Z. (2026, April 3). China edges past U.S. in Global approval ratings. *Gallup News*. Gallup. Retrieved June 13, 2026, from https://news.gallup.com/poll/707945/china-edges-past-global-approval-ratings.aspx

Reports Without Borders. (2025). *RSF World Press Freedom Index 2025*. Retrieved February 9, 2026, from https://rsf.org/en/index

Scott-Smith, G. (2023). International exchanges. In E. Gilboa (Ed.), *A research agenda for public diplomacy* (pp. 251–266). Elgar. https://doi.org/10.4337/9781802207323.00025

Secretaría de la Defensa Nacional. (2026, February 22). *La Secretaría de la Defensa Nacional informa sobre una operación para la detención de Rubén "N" (a) Mencho* (Press release). Retrieved February 9, 2026, from https://www.gob.mx/defensa/prensa/la-secretaria-de-la-defensa-nacional-informa-sobre-una-operacion-para-la-detencion-de-ruben-n-a-mencho

Slaughter, A.-M. (2004). *A new world order*. Princeton University Press.

Spalding, A. (2012). Four unchartered corners of anti-corruption law: In search of remedies to the sanctioning effect. *Wisconsin Law Review, 2*, 661–688.

Spykman, N. (1942). *America's strategy in world politics*. Harcourt, Brace and Company.

Stephenson, M. (2017). France's new anticorruption law: What does it change? *The Global Anticorruption Blog*. Retrieved February 9, 2026, from https://globalanticorruptionblog.com/2017/03/02/frances-new-anticorruption-law-what-does-it-change/

Stott, M., & Stabe, M. (2026, February 13). Venezuelans optimistic after US intervention, poll finds. *Financial Times*. Retrieved February 9, 2026, from https://www.ft.com/content/d9936aff-98e8-436e-ad68-50d883513509

Teachout, Z. (2014). *Corruption in America*. Harvard University Press.

Thomas, K. (2021). *Murder by contract*. The Global Initiative Against Transnational Organized Crime. Retrieved February 9, 2026, from https://globalinitiative.net/wp-content/uploads/2021/09/GITOC-Murder-by-Contract-Targeted-Killings-in-eastern-and-southern-Africa-.pdf

Transparency International (TI). (2013). *Global corruption barometer 2013*. Retrieved February 9, 2026, from https://images.transparencycdn.org/images/2013_GlobalCorruptionBarometer_EN_200525_112757.pdf

Transparency International (TI). (2023). *Financial statements for the year ended 31 December 2022*. Transparency International. Retrieved February 9, 2026, from https://files.transparencycdn.org/images/2022-Financial-Statements.pdf

Trump, D. (2017, September 19). *Remarks by President Trump to the 72nd Session of the United Nations General Assembly*. Retrieved February 9, 2026, from https://trumpwhitehouse.archives.gov/briefings-statements/remarks-president-trump-72nd-session-united-nations-general-assembly/

United Nations Development Programme. (2023). *Human Development Index (HDI)*. Retrieved July 11, 2025, from https://hdr.undp.org/data-center/human-development-index#/indicies/HDI

United Nations Office on Drugs and Crime (UNODC). (2012). *Country review report of the United States of America*. Retrieved February 9, 2026, from https://www.unodc.org/documents/treaties/UNCAC/WorkingGroups/ImplementationReviewGroup/ExecutiveSummaries/V1251970e.pdf

United Nations Office on Drugs and Crime (UNODC). (2018, November 28). *UNCAC second cycle*. Retrieved February 9, 2026, from https://www.unodc.org/documents/treaties/UNCAC/SA-Report/2019_07_05_USA_SACL.pdf

United Nations Office on Drugs and Crime (UNODC). (2023a). *The global study on homicide 2023*. United Nations.

United Nations Office on Drugs and Crime (UNODC). (2023b). *Implementation review group: Executive summary of the United States of America*. Retrieved February 9, 2026, from https://www.unodc.org/documents/treaties/UNCAC/WorkingGroups/ImplementationReviewGroup/12-16June2023/CAC-COSP-IRG-II-3-1-Add.10/2307244E.pdf

United Nations Office on Drugs and Crime (UNODC). (2026). *Preventing and countering organized crime*. Retrieved February 9, 2026, from https://www.unodc.org/unodc/en/humanrights/areas/organized-crime.html

United Nations. (2024). *Status of ratification*. Retrieved July 11, 2025, from https://indicators.ohchr.org

United States of America v. Nicolás Maduro Moros, Diosdado Cabello Rondón, Ramón Rodríguez Chacín, Cilia Adelia Flores de Maduro, Nicolás Ernesto Maduro Guerra, & Hector Rusthenford Guerrero Flores. (2011). United States District Court Southern District of New York, S4 11 Cr. 205 (AKH). Retrieved February 9, 2026, from https://www.justice.gov/opa/media/1422326/dl

United States. (1776). *Declaration of Independence*. Retrieved February 9, 2026, from https://www.archives.gov/founding-docs/declaration

United States. (2015). *USA response*. Retrieved July 11, 2025, from https://www.unodc.org/documents/treaties/UNCAC/WorkingGroups/ImplementationReviewGroup/14-16November2016/GoodPractices/2015.46/United_States_of_America.pdf

Vveinhardt, J., & Bendaraviciene, R. (2022). How do nepotism and favouritism affect organisational climate? *Frontiers in Psychology, 12*, 1–10. https://doi.org/10.3389/fpsyg.2021.710140

Wendt, A. (1999). *Social theory of international politics*. Cambridge University Press.

White House. (2013, December 5). *The open government partnership*. Retrieved February 9, 2026, from https://www.opengovpartnership.org/wp-content/uploads/2019/06/US-National-Action-Plan.pdf

White House. (2021, December). *United States strategy on countering corruption*. Retrieved February 9, 2026, from https://bidenwhitehouse.archives.gov/wp-content/uploads/2021/12/United-States-Strategy-on-Countering-Corruption.pdf

White House. (2022, October). *National security strategy*. Retrieved February 9, 2026, from https://bidenwhitehouse.archives.gov/wp-content/uploads/2022/11/8-November-Combined-PDF-for-Upload.pdf

White House. (2025a, November). *National Security Strategy of The United States of America*. Retrieved February 9, 2026, from https://www.whitehouse.gov/wp-content/uploads/2025/12/2025-National-Security-Strategy.pdf

White House. (2025b, February 10). *Pausing foreign corrupt practices act enforcement to further American economic and national security*. Retrieved February 9, 2026, from https://www.whitehouse.gov/presidential-actions/2025/02/pausing-foreign-corrupt-practices-act-enforcement-to-further-american-economic-and-national-security/

Wike, R., Poushter, J., Silver, L., & Fetterolf, J. (2025). *U.S. image declines in many nations amid low confidence in Trump*. Pew Research Center. Retrieved June 13, 2026, from https://www.pewresearch.org/global/2025/06/11/us-image-declines-in-many-nations-amid-low-confidence-in-trump/

Wiseman, G., & Scott, A. (2026). Engaging citizens in a polarised society: The choices for US diplomacy. In J. Melissen, H. Kim, & G. Chandrasekara (Eds.), *Home engagement in diplomacy* (pp. 210–248). Brill. https://doi.org/10.1163/9789004738324_010

World Bank & United Nations Office on Drugs and Crime (UNODC). (2010). *No safe havens: A global forum on stolen asset recovery and development*. Retrieved February 9, 2026, from https://documents1.worldbank.org/curated/en/545101468251699476/pdf/645930WP0No0Sa00Box0361540B0PUBLIC0.pdf

World Bank. (2024a). *GDP (current US$)*. Retrieved February 9, 2026, from https://data.worldbank.org/indicator/NY.GDP.MKTP.CD?most_recent_value_desc=true

World Bank. (2024b). *Gini Index*. Retrieved July 11, 2025, from https://data.worldbank.org/indicator/SI.POV.GINI?most_recent_value_desc=true

World Intellectual Property Organization (WIPO). (2024). *Global innovation index 2025*. WIPO. Retrieved July 11, 2025, from https://www.wipo.int/web-publications/global-innovation-index-2025/assets/89507/global-innovation-index-2025-en.pdf

World Justice Project. (2025). *WJP Rule of Law Index*. Retrieved February 9, 2026, from https://worldjusticeproject.org/rule-of-law-index/global

Zaharna, R. (2022). *Boundary spanners of humanity*. Oxford University Press. https://doi.org/10.1093/oso/9780190930271.001.0001

Zürn, M. (2018). *A theory of global governance*. Oxford University Press. https://doi.org/10.1093/oso/9780198819974.001.0001

CHAPTER 6

South Korea: Eradicating Deeply Rooted Evils

6.1 Contextualising Integrity in a Developmental State

Few countries illustrate as clearly as South Korea the entanglement between rapid economic development, democratic consolidation, and anticorruption norm-building. Established in 1948 after the division of the Korean Peninsula along the 38th parallel, the Republic of Korea emerged in the southern zone under United States auspices. The Soviet Union supported the establishment of the Democratic People's Republic of Korea in the North. This geopolitical bifurcation created a persistent security dilemma that continues to shape the peninsula's political landscape. Soon afterwards, the Republic of Korea endured the devastation of the Korean War (1950–1953) (Ho-jung et al., 2019). In its aftermath, South Korea experienced two decades of acute poverty and institutional fragility. Within a generation, however, it became one of the world's major economies.

From the 1960s onwards, successive governments prioritised rapid industrialisation (Ho-jung et al., 2019). Through an interventionist developmental model, the state channelled credit, regulatory protection, and strategic coordination to large family-owned conglomerates known as *chaebols* (재벌), including Samsung, Hyundai, LG, and Lotte (Transparency International, 2006). Sustained annual growth rates of 7–8% between 1960

N. de A. e S. F. dos Santos, *Anticorruption Public Diplomacy*, Palgrave Macmillan Series in Global Public Diplomacy,
https://doi.org/10.1007/978-3-032-28668-0_6

and 1990 positioned South Korea among the world's fifteen largest economies (World Bank, 2024), eventually enabling its transition from Official Development Assistance (ODA) recipient to donor (ACRC, 2023a). This transformation consolidated the *chaebols* as central pillars of the national economy. Industrial expansion, export competitiveness, and geopolitical resilience became closely intertwined with corporate concentration. Yet this developmental success carried an inherent tension: the same state–business nexus that accelerated growth simultaneously created conditions for systemic corruption.

Privileges granted to conglomerates entrenched opaque networks linking political authority and corporate leadership (Transparency International, 2006). Presidential administrations repeatedly became embroiled in corruption scandals involving *chaebols* (Sang-Hun, 2018). The release of a Samsung executive in 2021 on economic grounds during the COVID-19 crisis (Dale & Yuk, 2021), and presidential pardons granted in 2022 to Lotte and Samsung executives (United States Department of State, 2022, p. 11) illustrate the enduring structural influence of these conglomerates.

Hence, corruption in South Korea cannot be reduced to isolated misconduct; it is historically rooted in the developmental governance model. This structural integration generated a recurring political dynamic. Revisionist movements denounced entrenched practices under the expression *jeokpye cheongsan* (적폐청산), meaning the eradication of accumulated deep-rooted evils (structural corruption) (Yoo-seok, 2019). The phrase became central in electoral campaigns and civic mobilisations, particularly during the protests that culminated in the impeachment of President Park Geun-hye (Kim, 2018). Yet, it also reveals a cycle in which political forces elected under anticorruption banners often became entangled in similar practices (Kim, 2023). This cyclical pattern gave rise to the popular saying *naeronambul* (내로남불), translated as "if I do it, it's a romance; if you do it, it's adultery" (Dale & Yuk, 2021). The expression captures public scepticism towards selective moralism and the politicisation of anticorruption discourse.

Despite these tensions, South Korea's route reflects measurable consolidation of its international reputation. The country rose from 52nd place in 2016 to 30th in 2024 in Transparency International's Corruption Perceptions Index, indicating improved international recognition of integrity performance. It also ranks in the top quartile of the World Bank's Control of Corruption indicator, the Index of Public Integrity developed by the European Research Centre for Anti-Corruption and State-Building, and the Bribery Risk Matrix produced by TRACE International.

At the same time, South Korea expanded its international normative engagement. It was among the early signatories of the OECD Anti-Bribery Convention in 1997 and ratified the United Nations Convention against Corruption (UNCAC) in 2003. It became a founding member of the Open Government Partnership (OGP) in 2011 (Cain, 2014) and hosts an active Transparency International chapter since 1999. Moreover, it plays a leading coordinating role in several anticorruption initiatives within the Asia–Pacific region (Anti-Corruption & Civil Rights Commission [ACRC], 2025) and has participated in the board of the International Anti-Corruption Academy (IACA) since 2012. This outward projection reflects a broader strategic orientation in the country's international positioning. The pursuit of international recognition through democratic governance and market credibility constitutes a core component of South Korea's national interest (Park, 2011). Integrity is increasingly framed not only as a domestic overhaul imperative but also as a reputational asset in global governance.

South Korea therefore represents a paradigmatic case in which anticorruption emerges simultaneously as structural vulnerability, reform discourse, and instrument of international positioning. The South Korean case is marked by visible contestation, scandal cycles, and active norm rearticulation. Because corruption has been historically intertwined in its development, projecting an integrity-based identity acquires heightened diplomatic significance. Anticorruption becomes part of a broader identity reconstruction process through which the state seeks to harmonise developmental nationalism, democratic consolidation, and global normative engagement. Understanding how integrity informs South Korea's external projection therefore requires examining how national interests and state identities within the South Korean developmental model shape emerging ACPD practices.

6.2 National Interests and Identities in the South Korean Model

South Korea occupies the southern half of the Korean Peninsula in Northeast Asia. It shares its only land border with North Korea and is surrounded by major maritime routes linking countries such as Japan and

China. This geographic location within one of the world's most geopolitically dense regions reinforces the structural centrality of security in its national outlook (Park, 2011). Ranked among the world's leading military powers (Global Firepower [GFP], 2026), its defence posture remains shaped by the enduring threat posed by North Korea (Park, 2011). The unresolved armistice and the region's strategic density situate national survival at the core of state identity. Security thus operates as a foundational organising principle of the South Korean model of statecraft.

South Korea operates under the 1987 Constitution, which institutionalised democratic governance after decades of authoritarian rule (Ho-jung et al., 2019). This transition marked a decisive moment of identity reconstruction, reframing the state from developmental authoritarianism to constitutional democracy. The presidential system vests executive authority in the president, while the judiciary follows a civil law tradition (Kim & Nam, 2025). South Korea maintains 187 diplomatic missions abroad and ranks 13th in the Global Diplomacy Index (Lowy Institute, 2024). This network reflects a sustained strategic commitment to international engagement.

South Korea ranks among the world's leading economies, possessing the world's 12th largest GDP (World Bank, 2024). With public debt at approximately 46% of GDP, well below the OECD average (OECD, 2024), the country preserves fiscal sustainability and policy space for strategic investment. It allocates roughly 0.2% of its gross national income to ODA and ranks as the 28th largest OECD donor (OECD, 2025), symbolising its transition from aid recipient to development partner.

South Korea's economy is innovation-driven. The country accounts for 2.8% of global exports, with manufactured goods and information and communication technologies comprising about 28% of total exports (Dell & McDevitt, 2022; United Nations Trade & Development, 2025). Investment in research and development reaches 4.9% of GDP, and the country ranks fourth globally in patent holdings (World Intellectual Property Organization [WIPO], 2024). These indicators forge a type identity (Wendt, 1999) centred on technological leadership, competitiveness, and knowledge production, while boosting a corporate identity defined by security orientation and institutional capacity.

Within this structural configuration, national interests converge around three pillars: security, prosperity, and international recognition. Democratic consolidation strengthens internal legitimacy, economic dynamism sustains developmental continuity, and participation in global governance enhances reputational security (Cull, 2024; Office of National Security, 2023; Park, 2011). Identity and interest thereby operate in a mutually reinforcing relationship. This alignment becomes particularly visible in the normative domain. Advocacy of democratic standards, rule of law, and transparency acts not only as an expression of values but also as strategic positioning within global governance. Integrity acquires dual meaning: domestically it addresses structural vulnerabilities inherited from the developmental state; internationally it supports the country's aspiration to be recognised as a responsible middle power (Cooper & Dal, 2017; Jordaan, 2003) aligned with universal norms.

In this sense, anticorruption policy is engraved within the South Korean model of statecraft as both governance remedy and reputational strategy. The security-oriented, capacity-driven, and developmentally coordinated corporate identity interacts with a type identity centred on technological modernity and democratic legitimacy. National interests, shaped by geopolitical vulnerability and economic interdependence, incentivise the projection of integrity as normative capital. These dynamics become clearer when examining how South Korea articulates its anticorruption identity, discussed in the following section.

6.3 Anticorruption Identity: Vulnerability, Reform, and Middle Power Aspiration

South Korea's anticorruption identity, forged amid geopolitical and security pressures, has become a central element of the country's reputational security (Cull, 2024). It underpins regional leadership, economic partnerships, and security alliances, all strategically integrated into national interests (Park, 2011). It also functions as an indicator of international credibility. The goal of ranking within the top thirty positions in Transparency International's Corruption Perceptions Index was explicitly set (ACRC, 2019, p. 6) and achieved in 2024, integrating international benchmarking into national governance objectives. Anticorruption thus becomes a site where external standards are translated into domestic performance criteria.

South Korea's anticorruption reforms consolidated relatively late, emerging primarily in the late twentieth century. Addressing corruption has proved complex, as it became structurally entrenched in the state–*chaebol* nexus sustaining the developmental model (Transparency

International, 2006; ACRC, 2023a). Integrity improvements did not occur through abrupt rupture but developed incrementally after the 1987 democratic transition (Transparency International, 2006). Legislative acts adopted during the 1990s illustrate this institutional recalibration. Revisions to the Public Ethics Act introduced asset registration and revolving-door restrictions, while the Public Officials Election Act targeted electoral irregularities. The Administrative Procedure Act and the Disclosure of Information by Public Agencies Act strengthened transparency and financial accountability. These instruments signalled the gradual consolidation of a role identity centred on legal modernisation, procedural accountability.

These endeavours have not followed a linear path. The creation of the Korea Independent Commission Against Corruption in 2002 marked a turning point in consolidating a specialised integrity system. Its merger in 2008 into the Anti-Corruption and Civil Rights Commission (ACRC) diluted its autonomy and narrowed enforcement capacity (OECD Working Group on Bribery, 2011; Transparency International, 2006). By contrast, the adoption of the Kim Young-ran Law (Improper Solicitation and Graft Act), which entered into force in 2016, constituted a renewed attempt to recalibrate public-sector integrity standards. The legislation tightened rules governing gifts, hospitality, and improper solicitation, signalling responsiveness to both domestic public pressure and evolving international anticorruption norms. Reform thus oscillates between consolidation and recalibration, reflecting ongoing processes of normative negotiation.

South Korea's national integrity system encompasses executive (president, prime minister, and state council), legislative, and judicial authorities, oversight and prosecutorial bodies, procurement mechanisms, the ACRC, the national election commission, the business sector, civil society, and international actors (Transparency International, 2006). Persistent vulnerabilities remain in political financing, prosecutorial independence, and corporate compliance, while strengths include inter-agency collaboration, whistleblower protection, and digital procurement transparency. This coexistence of alignment and fragility underscores the uneven process of norm internalisation.

Digital innovation constitutes a defining feature of South Korea's anticorruption identity. The country adopted pioneering e-government legislation in 2011 and developed advanced e-procurement systems recognised internationally for enhancing transparency (Transparency International,

2006). Technology is deeply integrated in integrity governance, reinforcing an anticorruption identity grounded in innovation.

Recurrent scandals have exposed enduring structural weaknesses linked to the political–corporate nexus. These include accounting fraud, illicit campaign contributions, military procurement manipulation, international bribery, and the scandal culminating in the impeachment of President Park Geun-hye in 2016 (Transparency International, 2006). Such episodes demonstrate persistent political–corporate entanglement despite ongoing reform efforts. South Koreans consistently report that corruption affects their lives and express expectations of rising corruption levels (Transparency International, 2003, 2007, 2013). Surveys also reveal sustained distrust towards political parties, the legislature, the judiciary, and the police. Public perception mediates the credibility of institutional renewal, revealing a gap between normative projection and lived societal experience.

Enforcement fragilities further complicate this scenario. Although foreign bribery was criminalised following adherence to the United Nations and OECD anticorruption conventions, South Korea was assessed between 2014 and 2022 as demonstrating "little or no enforcement" of the latter (Heimann et al., 2014; Dell & McDevitt, 2022). Limited investigative resources, coordination gaps, and lenient sanctions have weakened deterrence. Yet this deficit coexists with sustained engagement in international monitoring. OECD and UNODC evaluations recognise legislative improvements and efforts to incorporate external recommendations into domestic law (OECD Working Group on Bribery, 2011, 2018; UNODC, 2023). The creation of the Corruption Investigation Office for High-Ranking Officials (CIO) further signals attempts to enhance accountability, despite controversy regarding potential political influence (Dale & Yuk, 2021). This coexistence of formal compliance and practical constraint reflects uneven norm internalisation and a continually negotiated anticorruption identity.

Internationally, South Korea positions itself as an active participant in global integrity regimes. Beyond adherence to multilateral anticorruption conventions, it engages in initiatives such as the OGP and the IACA. Although it does not substantially finance transnational norm entrepreneurs, it contributes modestly to international anticorruption bodies, suggesting normative alignment rather than material leadership. This configuration produces a collective identity anchored in a rule-based multilateral order where South Korea seeks recognition as a responsible agent.

South Korea's anticorruption identity is both normative and instrumental, reflecting the interplay between structural vulnerabilities, democratic consolidation pressures, geopolitical insecurity, and aspirations for regional leadership. In this context, ACPD emerges as intertwined with the broader project of democratic consolidation and institutional credibility. It serves as a mechanism through which South Korea performs a reform-oriented, technologically advanced, and multilateral role identity while strengthening its position within the global anticorruption regime.

6.4 Resource Design and Identity Projection in South Korea's Public Diplomacy

South Korea's ACPD rests on a diversified yet strategically articulated set of resources. Rather than operating as isolated assets, these resources form an integrated structure through which the state projects authority and credibility. Analytically, they can be organised across six domains: economic capacity; policy frameworks; cultural and value-based projection; global connectivity; technological leadership; and military capability. They constitute the foundational infrastructure underpinning South Korea's identity projection.

Economic performance is one of the backbones of this configuration. Ranked among the world's fifteen largest economies (World Bank, 2024) and maintaining comparatively low public debt (OECD, 2024), South Korea sustains an export-oriented development model centred on manufactured goods and advanced services (United Nations Trade & Development, 2025). Its prominence in high-technology sectors (Dell & McDevitt, 2022) reinforces a self-image of industrial sophistication and innovation-driven modernity. A business-friendly regulatory environment (World Bank, 2020) further strengthens perceptions of institutional reliability. Hence, economic capacity functions as material power and reputational capital. Within ACPD, economic credibility strengthens integrity claims by linking transparency to competitiveness, regulatory stability, and global market integration. Financial strength supports sustained engagement with foreign publics, international organisations, and multilateral initiatives.

Policy and governance resources further consolidate this configuration. Following democratic consolidation, regulatory quality remains robust (WIPO, 2024) despite concerns regarding judicial independence (Schwab, 2019). High human development indicators, including life expectancy (United Nations Development Programme [UNDP], 2025) and social protection systems (International Labour Organization, 2024), reinforce an image of institutional stability and state capacity. South Korea maintains sustained engagement with international human rights frameworks (United Nations, 2024). Collectively, these attributes sustain a role identity associated with democratic governance and rule-based administration. In ACPD, they function as normative signals framing integrity as embedded within democratic resilience rather than as technical compliance.

Cultural projection constitutes another pillar of South Korea's public diplomacy. The transnational expansion of South Korean creative industries, including K-pop, cinema, television dramas, fashion, design, and gaming, has generated substantial symbolic capital and global recognition (United Nations Trade & Development, 2024; Jin, 2016). Digital streaming platforms have accelerated this circulation, transforming South Korean audiovisual production into global cultural phenomena (Jin, 2016). This expansive cultural influence is widely referred to as *Hallyu*, or the Korean Wave (Nye & Kim, 2013). Beyond entertainment value, these industries operate as strategic assets linking cultural exports to national branding and diplomatic outreach (Nye & Kim, 2013). Cultural production thus functions as a source of soft power in Nyean terms and as an institutionalised mechanism of identity performance. In this ACPD configuration, cultural visibility fosters receptive transnational audiences, enabling integrity narratives to circulate through reputational channels associated with modernity and innovation.

South Korea's connectivity further enhances its diplomatic reach. The country maintains an extensive diplomatic network (Lowy Institute, 2024) and a dense position within transnational governance networks (Transparency International, 2006). High passport mobility (Henley & Partners, 2025) signals international openness, while widespread social media reflects deep digital embeddedness (Kemp, 2025). Connectivity strengthens the relational dimension of public diplomacy, facilitating interaction with foreign publics, international organisations, and transnational civil society actors.

Technological leadership is one of South Korea's most distinctive identity markers. Strong educational performance (OECD, 2023), near-universal internet access (Kemp, 2025), high scientific productivity (Scimago, 2025), sustained investment in research and development, and robust patent registration (WIPO, 2024) consolidate its status as an innovation hub. Importantly, technological capacity is deeply woven into governance practices and carries direct implications for ACPD. Digital governance systems reinforce this identity by linking administrative efficiency with transparency. In ACPD, technology functions as both governance infrastructure and evidence of operational integrity.

Military capability constitutes the final pillar of this resource architecture. Ranked among the world's leading military powers (GFP, 2026), South Korea has developed a strategic role as a defence partner (Ministry of National Defense, 2025), boosting its credibility within regional and global security arrangements. While traditionally associated with hard power, military capabilities also contribute to an identity as a responsible security provider. Stability and deterrence underpin the confidence and autonomy necessary for sustained international engagement.

Jointly, these domains reveal a composite identity. Economic dynamism, democratic governance, cultural influence, technological innovation, global connectivity, and military capability converge to project the image of a technologically advanced, globally engaged democracy. In ACPD, these resources are configured through a smart power arrangement integrating material capacity with normative aspiration. Anticorruption claims gain plausibility when anchored in economic competitiveness, digital governance, institutional optimisation, and multilateral engagement. Resource design thus supports the projection of South Korea's integrity identity in ACPD. The following section examines how this resource base is operationalised through concrete practices of ACPD.

6.5 The Operational Repertoire of Anticorruption Public Diplomacy

Under the broader *jeokpye cheongsan* narrative, South Korea's ACPD enacts, communicates, and stabilises integrity as a component of its international identity. The ACPD repertoire unfolds sequentially, moving from information gathering to dialogical engagement and advocacy, followed by cultural and educational diplomacy, collaborative exchange, and international broadcasting. It culminates in strategic planning, evaluation, and lessons learned, forming an adaptive governance cycle in which communication and reform mutually reinforce one another. Together, these dimensions illustrate how South Korea performs integrity within processes of international socialisation.

Listening and Information Gathering Through Global Networks

Listening is a foundational dimension of public diplomacy (Cull, 2019). In South Korea's ACPD, listening extends beyond passive information collection. It operates as a structured mechanism through which the state captures expectations, identifies reputational risks, and adjusts integrity narratives.

Seven channels operationalise this listening function. First, digital whistleblowing platforms enable corruption reporting through dedicated online systems. The ACRC administers the Clean Portal, facilitating protected reporting and signalling openness to scrutiny (UNODC, 2023). Embedding whistleblowing in accessible digital infrastructure promotes responsiveness while bolstering enforcement capacity. Second, systematic foreign media monitoring allows authorities to detect corruption trends and reputational vulnerabilities (OECD Working Group on Bribery, 2018). Incorporating journalistic reporting into institutional assessment recognises the media as watchdog and agenda-setter within the global integrity field. Third, social media platforms such as X and Facebook function as informal listening arenas in which authorities monitor reactions to anticorruption initiatives (UNODC, 2022, p. 18). Especially in a post-reality environment (Manor & Bjola, 2021), integrity reputations are increasingly shaped in real-time discursive spaces.

Fourth, South Korean embassies and overseas missions contribute through structured reporting on corruption involving national companies abroad (OECD Working Group on Bribery, 2018), thereby linking corporate conduct abroad to national credibility. Fifth, benchmarking with foreign anticorruption bodies, including those of Finland, Sweden, and France, serves technical cooperation and norm absorption (OGP, 2020). In this sense, listening becomes a pathway for norm internalisation (Finnemore & Sikkink, 2001). Sixth, the ACRC holds annual consultations with leaders of foreign companies operating in South Korea, as well as with representatives of foreign chambers of commerce and diplomatic missions (ACRC, 2020). These gatherings institutionalise economic listening by capturing concerns related to regulatory transparency and compliance.

Finally, the Center for Participatory Diplomacy at the Ministry of Foreign Affairs (MOFA) developed a mobile application enabling citizens to contribute to foreign policy discussions. Beyond expanding consultation mechanisms, this instrument reflects the broader societalisation of diplomacy and challenges elite-centred conceptions of foreign policymaking (Melissen & Chandrasekara, 2026). By institutionalising home engagement, South Korea recognises citizens as both audiences and co-constitutive agents in the diplomatic process, reaffirming the bidirectional character of ACPD.

These practices combine material infrastructures, namely digital platforms, reporting systems, and technological investment, with immaterial resources such as institutional procedures, transparency, and participatory norms. Listening operates at the intersection of soft and hard power, signalling openness while strengthening enforcement capacity and regulatory credibility.

Institutionally, coordination rests with the ACRC, the MOFA, and the Supreme Prosecutors' Office (SPO) whose authority derives from formal institutional mandates and technical competence. Non state agents engage through defined gateways. South Korean companies operating abroad contribute to reporting mechanisms; journalists shape monitoring processes through investigative coverage; citizens engage via participatory platforms; and foreign agencies, diplomats, and corporate actors participate through invitations to consultations and benchmarking exercises. Listening is therefore structured rather than spontaneous and is mediated through institutionalised representation ties.

Within the broader framework of *jeokpye cheongsan*, listening performs a dual function. Domestically, it integrates scrutiny into administrative routines. Internationally, it projects procedural openness and adaptive governance. Consequently, structured listening becomes a performative component of South Korea's integrity identity.

Dialogical Engagement: From Norm Absorption to Regional Leadership

Dialogical engagement lies at the heart of South Korea's ACPD as a space where norms are negotiated, internalised, and projected internationally. It positions the country at once as a norm recipient and an advocate of integrity reform. This engagement unfolds across eight modalities. First, bilateral cooperation in enforcement, covering investigations, mutual legal assistance, information-sharing, and asset recovery, demonstrates a commitment to upholding anticorruption norms across borders. One example is the memorandum of understanding coordinated by the SPO to facilitate cooperation with the United States (OECD Working Group on Bribery, 2011). Through such arrangements, enforcement becomes both a domestic instrument and an international responsibility. Dialogue combines communicative soft power with enabling hard power institutional infrastructures.

South Korea's dialogical engagement reflects a dual movement of learning and mentoring. The second modality involves the pursuit of technical assistance from states perceived as more advanced in such matters. Collaboration with the United Kingdom on legislative and regulatory frameworks illustrates this learning-oriented engagement (ACRC, 2016). Third, South Korea also transfers its expertise to developing countries, particularly in the Asia–Pacific region. Technical cooperation with countries such as Indonesia, Mongolia, Myanmar, Thailand, Vietnam, and Kuwait exemplifies this outward projection (ACRC, 2010, 2019). Generally coordinated by the ACRC, this circulation of knowledge functions as diplomatic capital rooted in institutional design, digital governance, and compliance mechanisms. Through soft capacities to listen, communicate, and influence, South Korea positions itself as both learner and mentor, enhancing its identity as a technically competent state.

Fourth, dialogical engagement unfolds through sustained participation in multilateral networks coordinated by the ACRC and the MOFA. Active involvement in the IACA, including board membership, integrates South Korea into global integrity epistemic communities. This has provided opportunities to deliver lectures and participate in educational programmes (ACRC, 2016; UNODC, 2023), expanding the country's visibility. Fifth, regional leadership materialises through initiatives such as negotiating the creation of the Asset Recovery Interagency Network Asia-Pacific (ARIN-AP), subsequently headquartered in Seoul (OECD Working Group on Bribery, 2018). Hosting it positions South Korea as a convening node within regional anticorruption cooperation. In these modalities, dialogical engagement takes the form of pedagogical collaboration and normative alignment, mobilising soft and collaborative power capacities.

Sixth, participation as a reviewing country in anticorruption frameworks reinforces collective standards. South Korea has acted as a UNCAC peer reviewer in states including Japan, Kuwait, Niue, and the Solomon Islands (ACRC, 2021). By doing so, it contributes directly to monitoring and strengthening the global anticorruption norm through listening, communicating, inspiring (soft power), and cooperating (collaborative power), thereby enhancing its role identity within the global anticorruption regime.

Seventh, dialogical engagement extends into digital spheres through online professional communities. The ACRC's Facebook network for alumni of international training programmes sustains long-term exchange and knowledge circulation (ACRC, 2018b). Social media thus extends institutional diplomacy into semi-formal transnational communities through soft and collaborative forms of power.

Finally, the eighth modality involves financial support for international initiatives. Funding projects aligned with priorities of the Association of Southeast Asian Nations (ASEAN), such as the "Strengthening regional cooperation and the capacity of ASEAN countries to counter corruption and other serious crimes (2020–2023)" (UNODC, 2020), adds a financial dimension to this dialogical engagement. Economic resources, technical expertise, and multilateral engagement reinforce signals of responsibility and integrity. In such cases, soft, collaborative, and enabling hard power converge to promote normative alignment.

Across these modalities, dialogue functions as learning, cooperation, and norm diffusion. Institutional coordination rests primarily with the ACRC, with additional roles played by the MOFA and the SPO. Participation by non state and foreign agents occurs through formal institutional channels, including memoranda of understanding, membership in international organisations, participation in peer review mechanisms, and professional training networks. Dialogical engagement therefore plays a central role within South Korea's ACPD. It enables the country to move progressively from norm-recipient to norm-shaper while consolidating its identity as a technically capable and regionally responsible actor within the global integrity governance.

Advocacy and Projection: Performing Integrity on the Global Stage

Through advocacy, South Korea positions itself as a responsible agent regarding the global anticorruption norm. In this process, domestic programmes are translated into internationally recognisable signals of institutional credibility. At the regulatory level, due diligence procedures applied by institutions such as Export–Import Bank of Korea (Eximbank), the

Korea International Cooperation Agency (KOICA), and the Korea Trade Insurance Corporation require exporters to demonstrate internal anticorruption control systems (OECD Working Group on Bribery, 2011). Compliance therefore extends beyond domestic governance to shape international economic exchanges and reinforce a commitment to integrity in global trade.

Advocacy also operates through international recognition of national best practices. The Korean Pact for Anti-Corruption and Transparency (K-Pact), a national alliance integrating civil society, political and private-sector actors, was highlighted as a model initiative by the Basel Institute on Governance (2020). Such recognition transforms national programmes into sources of international legitimacy. Narrative construction is another key dimension of advocacy. Programmes such as the Integrity Assessment, the e-People System, the Corruption Impact Assessment, and the Clean Portal are regularly presented through speeches, publications, interviews, and digital platforms (ACRC, 2014, 2018b; UNODC, 2022). Through these channels, governance instruments are reframed as narratives of transformation and innovation. External validation further amplifies these narratives. Statements by foreign experts, including the American scholar Andrew Spalding, praising South Korea's anticorruption achievements (ACRC, 2018a), are incorporated into official communication, boosting the credibility of integrity claims.

International awards and high-level speeches also play a performative role. The United Nations Public Service Award granted in 2003 to the e-Procurement System reinforced the country's reputation as an innovator in transparency governance (Transparency International, 2006). Speeches delivered in global forums serve as normative reaffirmation. One example is the address at the Conference of the States Parties to the UNCAC in 2017, attended by approximately 1,600 representatives from 158 countries (ACRC, 2018b). By addressing the corruption scandal involving a former president, South Korea projected transparency and reform-oriented resilience.

Communication and branding campaigns further deepen the performative advocacy. The campaign "World of Integrity" sought to align South Korea's global economic standing with an equivalent integrity reputation (UNODC, 2022). Promotional materials and participation in international networks positioned the country among the world's most transparent states. Similarly, the slogan "Korea, a country of integrity"

(ACRC, 2010, p. 71) condenses abstract values into a recognisable national integrity brand.

Partnerships with global norm entrepreneurs further expand this landscape. Cooperation with UNDP in producing an e-book spotlighting South Korean anticorruption policy (Lee & Lee, 2016) illustrates how alliances enhance normative diffusion. Visits by the ACRC president to organisations involved in anticorruption evaluation, including the UNODC, Transparency International, Bertelsmann Stiftung, and the Economist Intelligence Unit (ACRC, 2014, 2022a) place ACPD within key governance nodes.

Digital platforms also amplify advocacy. Social media accounts enable interactive dissemination of anticorruption information, presenting transparency as both institutional practice and communicative commitment. The creation of the International Cooperation Centre within the SPO extends advocacy into asset recovery cooperation, converting technical expertise into globally visible services. Technological innovation adds another dimension. The international patent of the e-People Global e-Petition System (ACRC, 2015) demonstrates administrative sophistication and a willingness to export governance technology. By promoting its digital complaint-handling system internationally, South Korea converts anticorruption infrastructure into a strategic differentiator.

Across these initiatives, resources including laws, institutions, digital systems, budgets, and international agreements interact with narratives, reputational capital, and symbolic branding. These elements generate international outcomes through combinations of soft, collaborative, and hard power. Communication, inspiration, negotiation, enablement, and resource allocation collectively attribute international meaning to national assets.

Institutional coordination remains centred on the ACRC, although the SPO leads specific initiatives, particularly in asset recovery and technological recognition, with both deriving legitimacy from their institutional mandates. Non state agents participate selectively, including non-governmental organisations (NGOs), private firms, the Federation of Korean Industries (FKI), expatriate experts, universities, designers, and communication specialists. International norm entrepreneurs, such as the United Nations, UNODC, UNDP, and the OECD, appear in partnership roles in a limited but symbolically significant number of actions. Representation ties vary across context-specific arrangements, ranging from formal invitations and partnership agreements to inclusion in a domestic policy process, publication of interviews, membership in international conventions, and recognition under international intellectual property regimes.

Advocacy thus performs a crucial diplomatic function. By projecting regulatory innovation, institutional resilience, and technological capacity, South Korea seeks not only to comply with global anticorruption norms but also to shape their interpretation, particularly within regional governance arenas.

Cultural and Educational Diplomacy for Institutional Integrity

Cultural diplomacy expresses integrity through shared collective experience. In South Korea's ACPD, such activities operate as arenas where integrity is demonstrated and shared internationally. Three patterns structure this dimension. The first involves hosting international conferences, transforming the country into a convening platform for global integrity dialogue. The organisation of the 19th International Anti-Corruption Conference in Seoul in December 2020, in partnership with Transparency International, exemplifies this approach (ACRC, 2021). Held virtually due to the pandemic, it gathered more than 500 speakers and 10,000 participants, generating about 1.7 million video views. It concluded with the Seoul Declaration, a post-pandemic anticorruption governance cooperative scheme. In this context, budgetary resources, digital infrastructure, and institutional coordination interacted with immaterial assets such as policy credibility and normative commitment.

Anticorruption training programmes delivered by the ACRC either in person or virtually are the second pattern. They target foreign senior public officials (ACRC, 2014, 2018b, 2020, 2021), mobilising policies, institutional assets, technical expertise, and budgets. Beyond transferring technical knowledge, these initiatives present models where digital and legal innovation converge with administrative accountability. By exposing participants to South Korea's integrity assessment systems, complaint-handling mechanisms, and corruption impact evaluation tools, the ACRC fosters shared professional understandings of integrity governance while demonstrating institutional capacity.

The third pattern involves animated videos featuring anticorruption mascots (ACRC, 2022b), introducing a creative layer to cultural diplomacy. These visual narratives translate complex governance principles into accessible imagery, promoting honesty, trust, and public integrity.

Technical skills and financial investment combine with narrative framing and symbolic design, projecting meanings of efficiency, transparency, and technological sophistication.

The ACRC coordinates this cultural diplomacy within ACPD, under its institutional mandate. Participation extends to non state agents, including NGOs and companies, as well as foreign actors, such as public officials, multinational executives, and anticorruption norm entrepreneurs, including Transparency International, the United Nations, and the OECD. Representation ties are formalised through international agreements and official invitations issued by the ACRC.

Across these patterns, cultural diplomacy functions as an experiential mechanism of norm consolidation, converting national institutional achievements into internationally shared reference points. Through the combination of soft, collaborative, and hard power, capacities to influence, inspire, cooperate, mediate, and enable generate culturally resonant messages of integrity. Reform narratives are extended into visible and participatory arenas. Integrity is asserted, enacted, and taught through South Korea's ACPD and its integration into the global anticorruption community.

Exchange, Collaborative Diplomacy, and Regional Leadership

Exchange mechanisms function as platforms for collaborative governance and regional norm consolidation. Four modalities define these exchange practices in South Korea's ACPD. The first involves participation in international networks, particularly regional platforms. For instance, the country plays an active role in the Asia-Pacific Economic Cooperation (APEC), particularly through the Anti-Corruption and Transparency Experts' Task Force (UNODC, 2022), thereby transforming network participation into an arena for normative influence. Within this structure, anticorruption policies, technical expertise, and institutional experience function as shared resources through which the country contributes to shaping regional standards while strengthening its credibility.

Hosting international missions constitutes a second dimension. The reception of the UNCAC peer review visit in 2011 (UNODC, 2022) exemplifies how opening institutions to external evaluation transforms compliance into a display of transparency and legitimacy. Infrastructure, legal frameworks, and institutional coordination facilitate this scrutiny. Participation in professional training abroad constitutes a third modality.

Between 2012 and 2017, ACRC officials and ministerial teams undertook specialised training at the IACA, following a memorandum of understanding between the two parties (ACRC, 2014, 2017). This outward engagement signals institutional reflexivity: South Korea positions itself not only as a model but also as a learner within the global anticorruption community. Exchange thus operates as a process of socialisation through which knowledge circulates bidirectionally.

The reception of foreign delegations to observe anticorruption practices constitutes a fourth and visible exchange modality. Since 2008, thousands of foreign officials and journalists have visited South Korea to examine its ombudsman system, digital complaint mechanisms, and integrity assessment frameworks (ACRC, 2017, 2022b). These visits transform infrastructure and policy design into showcase assets. Exchange thus becomes experiential diplomacy: participants encounter anticorruption governance not merely as an abstract norm but as an operational reality.

Institutional coordination lies primarily with the ACRC, with MOFA leading initiatives such as review missions. Norm entrepreneurs, including the United Nations, UNODC, IACA, and APEC, participate through their mandates and expertise. International agents, ranging from government officials and scholars to expert reviewers, engage through formal invitations, organisational membership, or international agreements. These exchanges combine soft, collaborative, and enabling hard power. Communication and mediation capacities interact with institutional resources, namely laws, organisations, infrastructure, and budgets, to produce shared meanings of transparency and commitment.

Collaborative diplomacy thus arises as a defining facet of South Korea's ACPD. Rather than imposing models, it facilitates participation in collective agenda-setting and the development of regional integrity programmes. Membership places the country within Asia–Pacific governance schemes, bolstering a responsible regional identity. By projecting anticorruption narratives in cooperative spaces, the country acts at once as contributor and beneficiary within the regional and global anticorruption norm. Regional leadership therefore emerges through sustained participation in shared governance forums. In sum, exchanges transform national institutional capacities into collaborative ACPD assets.

Broadcasting Trust: Narrative and Digital Engagement

The dissemination of messages in South Korea's ACPD functions as a strategic effort to cultivate trust among transnational publics. Through broadcasting practices, the country structures narratives, harmonises terminology, and enhances institutional visibility within the global anticorruption regime. This activity encompasses eight techniques, ranging from printed materials to digital platforms and knowledge-sharing hubs.

Online manuals are the first layer. The Guidebook for Anti-corruption Business Management, for example, provides guidance on trends such as ISO 37001, a global standard for anti-bribery management systems (OECD Working Group on Bribery, 2007). Through this guide, South Korea presents its regulatory experience as both technically sophisticated and internationally aligned. A second layer consists of printed and digital leaflets. The leaflet K-Integrity Wave, produced in English for foreign audiences, frames domestic anticorruption achievements as components of broader national excellence (ACRC, 2022b), thereby aligning institutional integrity with economic modernity. Academic and policy-oriented publications constitute the third layer. Examples include papers on anticorruption conventions published in foreign journals and circulated among government agencies, universities, companies, and political parties (OECD Working Group on Bribery, 2004). The MOFA selects contributions, engaging specialised epistemic communities and converting scholarly production into diplomatic capital.

Regular English-language newsletters constitute a fourth layer. The ACRC Korea Transparency Newsletter (ACRC, 2016), for instance, disseminates monthly online updates to foreign professional and governmental networks. These newsletters function as instruments of ongoing narrative reinforcement. Similarly, occasional pamphlets promoting specific policies (fifth technique), such as the Public Interest Whistleblower Protection Act, translate legislative acts into accessible communication (ACRC, 2023b). Legal innovation thus becomes communicative evidence of normative commitment.

Direct engagement with foreign media is the sixth layer. Interviews granted by the President of the ACRC to international outlets (ACRC, 2021) personalise institutional messaging and attribute a recognisable voice to ACPD, promoting trust. The seventh technique involves digital broadcasting via the YouTube channel ACRC Vision, which expands outreach to broader audiences (ACRC, 2021). Audiovisual storytelling disseminates anticorruption narratives beyond traditional diplomatic circles, reframing institutional processes as accessible public goods. An eighth technique involves the creation of collective websites, such as that of the Asia-Pacific anticorruption forum (ACRC, 2010). This introduces a collaborative dimension to broadcasting, enabling Asian participant governments to share best practices digitally.

Resources including policies, institutions, technical expertise, communication tools, social media, international agreements, network membership, and budgets acquire meaning via soft, collaborative, and hard power. Through communication, influence, cooperation, and coordination, ideational significance is attached to governance tools. Trust thus emerges not as an abstract claim but as a narratively reinforced expectation.

Institutional coordination lies primarily with the ACRC, with selective involvement of the MOFA. Participation by norm entrepreneurs and non state agents remains limited, appearing mainly in academic publications. International agents span a broad spectrum, including foreign governments, academic institutions, companies, NGOs, chambers of commerce, evaluation bodies, and media outlets. Such agents participate through international membership, network affiliation, invitations, and academic collaboration.

In these activities, ACPD functions as a narrative consolidation of *jeok-pye cheongsan*, transforming it into communicative capital. Broadcasting trust therefore represents the communicative culmination of ACPD: the strategic circulation of integrity narratives designed to stabilise credibility within the global anticorruption regime.

Strategic Planning, Monitoring, and Reflexive Adaptation

The outward projection of South Korea's ACPD is anchored in strategic planning, systematic evaluation, and continuous learning. The ACRC's five-year anticorruption plan for 2018–2022 explicitly aimed to place the country within the top 30 positions in Transparency International's Corruption Perceptions Index (ACRC, 2019). This illustrates how policy design aligns with international benchmarks and broader reputational positioning. The plan was organised around four priorities, translating aspirations into measurable commitments: global integrity policies, corruption-free public service, corporate transparency, and integrity governance. In preparing the plan, the ACRC established an online consultation platform and implemented the Public–Private Consultative Council for a Transparent Society, gathering actors from the public and private sectors. Such initiatives reinforce policy legitimacy through inclusive participation.

Monitoring and evaluation constitute the second pillar of ACPD adaptation. The ACRC (2026) publishes annual reports containing qualitative and quantitative indicators, including metrics on media exposure, digital communication performance, and distribution of publications. These indicators reflect the recognition that ACPD operates across institutional and communicative domains. In addition, the quarterly reviews of the action plan are submitted to the Anti-Corruption Policy Consultation Council (ACRC, 2019). Such actions have produced concrete outcomes, such as the Prevention of Conflict of Interest Related to Duties of Public Servants Act, adopted in 2021 (ACRC, 2023b). Evaluation thus becomes a policy-generating rather than merely descriptive practice.

Institutional learning demonstrates how reflexivity extends beyond internal reporting to dialogue with international partners. During the 19th International Anti-Corruption Conference in Seoul, South Korea co-organised a workshop analysing the transfer of integrity policies in partnership with UNDP (ACRC, 2023b). The event assessed experiences derived from bilateral anticorruption technical assistance agreements and incorporated feedback from participating countries. Through such events, experiential knowledge is collectively examined. Reflexivity thus becomes diplomatically shared. Lessons learned become transnationally negotiated insights, corroborating South Korea's image as both proactive and self-critical.

Across these dimensions, resources such as policy plans, legislation, reporting systems, and institutional councils interact with immaterial elements including reputational ambition and transparency norms. These resources are activated primarily through soft and collaborative power capacities, including communication, consultation, and enablement. Hard power elements emerge when planning translates into legislative improvement.

Institutional coordination remains centred in the ACRC, reflecting its governmental mandate. International agents participate particularly in lessons learned via collaboration with UNDP and bilateral counterparts. Representation ties derive from membership in consultative bodies or participation in formally convened workshops.

Strategic planning and evaluation institutionalise integrity through iterative cycles of planning, monitoring, and recalibration. ACPD thus evolves into a form of adaptive governance through which South Korea continually recalibrates its integrity identity in response to domestic dynamics and international expectations.

6.6 Analysing South Korea's Anticorruption Public Diplomacy

Having examined the operational repertoire of South Korea's ACPD, the analysis now turns to how these practices are structurally integrated into domestic institutions. South Korea's ACPD works as a coordinated yet distributed system of international engagement encompassing normative circulation, role performance, and governance networks (Finnemore & Sikkink, 1998; Slaughter, 2004; Wendt, 1999). Domestic institutional reforms are translated into internationally recognisable practices that embody and shape the global anticorruption norm. The following subsections examine four key dimensions of this system: the configuration of agents and representational authority; the operational design; the resources sustaining ACPD engagement; and the smart power configuration through which these elements generate international effects. Jointly, these dimensions show how the country projects an anticorruption identity internationally while also contributing to the co-production of global integrity norms.

Agents, Representational Authority, and Coordination

South Korea's ACPD configuration brings together state, non state, and international agents. These agents perform social roles through which anticorruption norms circulate within international society (Wendt, 1999; Adler, 2005). In South Korea's ACPD, agents carry forms of representational authority through which state identities, interests, and normative status become internationally observable. Coordination remains predominantly state-centred. Analytically, the system resembles a multi-level diplomatic structure in which authority, participation, and influence emerge through interaction across three levels: the state core, mediated non state agents, and institutionalised international partners. These levels sustain processes of international socialisation and norm diffusion (Finnemore & Sikkink, 1998) in regional and global governance networks.

At the centre stands a state-anchored coordination structure. The ACRC acts as the system's principal orchestrator, coordinating initiatives, convening international partners, and aligning anticorruption activities with South Korea's broader public diplomacy strategy. Representational authority derives from institutional mandates embedded in the state's legal framework. The ACRC also centralises strategic planning and evaluation.

At the first level, additional state agents participate within their institutional competences. These include the MOFA, diplomatic missions abroad, the SPO, law enforcement authorities, Eximbank, KOICA, and specialised ministries. Within this configuration, representational ties arise from formal legal mandates. State institutions act internationally through their jurisdictional mandates, transforming domestic administrative authority into diplomatically recognised roles. Such authority enables institutions to project domestic governance practices internationally, thereby converting administrative competence into a source of diplomatic legitimacy (Sending et al., 2015). Individually, ACPD actions remain coordinated by a state agent, typically the ACRC, MOFA, or the SPO, preserving a structurally state-centred model of ACPD.

A second level consists of domestic non state agents. It includes major conglomerates such as Samsung, Hyundai, LG, and Lotte; state-owned enterprises; business associations such as the FKI; political parties; the Korean chapter of Transparency International; academic institutions; journalists; designers and communication experts (ACRC, 2010; OECD Working Group on Bribery, 2004). Collective ventures also play a role, including the Council for the Korean Pact on Anti-Corruption and Transparency, which assembles public and private actors within national integrity actions (Basel Institute on Governance, 2020). This reflects broader dynamics of transgovernmental cooperation (Slaughter, 2004), in which non state agents participate in international governance networks. Importantly, diasporas often operate as transnational intermediaries linking domestic policy debates with foreign publics and governance networks (Shain & Barth, 2003). In this regard, South Korean anticorruption specialists living abroad (ACRC, 2015) contribute to the circulation of expertise and narratives across transnational networks.

Although these agents do not exercise sovereign authority, they become integrated into ACPD through mediated representational ties structured by governmental engagement. These include governmental invitations, partnerships with public agencies, inclusion in anticorruption policy, media contributions, participation in ACRC training programmes, and engagement through official digital platforms. Through these mechanisms, non state agents amplify state-led integrity narratives, mobilising communicative, economic, and reputational resources internationally. In this sense, they reproduce dynamics characteristic of transnational advocacy and governance networks that facilitate the diffusion of international norms (Finnemore & Sikkink, 1998, 2001), extending the reach of ACPD across societal and transnational communication spaces.

A third level consists of international actors interacting with South Korea within multilateral governance frameworks. These include organisations such as the OECD, UNODC, the United Nations, UNDP, the IACA, the ARIN-AP, and ASEAN. Such organisations function as platforms for the diffusion and institutionalisation of global norms (Finnemore, 1996). Beyond them, a range of international agents also participates in ACPD activities, including multinational companies, foreign governments, and their agencies, as well as foreign chambers of commerce.

Bilateral channels play a similar role, enabling the participation of diplomats stationed in South Korea, as well as specialised authorities such as the United Kingdom's Foreign and Commonwealth Office (ACRC, 2016; OECD Working Group on Bribery, 2011). Officials from diverse regions, particularly from the Asia–Pacific, also engage through ACRC anticorruption training programmes (ACRC, 2014, 2017, 2022b). Epistemic communities contribute as knowledge brokers in the international transmission of governance models (Haas, 1992). Academic institutions and expert networks therefore expand this level in the South Korean case, contributing to the circulation of anticorruption knowledge and policy practices. International NGOs, assessment bodies, foreign journalists, intellectual property authorities, and foreign residents in South Korea also interact with South Korean ACPD.

ACPD's lessons learned also illustrate the breadth of this international engagement. A notable example occurred in 2021, when the ACRC organised a workshop with UNDP entitled "Successful Cases and Lessons in Cross-Country Transfer of Integrity Policies" (ACRC, 2023b). Representational ties within this layer emerge through institutionalised mechanisms: official invitations, participation in ACRC training programmes, authorship of international publications, membership in international networks, the signing of cooperation agreements, or engagement with South Korean regulatory and intellectual property frameworks. Through these channels, ACPD operates as a process of reciprocal international socialisation (Checkel, 2005), in which South Korea simultaneously contributes to and learns from global integrity governance structures.

Operational Design of South Korean Anticorruption Public Diplomacy

South Korean ACPD is characterised by a highly institutionalised operational structure in which external engagement emerges as a direct extension of domestic anticorruption governance coordinated by the ACRC. Although some initiatives are independently led by bodies such as the SPO and the MOFA, international anticorruption engagement is largely organised through a national anticorruption action plan (ACRC, 2019) that connects domestic policy with international interaction. This configuration allows ACPD to operate as an integrated component of the national integrity system, aligning domestic governance with internationally recognised integrity standards.

The coordination of anticorruption governance under the auspices of the ACRC lies at the core of this operationalisation. By integrating domestic regulatory authority with international engagement, the South Korean model reduces the fragmentation that often characterises ACPD in other contexts. In institutional terms, the same bodies responsible for integrity policies domestically also serve as primary interlocutors in ACPD. This arrangement blurs the boundary between internal administrative processes and external diplomatic communication, transforming international engagement into a continuum shaped by domestic institutional priorities and expectations embedded in global governance frameworks.

These institutional arrangements enable the performance and reproduction of anticorruption identity in international arenas. State identities are not fixed; they are continuously constituted through interaction, recognition, and shared expectations (Wendt, 1999). By incorporating ACPD within domestic governance institutions, South Korea presents integrity as a normative commitment and an organisational principle structuring state practice. The adoption and projection of integrity standards also contribute to positioning the country as a reliable and responsible actor within the international system, particularly in a region shaped by security competition and geopolitical tensions.

This structure also facilitates processes of norm diffusion and international socialisation. Norms rarely spread solely through formal legal adoption; they also circulate through persuasion, emulation, contestation, and learning within transnational governance networks (Finnemore & Sikkink, 1998, 2001; Wiener, 2004). Institutionalised channels of interaction increase the frequency and stability of these exchanges, allowing actors to observe, interpret, and adapt governance practices over time (Checkel, 2005). By situating ACPD within stable bureaucratic routines, South Korea sustains recurring sites of international engagement.

Another defining feature of this operational design is its emphasis on administrative continuity and bureaucratic coordination within established governance routines. South Korean ACPD does not rely primarily on episodic diplomatic campaigns or short-term initiatives. It is sustained through administrative processes that enable long-term engagement with international and regional partners and multilateral governance platforms. Notably, bureaucratic structures rely on established routines and standard operating procedures that help stabilise policy implementation over time (March & Olsen, 1989). Within international governance settings, repeated interaction through institutional frameworks facilitates processes of socialisation through which norms become gradually strengthened and internalised (Checkel, 2005). In this context, institutionalising ACPD within administrative structures reduces reliance on ad hoc political initiatives and promotes consistent patterns of international interaction, enhancing the credibility of South Korea's anticorruption commitments while limiting the volatility associated with politically driven initiatives.

The operational model therefore does not rely predominantly on symbolic advocacy or reputational signalling. While normative messaging remains present, South Korea's ACPD is primarily embedded in administrative governance structures linking internal policy development with international engagement. In this configuration, diplomacy is enacted primarily through institutional practices rather than through discourse alone. Practice-oriented approaches to international relations emphasise that state action in global governance is structured through routine institutional interactions and bureaucratic procedures that organise how actors engage with international norms and institutions (Adler & Pouliot, 2011; Sending et al., 2015). In this context, ACPD becomes part of the operational routines of governance. Integrity becomes institutionalised as an organisational principle that structures administrative practice. These practices also function as diplomatic interfaces through which the state engages with global anticorruption institutions and strengthens its standing within international governance networks.

Taken together, these elements suggest that South Korea's ACPD operates through an institutionally embedded model of governance projection, in which domestic administrative structures and international engagement form mutually reinforcing dimensions of the same policy framework. This operational design enables the country to maintain coherence between internal integrity reforms and its external diplomatic presence, positioning integrity governance as a stable component of its participation in the global anticorruption regime and of its broader strategy of international integration.

The Resource Configuration

South Korean ACPD operates within a resource environment shaped by strong institutional coordination, technological capacity, and a growing reservoir of reputational capital linked to the country's governance modernisation. In international relations, material and immaterial resources constitute structural foundations through which states project influence and participate in global governance (Barnett & Duvall, 2005; Nye, 2011). In the global arena, these resources become sources of attraction and credibility sustaining a state's capacity to influence foreign publics (Nye, 2011; Cull, 2019). Within ACPD, they function as enabling conditions through which states communicate governance models and diffuse integrity standards internationally.

Material and institutional resources form the most visible pillar of South Korean ACPD. Anticorruption governance is anchored in a system of policies, institutions, monitoring mechanisms, and integrity instruments coordinated by the ACRC. This centralised structure provides organisational continuity and administrative capacity for both domestic governance and international engagement. Such institutional consolidation enhances the state's capacity to coordinate complex policy domains while sustaining policy credibility. More broadly, this organisation reflects the capacity of the modern state to translate policy commitments into routinised administrative practices over time (Adler-Nissen, 2023; Evans, 1995). Within ACPD, these arrangements provide the organisational basis for initiatives such as training programmes, international conferences, and cooperation frameworks, ensuring that external engagement rests on stable policy programmes and public funding.

Technological capacity further reinforces this resource environment. Over recent decades, the country has developed digital governance infrastructures to increase transparency, facilitate citizen participation, and strengthen administrative integrity. Platforms such as electronic petition systems, digital complaint mechanisms, and online integrity assessment tools provide practical instruments for domestic anticorruption governance (ACRC, 2010, 2017, 2025). These technologies also serve as demonstrable assets in the international arena. In a context increasingly marked by networked governance and information flows, technological infrastructures constitute sources of administrative power (Slaughter, 2004; Zaharna, 2022). By presenting digital transparency tools and governance platforms in training programmes, technical cooperation initiatives, and international forums, South Korea transforms administrative innovation into a communicable component of its ACPD. Hence, technological expertise functions both as a governance instrument and as a diplomatic asset across transnational policy networks.

South Korea also benefits from immaterial assets derived from its trajectory of institutional modernisation and technological leadership. Reputation constitutes a form of symbolic capital that enhances the credibility and persuasive capacity of states in international society (Adler-Nissen, 2014). Influence in global governance frequently depends on the ability of states to transform institutional achievements into recognised markers of legitimacy and authority (Adler-Nissen, 2014). The country's rapid economic development and digital transformation have contributed to an international image of administrative efficiency and policy innovation (Amsden, 1989). Within ACPD, this reputation strengthens the legitimacy of South Korean governance practices when presented as reference points for institutional reform. These initiatives are therefore interpreted as expressions of broader state capacity rather than as isolated policy measures.

Geopolitical considerations further shape the resource environment surrounding South Korean ACPD by situating these material and immaterial factors within wider strategic networks of global governance. As a middle power, South Korea faces structural incentives to demonstrate international credibility and institutional reliability. Middle powers frequently seek influence by integrating themselves into international institutions and governance networks (Cooper & Dal, 2017). Participation in international governance networks, including multilateral anticorruption initiatives and specialised policy communities, operates as a relational resource that reinforces governance objectives and broader strategic interests. By aligning domestic integrity reforms with international standards and actively participating in multilateral anticorruption initiatives, the country strengthens its identity as a reliable partner on the international stage. South Korea's ACPD emerges from the interaction of administrative capacity, digital governance expertise, symbolic legitimacy, and strategic positioning. These resources shape the manner in which South Korea participates in the global diffusion of integrity norms.

Smart Power and the Politics of Influence in Anticorruption Public Diplomacy

Smart power refers to the strategic combination of different styles of power and multiple resources within a coherent diplomatic strategy designed to achieve political objectives (Nye, 2011; Wilson, 2008). In this perspective, power is not simply possessed but performed through processes that assign political meaning to domestic resources. In the South Korean case, governance arrangements, practices, and technological innovations become sources of influence only when they are communicated and recognised within international arenas (Adler-Nissen, 2014, 2023; Wendt, 1999). Influence emerges through processes of socialisation and recognition that shape states' identities and expectations (Finnemore & Sikkink, 1998; Wendt, 1999). In South Korea's ACPD, domestic governance resources are strategically mobilised and reframed as instruments of diplomatic influence within the global anticorruption regime.

The first component of this smart power configuration corresponds to soft power (Nye, 2011). In the South Korean case, attraction derives from the international visibility of domestic governance reforms and administrative innovation. Integrity policies are communicated through advocacy initiatives, international conferences, digital transparency platforms, and educational programmes. These practices transform anticorruption governance into narratives of institutional competence and administrative modernisation. The credibility of these narratives depends not only on communication but also on the perceived legitimacy and effectiveness of the institutions sustaining them (Melissen, 2005; Cull, 2019). South Korea's soft power in ACPD rests on the capacity to translate domestic governance reforms into internationally intelligible signals of technological sophistication, transparency, and institutional reliability.

The second dimension corresponds to hard power, although in a form that differs from enforcement-oriented models of ACPD. While hard power is commonly associated with coercive instruments such as economic pressure (Nye, 2011), in the South Korean case, it operates primarily through structural and institutional resources. Integrity commitments are supported by enforceable institutional mechanisms and by economic and technological capacity that enable governance tools such as digital transparency systems. These resources generate what may be described as productive capacity: the ability to generate governance technologies, administrative expertise, and policy instruments that can be shared or adapted in international cooperation programmes (Barnett & Duvall, 2005; Evans, 1995). Such capacity strengthens diplomatic credibility by anchoring normative claims in demonstrable administrative capability.

A third dimension of South Korean smart power emerges through collaborative power, understood as the capacity to generate influence through cooperation, joint problem-solving, and networked interaction (Cooper & Dal, 2017; Hocking et al., 2012). In contemporary diplomacy, influence often develops within transnational policy networks where governments, international organisations, and civil society co-produce governance practices and policy knowledge (Slaughter, 2004). South Korea actively participates in such networked diplomacy through training programmes for foreign officials, technical assistance initiatives, multilateral conferences, and regional policy dialogues. These activities create institutional spaces where policies and practices are exchanged, evaluated, and adapted, transforming domestic policy expertise into a shared resource (Adler-Nissen, 2023). Collaborative power allows South Korea to operate as a connector between domestic policy expertise and international governance networks, facilitating the diffusion of integrity norms while reinforcing its diplomatic presence.

The interaction between soft, hard, and collaborative power constitutes the core of South Korea's smart power configuration. Soft power generates attraction and normative appeal around the country's governance model; hard power provides the institutional credibility and material resources that sustain this projection; and collaborative power embeds these practices within transnational networks of policy exchange. Smart power is most effective when instruments of influence reinforce one another rather than operating in isolation (Nye, 2011). Influence therefore emerges not from a single resource but from the strategic combination of multiple forms of power within a coherent diplomatic strategy.

This configuration is particularly relevant for a middle power operating in a geopolitically sensitive environment. Such countries often anchor their diplomacy in policy expertise, norm entrepreneurship, and institutional strengths (Cooper & Dal, 2017; Jordaan, 2003). ACPD therefore becomes part of a broader strategy through which South Korea enhances its international influence while presenting itself as a modern, capable, and cooperative actor. Seen in this light, South Korean ACPD represents a structured politics of influence in which domestic governance resources are translated into internationally meaningful signals through the coordinated use of power. Smart power provides the strategic logic connecting these resources, enabling South Korea to participate in the diffusion of the global anticorruption norm while consolidating its global position. This configuration foreshadows a form of technocratic diplomacy in which administrative expertise, digital governance, and institutional capacity become central resources of international influence.

6.7 Synthesis: Technocratic Integrity and Networked Influence

South Korea's ACPD illustrates how integrity governance can become a strategic instrument of international influence. In the South Korean case, ACPD operates as a structured diplomatic practice through which domestic reforms are translated into internationally recognisable signals of institutional proficiency, technological sophistication, and democratic resilience. The trajectory from a developmental state historically marked by political–business entanglement to an internationally engaged advocate of integrity governance illustrates how anticorruption policies address domestic vulnerabilities while reinforcing international positioning.

Three central dynamics characterise this model. First, integrity discourse emerges from structural vulnerability. The historical entanglement between political authority and *chaebol*-centred development generated enduring legitimacy challenges that continue to shape public perceptions of corruption. The narrative of *jeokpye cheongsan,* originally a domestic political call to eradicate structural corruption, provided a symbolic framework through which anticorruption reforms were articulated as part of a broader project of democratic renewal. Over time, this discourse evolved beyond domestic mobilisation and became integrated into South Korea's external projection through ACPD.

Second, South Korea's ACPD is characterised by a highly institutionalised operational scheme in which diplomatic engagement extends domestic governance routines. Unlike models that rely predominantly on episodic diplomatic campaigns or normative rhetoric, the South Korean approach integrates ACPD into administrative structures coordinated by the ACRC. This institutionalisation transforms routine administrative practices, such as digital transparency systems, integrity assessments, and complaint-handling platforms, into instruments of diplomatic engagement. In doing so, it blurs the conventional boundary between domestic administration and international diplomacy, allowing them to function as vehicles of international communication.

Third, the case illustrates how a middle power can mobilise diverse resources through a smart power combination. Soft power operates through the communicative visibility of national practices and policies, projecting an identity of institutional competence and modern governance. Hard power manifests through the structural capacity underpinning this governance model, particularly through economic and technological assets. Collaborative power complements these elements by embedding South Korea within transnational policy networks and regional governance platforms. Through these configurations, expertise becomes a shared resource across global governance communities.

These three dimensions converge in a distinctive form of technocratic diplomacy. South Korea's ACPD projects integrity through administrative competence and technological development. Digital governance tools, e-government systems, and integrity assessment mechanisms serve as practical illustrations of how transparency can be operationalised in complex administrative environments. In this sense, integrity becomes performative: it is enacted through policy instruments, institutional routines, and demonstrable governance practices that circulate across international networks.

Precisely because of this projection, the case also reveals the tensions inherent in projecting integrity internationally while confronting persistent structural constraints. Recurrent political scandals, the enduring influence of large conglomerates, and uneven enforcement of foreign bribery regulations highlight the continuing gap between normative aspiration and institutional practice. South Korea's ACPD is built precisely on this delicate balance: persistent domestic vulnerabilities coexist with a remarkably successful international trajectory of norm alignment, institutional innovation, and regional leadership. Rather than undermining the country's ACPD, these tensions define the conditions under which its integrity projection acquires diplomatic significance.

This configuration is closely linked to South Korea's wider national identity and strategic environment. Situated in a geopolitically contested region and historically compelled to navigate between major powers, the country uses ACPD to strengthen its room for manoeuvre as a state seeking regional relevance, economic reliability, and security partnerships. Within the broader comparative framework of this book, South Korea therefore represents a distinctive configuration of ACPD that foregrounds technocratic governance capacity combined with networked cooperation. Integrity is projected not only as a normative commitment but also as administrative expertise supported by digital innovation, institutional coordination, and sustained participation in multilateral governance networks.

References

Adler-Nissen, R. (2014). Symbolic power in European diplomacy: The struggle between national foreign services and the EU's external action service. *Review of International Studies, 40*(4), 657–681. https://doi.org/10.1017/S0260210513000326

Adler-Nissen, R. (2023). Practice. In S. Goddard, G. Lawson, & J. Sending (Eds.), *The Oxford handbook of international political sociology* (pp. 177–198). Oxford University Press.

Adler, E. (2005). *Communitarian international relations*. Routledge.

Adler, E., & Pouliot, V. (2011). International practices. *International Theory, 3*(1), 1–36. https://doi.org/10.1017/S175297191000031X

Amsden, A. (1989). *Asia's next giant*. Oxford University Press.

Anti-Corruption and Civil Rights Commission (ACRC). (2010). *Annual report 2010*. Retrieved February 9, 2026, from https://www.acrc.go.kr/boardDownload.es?bid=64&list_no=13278&seq=1

Anti-Corruption and Civil Rights Commission (ACRC). (2014). *Annual report 2013*. Retrieved February 9, 2026, from https://www.acrc.go.kr/boardDownload.es?bid=64&list_no=13287&seq=1

Anti-Corruption and Civil Rights Commission (ACRC). (2015). *Annual report 2014*. Retrieved February 9, 2026, from https://www.acrc.go.kr/boardDownload.es?bid=64&list_no=13293&seq=2

Anti-Corruption and Civil Rights Commission (ACRC). (2016). *Annual report 2015*. Retrieved February 9, 2026, from https://www.acrc.go.kr/boardDownload.es?bid=64&list_no=13298&seq=1

Anti-Corruption and Civil Rights Commission (ACRC). (2017). *Annual report 2016*. Retrieved February 9, 2026, from https://www.acrc.go.kr/boardDownload.es?bid=64&list_no=13309&seq=1

Anti-Corruption and Civil Rights Commission (ACRC). (2018a). *An anti-corruption expert said, "Korea is a leader in the global anti-corruption movement"* (Press release). Retrieved February 9, 2026, from https://www.acrc.go.kr/board.es?mid=a20301000000&bid=62&act=view&list_no=12900

Anti-Corruption and Civil Rights Commission (ACRC). (2018b). *Annual report 2017.* Retrieved February 9, 2026, from https://www.acrc.go.kr/boardDownload.es?bid=64&list_no=13317&seq=1

Anti-Corruption and Civil Rights Commission (ACRC). (2019). *Annual report 2018.* Retrieved February 9, 2026, from https://www.acrc.go.kr/boardDownload.es?bid=64&list_no=13322&seq=1

Anti-Corruption and Civil Rights Commission (ACRC). (2020). *Annual report 2019.* Retrieved February 9, 2026, from https://www.acrc.go.kr/boardDownload.es?bid=64&list_no=13330&seq=1

Anti-Corruption and Civil Rights Commission (ACRC). (2021). *Annual report 2020.* Retrieved February 9, 2026, from https://www.acrc.go.kr/boardDownload.es?bid=64&list_no=13332&seq=1

Anti-Corruption and Civil Rights Commission (ACRC). (2022a). *ACRC actively promotes anti-corruption policy achievements in international community.* Retrieved February 9, 2026, from https://acrc.go.kr/board.es?mid=a20301000000&bid=62&list_no=39725&act=view

Anti-Corruption and Civil Rights Commission (ACRC). (2022b). *Annual report 2021.* Retrieved February 9, 2026, from https://www.acrc.go.kr/boardDownload.es?bid=64&list_no=39554&seq=1

Anti-Corruption and Civil Rights Commission (ACRC). (2023a). *History of Korea's anti-corruption policy.* Retrieved February 9, 2026, from https://www.clean.go.kr/menu.es?mid=a20106020000

Anti-Corruption and Civil Rights Commission (ACRC). (2023b). *Annual report 2022.* Retrieved February 9, 2026, from https://www.acrc.go.kr/boardDownload.es?bid=64&list_no=46007&seq=4

Anti-Corruption and Civil Rights Commission (ACRC). (2025). *Annual report 2024.* Retrieved February 9, 2026, from https://www.acrc.go.kr/boardDownload.es?bid=64&list_no=95833&seq=6

Anti-Corruption and Civil Rights Commission (ACRC). (2026). *Publications.* Retrieved February 9, 2026, from https://www.acrc.go.kr/board.es?mid=a20302000000&bid=64&cg_all=all&cg_code=C02

Barnett, M., & Duvall, R. (2005). Power in international politics. *International Organization, 59*(1), 39–75. https://doi.org/10.1017/S0020818305050010

Basel Institute on Governance. (2020, May 13). *Korean pact for anti-corruption and transparency.* Retrieved February 9, 2026, from https://collective-action.com/explore/initiatives/1401

Cain, G. (2014, January 1). *Independent reporting mechanism Republic of Korea.* Retrieved February 9, 2026, from https://www.opengovpartnership.org/documents/south-korea-irm-progress-report-2012–2013/

Checkel, J. (2005). International institutions and socialization in Europe: Introduction and framework. *International Organization, 59*(4), 801–826. https://doi.org/10.1017/S0020818305050289

Cooper, A., & Dal, E. (2017). Positioning the third wave of middle power diplomacy: Institutional elevation, practice limitations. *Canada's Journal of Global Policy Analysis, 71*(4), 561–582. https://doi.org/10.1177/0020702016686385

Cull, N. (2019). *Public diplomacy: Foundations for global engagement in the digital age.* Polity.

Cull, N. (2024). *Reputational security.* Polity.

Dale, A., & Yuk, C. (2021, August 27). *South Korea's anti-corruption campaign so far: an honest crusade or is it 'naeronambul'?* Retrieved February 9, 2026, from https://www.ropesgray.com/en/-/media/files/publications/2021/08/20210827_ee_alert.pdf

Dell, G., & McDevitt, A. (2022). *Exporting corruption 2022.* Transparency International. Retrieved February 9, 2026, from https://files.transparencycdn.org/images/2022_Report-Full_Exporting-Corruption_English.pdf

Evans, P. (1995). *Embedded autonomy.* Princeton University Press.

Finnemore, M. (1996). *National interests in international society.* Cornell University Press.

Finnemore, M., & Sikkink, K. (1998). International norm dynamics and political change. *International Organization, 52*(4), 887–917. https://doi.org/10.1162/002081898550789

Finnemore, M., & Sikkink, K. (2001). Taking stock: The constructivist research program in international relations and comparative politics. *Annual Review of Political Science, 4,* 391–416. https://doi.org/10.1146/annurev.polisci.4.1.391

Global Firepower (GFP). (2026). *2026 Military Strength Ranking.* Retrieved February 9, 2026, from https://www.globalfirepower.com/countries-listing.php

Haas, P. (1992). Epistemic communities and international policy coordination. *International Organization, 46*(1), 1–35. https://doi.org/10.1017/S0020818300001442

Heimann, F., Földes, Á., & Báthory, G. (2014). Exporting corruption. *Transparency International.* Retrieved February 9, 2026, from https://images.transparencycdn.org/images/2014_ExportingCorruption_OECDProgressReport_EN.pdf

Henley & Partners. (2025). *The Henley Passport Index 2024.* Retrieved February 9, 2026, from https://www.henleyglobal.com/passport-index/ranking

Ho-jung, S., Deog-jae, J., Ki-hwan, L., In-ho, K., Kang-hahn, L., E-don, C., Yeon-sik, C., Woo-yong, C., Monica, H., & Chang-hyun, C. (2019). *A history of Korea* (D. Kane, J.-C. An, & K. Seidel, Transl.). Academy of Korean Studies.

Hocking, B., Melissen, J., Riordan, S., & Sharp, P. (2012, October). *Futures for diplomacy (Clingendael - report 1)*. Clingendael. Retrieved February 9, 2026, from https://www.clingendael.org/sites/default/files/pdfs/20121030_research_melissen.pdf

International Labour Organization. (2024). *World social protection report 2024–26*. ILO. Retrieved February 9, 2026, from https://www.ilo.org/sites/default/files/2024-09/WSPR_2024_EN_WEB_1.pdf

Jin, D. (2016). *New Korean wave*. University of Illinois Press.

Jordaan, E. (2003). The concept of a middle power in international relations: Distinguishing between emerging and traditional middle powers. *Politikon, 30*(1), 165–181. https://doi.org/10.1080/0258934032000147282

Kemp, S. (2025). *Digital 2026: South Korea*. Retrieved February 9, 2026, from https://datareportal.com/reports/digital-2026-south-korea

Kim, D.-Y. (2023, January 20). 文정권 적폐청산과 내로남불이 키운 '검찰국가' [The 'prosecution state' in the Moon administration fostered by the eradication of corruption and naeronambul]. *Media Today*. Retrieved February 9, 2026, from https://www.mediatoday.co.kr/news/articleView.html?idxno=308089

Kim, G.-o. (2018). The direction of a social movement toward reconciliation and communication in the times of deep-rooted social evils eradication. *The Journal of the Humanities for Unification, 76*(12), 123–159. https://doi.org/10.21185/jhu.2018.12.76.123

Kim, J.-U., & Nam, G. (2025). Legal systems in South Korea: Overview. In Thomson Reuters Practical Law (Ed.). *Thomson Reuters*. Retrieved February 9, 2026, from https://uk.practicallaw.thomsonreuters.com/w-031-9598

Lee, J.-M. & Lee, A. (2016). *Introduction to Korea's anti-corruption initiative assessment*. Retrieved February 9, 2026, from https://www.undp.org/policy-centre/seoul/publications/introduction-koreas-anti-corruption-initiative-assessment#

Lowy Institute. (2024). *Global Diplomacy Index 2024*. Retrieved February 9, 2026, from https://globaldiplomacyindex.lowyinstitute.org

Manor, I., & Bjola, C. (2021). Public diplomacy in the age of 'post-reality'. In P. Surowiec & I. Manor (Eds.), *Public diplomacy and the politics of uncertainty* (pp. 111–143). Palgrave Macmillan. https://doi.org/10.1007/978-3-030-54552-9

March, J., & Olsen, J. (1989). *Rediscovering institutions*. Free Press.

Melissen, J. (2005). The new public diplomacy: Between theory and practice. In J. Melissen (Ed.), *The new public diplomacy* (pp. 3–27). Palgrave Macmillan.

Melissen, J., & Chandrasekara, G. (2026). Theorising and debating the domestic deficit in IR and diplomatic studies. In J. Melissen, H. Kim, & G. Chandrasekara (Eds.), *Home engagement in diplomacy* (pp. 5–38). Brill. https://doi.org/10.1163/9789004738324_003

Ministry of National Defense. (2025). *International peace-keeping operations.* Retrieved February 9, 2026, from https://www.mnd.go.kr/mbshome/mbs/mndEN/subview.jsp?id=mndEN_030300000000

Nye, J. (2011). *The future of power*. Public Affairs.

Nye, J., & Kim, Y. (2013). Soft power and the Korean wave. In Y. Kim (Ed.), *The Korean wave* (pp. 31–42). Routledge. https://doi.org/10.4324/9781315859064

OECD Working Group on Bribery. (2004, November 5). *Implementing the OECD Anti-Bribery Convention.* OECD. https://doi.org/10.1787/9789264031647-en

OECD Working Group on Bribery. (2007, March). *Phase 2 report: Korea.* OECD. https://doi.org/10.1787/c1159834-en

OECD Working Group on Bribery. (2011, October). *Phase 3 report on implementing the OECD anti-bribery convention in Korea.* OECD. https://doi.org/10.1787/f2918556-en

OECD Working Group on Bribery. (2018, December 13). *Implementing the OECD Anti-Bribery Convention.* OECD. https://doi.org/10.1787/643e0385-en

Office of National Security. (2023). *The Yoon Suk Yeol administration's national security strategy.* Retrieved February 9, 2026, from https://assets.korearisk.com/uploads/2023/06/Yoon-Suk-yeol-Administrations-National-Security-Strategy-June-2023.pdf

Open Government Partnership (OGP). (2020). *Independent Reporting Mechanism (IRM): Republic of Korea transitional results report 2018–2020.* Retrieved February 9, 2026, from https://www.opengovpartnership.org/wp-content/uploads/2021/10/South-Korea_Transitional-Results-Report_2018-2020_EN.pdf

Organisation for Economic Co-operation and Development (OECD). (2023). *Population with tertiary education.* Retrieved February 9, 2026, from https://www.oecd.org/en/data/indicators/population-with-tertiary-education.html

Organisation for Economic Co-operation and Development (OECD). (2024). *General government debt.* Retrieved July 11, 2025, from https://www.oecd.org/en/data/indicators/general-government-debt.html#indicator-chart

Organisation for Economic Co-operation and Development (OECD). (2025). *Development co-operation profiles: Korea.* Retrieved February 9, 2026, from https://www.oecd.org/content/dam/oecd/en/publications/reports/2025/06/development-co-operation-profiles_02ffa45c/korea_9fa7fe3c/d358baed-en.pdf

Park, I.-h. (2011). Korea's national interests and security conditions in the age of globalization. *The Korean Journal of International Studies, 9*(2), 207–231.

Sang-Hun, C. (2018, April 6). Park Geun-hye, South Korea's ousted president, gets 24 years in prison. *The New York Times.* Retrieved February 9, 2026, from https://www.nytimes.com/2018/04/06/world/asia/park-geun-hye-south-korea.html

Schwab, K. (2019). *The global competitiveness report 2019*. World Economic Forum. Retrieved July 11, 2025, from https://www3.weforum.org/docs/WEF_TheGlobalCompetitivenessReport2019.pdf

Scimago. (2025). *Journal & country rank*. Retrieved February 9, 2026, from https://www.scimagojr.com/countryrank.php

Sending, O., Pouliot, V., & Neumann, I. (2015). Introduction. In O. Sending, V. Pouliot, & I. Neumann (Eds.), *Diplomacy and the making of world politics* (pp. 1–30). Cambridge University Press.

Shain, Y., & Barth, A. (2003). Diasporas and international relations theory. *International Organization, 57*(3), 449–479. https://doi.org/10.1017/S0020818303573015

Slaughter, A.-M. (2004). *A new world order*. Princeton University Press.

Transparency International. (2003). *Global corruption barometer*. Transparency International. Retrieved February 9, 2026, from https://images.transparencycdn.org/images/2003_GCB_EN.pdf

Transparency International. (2006). *National Integrity Systems*. Retrieved February 9, 2026, from https://csis-website-prod.s3.amazonaws.com/s3fs-public/06Korea_NationalIntegritySystems.pdf

Transparency International. (2007). *Global corruption barometer 2007*. Transparency International. Retrieved February 9, 2026, from https://files.transparencycdn.org/images/2007_GCB_EN.pdf.

Transparency International. (2013). *Global corruption barometer 2013*. Transparency International. Retrieved February 9, 2026, from https://images.transparencycdn.org/images/2013_GlobalCorruptionBarometer_EN_200525_112757.pdf.

United Nations Development Programme. (2025). *Human development reports*. Retrieved February 9, 2026, from https://hdr.undp.org/data-center/country-insights#/ranks

United Nations Office on Drugs and Crime (UNODC). (2020, December 15). *UNODC and the Republic of Korea Strengthen Cooperation to Prevent & Respond to Corruption*. Retrieved February 9, 2026, from https://www.unodc.org/unodc/en/frontpage/2020/December/unodc-and-the-republic-of-korea-strengthen-cooperation-to-prevent-and-respond-to-corruption.html

United Nations Office on Drugs and Crime (UNODC). (2022). *Thematic compilation of relevant information submitted by Republic of Korea*. Retrieved February 9, 2026, from https://www.unodc.org/documents/corruption/WG-Prevention/Art_13_Awareness-raising_measures_and_Education/Republic_of_Korea.pdf

United Nations Office on Drugs and Crime (UNODC). (2023, June). *Implementation review group: Executive summary of the Republic of Korea*. Retrieved February 9, 2026, from https://www.unodc.org/documents/treaties/UNCAC/WorkingGroups/ImplementationReviewGroup/12-16June2023/CAC-COSP-IRG-II-4-1-Add.2/2304564E.pdf

United Nations Trade & Development. (2024). *Creative economy outlook 2024.* UN. Retrieved February 9, 2026, from https://unctad.org/system/files/official-document/ditctsce2024d2_en.pdf

United Nations Trade & Development. (2025). *General profile: Republic of Korea.* Retrieved February 9, 2026, from https://unctadstat.unctad.org/CountryProfile/GeneralProfile/en-GB/410/index.html#

United Nations. (2024). *Status of ratification.* Retrieved July 11, 2025, from https://indicators.ohchr.org

United States Department of State. (2022). *Republic of Korea.* Retrieved February 9, 2026, from https://www.state.gov/wp-content/uploads/2023/03/KOREA-REP-2022-HUMAN-RIGHTS-REPORT-ed.pdf

Wendt, A. (1999). *Social theory of international politics.* Cambridge University Press.

Wiener, A. (2004). Contested compliance: Interventions on the normative structure of world politics. *European Journal of International Relations, 10*(2), 189–234. https://doi.org/10.1177/1354066104042934

Wilson, E. (2008). Hard power, soft power, smart power. *The Annals of the American Academy of Political and Social Science, 616*(1), 110–124. https://doi.org/10.1177/0002716207312618

World Bank. (2020). *Ease of doing business ranking.* Retrieved July 11, 2025, from https://archive.doingbusiness.org/en/rankings

World Bank. (2024). *GDP (current US$).* Retrieved February 9, 2026, from https://data.worldbank.org/indicator/NY.GDP.MKTP.CD?locations=KR

World Intellectual Property Organization (WIPO). (2024). *Global innovation index 2025.* WIPO. Retrieved July 11, 2025, from https://www.wipo.int/web-publications/global-innovation-index-2025/en/index.html

Yoo-seok, O. (2019). A study on politics of liquidate of 'deep-rooted' corruption in the past seventy years. *Economy and Society, 121*(3), 37–60. https://doi.org/10.18207/criso.2019.121.37

Zaharna, R. (2022). *Boundary spanners of humanity.* Oxford University Press. https://doi.org/10.1093/oso/9780190930271.001.0001

CHAPTER 7

Comparing Anticorruption as Shared Language of International Socialisation

7.1 Framing the Comparative Inquiry

This chapter offers a systematic comparative synthesis of anticorruption public diplomacy (ACPD), bringing the Danish, New Zealand, American, and South Korean trajectories into dialogue. It identifies recurring patterns, salient contrasts, and the means by which anticorruption becomes a socially recognised diplomatic asset. ACPD is conceived as an iterative and intersubjective process through which states construct, project, negotiate, and adjust meanings of integrity. Through international socialisation, shared understandings reshape identities and reconfigure interests, orienting behaviour and engagement with foreign publics. States seek recognition, respond to expectations, and participate in the co-production, contestation, and stabilisation of the global anticorruption norm. From this angle, anticorruption emerges as a relational marker of legitimacy, responsibility, and standing in international society.

ACPD unfolds within a shared normative environment in which states interpret, enact, and communicate integrity commitments in line with their identities, strategic horizons, and institutional capacities. Although national approaches differ in ambition, organisational design, and communicative style, the cases collectively show that anticorruption has become an intelligible diplomatic language, structuring expectations in global governance. It creates opportunities for cooperation, competition,

N. de A. e S. F. dos Santos, *Anticorruption Public Diplomacy*, Palgrave Macmillan Series in Global Public Diplomacy, https://doi.org/10.1007/978-3-032-28668-0_7

persuasion, and reputational differentiation, linking domestic governance performance to international interpretation, validation, and recalibration.

At a comparative glance, the selected cases offer analytically productive combinations of convergence and contrast. All are internationally recognised for significant integrity commitments and sustained adherence to the global anticorruption norm, yet they differ markedly in political culture, foreign-policy orientation, and modes of diplomatic projection. Denmark and New Zealand are often associated with high levels of public trust and soft-power credibility, albeit expressed through distinct strategic logics. The United States combines extensive institutional capacity with a more overtly strategic and regulatory approach to international anticorruption engagement. South Korea illustrates how reform trajectories and technological innovation can support diplomatic repositioning within regional and global governance networks.

Four dimensions of socialisation emerge: cognitive, relational, normative, and ethical. The cognitive dimension appears in the diplomatic capital derived from governance models. Institutional traditions, legal frameworks, reforms, and reputational rankings gain international relevance only when recognised by external audiences (Adler, 2013). Indonesia's request for technical assistance from South Korea on anticorruption matters (Anti-Corruption and Civil Rights Commission [ACRC], 2019), for example, signals acknowledgement of the latter's reform trajectory.

The relational aspect is visible in cooperative and trust-building practices (Adler & Pouliot, 2011) such as dialogical engagement, coordination patterns, and collaborative power, which sustain integrity as a shared diplomatic concern. The agreement between South Korea and the United States to facilitate cooperation in anticorruption proceedings illustrates this dynamic (OECD Working Group on Bribery, 2011). The normative aspect lies in the diffusion and gradual internalisation of shared standards, including policies and regulatory instruments (Mccoy & Heckel, 2001), as evidenced by the adherence of all four countries to the United Nations and OECD anticorruption conventions.

The ethical aspect shows tensions between moral authority and legitimacy, including the potential instrumental use of ACPD as a moral façade for contested projects (Alexander, 2021). Sharp power dynamics make these tensions particularly visible. Examples include the extraterritorial enforcement of the American Foreign Corrupt Practices Act (FCPA), which may challenge perceptions of sovereign limits, and the financial leverage used by Denmark, which can generate relational asymmetries or expectations of reciprocity that temper overt criticism (Transparency International Danmark [TI Danmark], 2012, pp. 163–171). These mechanisms position ACPD as a recursive social process through which governance performance is interpreted, enacted, and evaluated in international arenas.

In this light, ACPD is best understood as co-constitutive. States do not merely use anticorruption to pursue predefined objectives; they also redefine identities, interests, and modes of recognition through anticorruption engagement. Domestic integrity may generate reputational assets, but these become diplomatically meaningful only through strategic framing and external recognition. ACPD thus entails projecting institutional achievements, attributing meaning to governance resources, and converting governance resources into influence through distinct configurations of power.

To unpack these dynamics, the chapter first examines how anticorruption identities and governance models generate diverse forms of diplomatic capital across political cultures. It then analyses how governments design and coordinate national repertoires of engagement, highlighting variation in strategic orientation, institutional leadership, coordination patterns, and policy instruments. A subsequent section explores ACPD's performative dimension, showing how integrity is enacted through listening, dialogical engagement, advocacy, cultural diplomacy, exchanges, and broadcasting. These activities illustrate how norms circulate, expectations are negotiated, and integrity is progressively internalised, adapted, or contested.

The analysis further considers how integrity initiatives enable distinct styles of influence, from attraction-based credibility and collaborative capacity-building to regulatory projection and more coercive forms of reputational pressure. The recurring patterns of international socialisation in ACPD provide evidence of an integrated analytical model explaining how domestic integrity capacity, identity construction, diplomatic practice, and external recognition interact over time. In this way, the comparison connects the empirical case studies to the book's broader theoretical argument.

7.2 Anticorruption Identity Across Political Cultures and Strategic Interests

In all cases, anticorruption emerges as a constitutive dimension of state identity linked to strategic interests and international positioning through processes of intersubjective socialisation and recognition (Wendt, 1999). ACPD embodies the state's interpretation of its own normative commitments in light of foreign-policy priorities. In seeking legitimacy and credibility among relevant international audiences (Adler & Barnett, 1998), states use ACPD to translate domestic governance issues into externally recognisable identity performances. Although operating within distinct political cultures and institutional traditions, the four states internalise integrity as a meaningful element of corporate, role, and collective identity. They do this through sustained participation in international normative frameworks and cooperative regimes (Checkel, 2005) while serving instrumental purposes related to credibility, influence, and status.

Interests behind anticorruption identities vary among the cases. Denmark pursues the defence of a rule-based Western governance model, competitiveness in global markets, and the preservation of its reputational authority. New Zealand seeks regional stability, cooperative influence in the Pacific, and wider security. The United States aspires to regulatory leadership, agenda-setting, and a global order aligned with its interests. South Korea seeks to enhance developmental legitimacy, advance regional status, and secure diplomatic recognition, in response to its specific security and geopolitical challenges. Importantly, the credibility dimension of ACPD remains uneven across cases, which may place these interests at risk. Episodic scandals, domestic political issues, selective enforcement patterns, or persistent structural fragilities continue to shape processes of social evaluation and perceptions of integrity in global governance arenas (Nye, 2004). This unevenness illustrates the contingent and negotiated character of ACPD.

In Denmark, anticorruption identity and economic interests are closely intertwined. Long-standing traditions of social trust, welfare provision, and administrative effectiveness sustain an identity associated with governance excellence and institutional reliability. The widely invoked notion of "Getting to Denmark" (Fukuyama, 2011) symbolises a governance ideal and a diplomatic benchmark that reinforces such expectations. Yet this picture remains more fragile than the language of exemplarity may suggest, as illustrated by the Danske Bank scandal (Bjerregaard & Kirchmaier,

2019). Reputational authority must thereby be continually reproduced and validated by external audiences and institutional partners (Adler, 2005), making ACPD highly dependent on external recognition. In this context, Denmark tends to prioritise maintaining the identity that underpins its international influence. Whether using soft, hard, or sharp power capabilities, Denmark advances integrity norms in ways that consolidate its credibility.

New Zealand presents a distinct model in which anticorruption identity is shaped by values of fairness, inclusiveness, and institutional trust derived from the fusion of Westminster traditions and Māori principles. When such identity meets interests related to regional stability, it translates into the promotion of governance resilience as a shared concern focused on the Pacific region while remaining attentive to global developments. ACPD operates as an extension of this relationship-based anticorruption identity, enabling the country to reinforce its positioning as a credible intermediary and facilitator of cooperative governance processes. It advances strategic interests by grounding stable partnerships and enhancing the country's trust-based capacity to shape regional policy agendas.

The United States displays a configuration characterised by strategic norm entrepreneurship oriented towards regulatory leadership, agenda-setting, and order-building in line with its preferences. The anticorruption identity derives from a legalistic and security-inflected profile linked to broader objectives related to market protection, geopolitical competition, and institutional alignment. The country has consistently mobilised ACPD to shape transnational compliance regimes and influence governance architectures through processes of norm diffusion and institutional entrepreneurship (Finnemore & Sikkink, 1998). By embedding anticorruption within narratives of democratic resilience and economic security (White House, 2021), the United States constructs a role identity centred on its interests (Wendt, 1999) while seeking to align international expectations with its own priorities. This anticorruption identity reflects its status as a central architect of global governance frameworks.

South Korea illustrates a reformist anticorruption identity characteristic of a middle power (Cooper & Dal, 2017). Heavily influenced by security and geopolitical concerns, South Korean interests have evolved to encompass economic development, international recognition, and regional leadership. Notably, this combination has been accompanied by close ties between politics and large corporate conglomerates (the chaebols), a context that has transformed the reformist impetus into a broader effort to consolidate democratic credibility as part of an attempt to reposition the country within regional and global arenas. ACPD enables South Korea to communicate narratives of institutional transformation and technological innovation, aligning domestic reform trajectories with strategic goals.

Despite these variations, the comparison reveals a significant convergence: anticorruption enables a shared normative reference, coordinating expectations and social learning among interacting states (Finnemore & Sikkink, 1998). Through public diplomacy activities grounded in anticorruption, states articulate diverse strategic interests in internationally intelligible terms. For Denmark, the anticorruption identity helps to preserve moral credibility, defend a governance model associated with Western institutional reliability, and respond to reputational shocks and international scrutiny. For New Zealand, it sustains a relational strategy centred on regional stability and cooperative resilience. For the United States, it reinforces regulatory authority and leadership in shaping international order. For South Korea, it supports status mobility, developmental legitimacy, and its recognition as a reforming power.

Corporate identities grounded in integrity performance shape how states perceive their legitimacy, while role identities inform expectations regarding ACPD, and collective identities emerge through participation in anticorruption networks and communities of practice (Adler, 2005; Adler-Nissen, 2023; Wendt, 1999). ACPD thus enables governments to transform internal governance experiences into credible signals of responsibility and competence capable of generating attraction and cooperative influence (Nye, 2004), thereby supporting broader strategic objectives related to influence, partnership-building, and positioning within international society.

The assumption of anticorruption as an identity has dual implications. Domestically, it legitimises reform agendas and administrative innovation. Internationally, it strengthens public diplomacy by linking strategic objectives to normative integrity commitments. Anticorruption thus becomes a symbolic resource and an instrument of international engagement at the crossroads between identity and interests, allowing states to align normative commitments with strategic objectives.

7.3 Governance Models as Diplomatic Capital

Domestic governance models condition states' capacity to secure favourable ACPD outcomes. Anticorruption operates simultaneously as a normative commitment and as a form of diplomatic capital whose influence depends on intersubjective validation through routinised interaction (Adler-Nissen, 2023; Finnemore & Sikkink, 2001). National resources acquire diplomatic relevance only when socially interpreted and recognised (Nye, 2011). Patterns of foreign recognition increasingly take into account domestic institutional configurations and political cultures (Melissen & Chandrasekara, 2026). In this context, diplomatic narratives may be hindered by national dynamics including populist capture, over-politicised environments (Wiseman & Scott, 2026), and persistent corruption. These conditions can limit access to norm-setting arenas (Jakobi, 2013), policy networks, and cooperative partnerships within ACPD. Governance models grounded in integrity thus function as reputational assets in their own right.

New Zealand exemplifies the relationship between governance reliability, integrity system robustness, and the capacity to shape expectations through ACPD. Institutional trust, policy continuity, and official professionalism underpin the country's reputation as a "high-integrity society" (Transparency International New Zealand, 2013, p. 8). This identity enables cooperative engagement in regional governance initiatives, particularly in the Pacific. Even in the absence of centralised national anticorruption bodies, consistent domestic performance generates diplomatic capital that sustains ACPD. Such legitimacy favours influence over coercion or regulatory projection, reinforcing relational pathways of socialisation grounded in trust and recognition (Bjola & Kornprobst, 2018). Here, influence derives from sustained perceptions of domestic trustworthiness.

Denmark offers another illustration. Strong institutional performance, grounded in long-term investments in public-sector accountability, regulatory consistency, and partnerships with global anticorruption institutions, has made "Getting to Denmark" synonymous with a governance benchmark (Jensen, 2014). This privileged position enabled Denmark to advance international initiatives in areas such as development cooperation, technical assistance, and due diligence. However, as gaps in domestic governance became more visible, ACPD also served as a mechanism to recalibrate external perceptions. The country increasingly relied on financial partnerships to boost favourable reputational dynamics (Norwegian Agency for Development Cooperation, 2010, p. 21), thereby sustaining its capacity to shape expectations and align partners.

The United States illustrates a highly institutionalised and strategic conversion of governance effectiveness into diplomatic leverage. In pursuing a policy of "denying safe haven" since at least the 1990s (Clinton White House, 1997), it developed a robust legal and institutional framework that influenced both OECD and United Nations anticorruption conventions (Pieth, 2012). Originally introduced as a domestic mechanism to curb corporate corruption, the FCPA was later expanded to address foreign bribery. This shift transformed governance capacity into a diplomatic asset, as extraterritorial enforcement, compliance regimes, and coordinated policy action were mobilised to shape international expectations and institutional architectures. The process reflects dynamics of norm entrepreneurship seeking to structure global standards of appropriate conduct (Finnemore & Sikkink, 2001). In this configuration, domestic governance models underpin a leadership role in global anticorruption governance, reinforcing both reputational authority and agenda-setting power.

In South Korea, improvements in domestic governance performance have been actively leveraged to reshape international perceptions through reform narratives that enable the state to renegotiate its role identity within governance communities (Wendt, 1999). Institutional reforms targeting bureaucratic integrity, public-service transparency, and digital governance innovation support a narrative of transformation underpinning the country's external projection. By aligning such reforms with regional cooperation initiatives and multilateral participation, South Korea converts them into developmental legitimacy. This process enables the country to position itself both as a reforming state and as a contributor to global integrity norms, strengthening its diplomatic standing while addressing persistent structural vulnerabilities.

Across the four cases, integrity reputation and governance effectiveness emerge as intangible resources capable of generating attraction and normative alignment within international socialisation processes (Finnemore & Sikkink, 2001; Nye, 2011). They function as key enablers of diplomatic influence in the international projection of anticorruption narratives and practices. When institutional performance aligns with diplomatic narratives, ACPD gains persuasive force, supporting cooperation, norm diffusion, and reputational consolidation. In this sense, domestic integrity and good governance operate as stabilising assets that underpin both strategic positioning and normative engagement. Yet this conversion is not automatic, as diplomatic influence depends on the continuous reproduction of legitimacy through recognised performance and consistent practice (Adler

& Pouliot, 2011). Legitimacy must therefore be continually enacted for integrity to translate into diplomatic power.

At the same time, ACPD can help mitigate asymmetries arising from shortcomings in domestic governance. In an era of intensified information flows, such failures, scrutinised by domestic spectators, can rapidly shape international perceptions. ACPD provides governments with a strategic mechanism to calibrate responses to global integrity expectations in line with evolving national realities. In this respect, ACPD mediates and co-constitutes the relationship between domestic developments and diplomatic practices, enabling the articulation, contestation, and adjustment of national identities (Wendt, 1999). Denmark, for instance, uses financial resources in this calibration process in line with national interests. The country remains one of the most significant financial contributors to anticorruption norm entrepreneurs, and this engagement generates expectations of reciprocity that may temper overt criticism (TI Danmark, 2012, pp. 163–171). Despite domestic controversies, including corruption scandals, such as the 2018 Danske Bank case, enforcement gaps, or perceptions of selective responsiveness, the country continues to rank among the least corrupt globally.

Domestic governance models are enabling conditions and strategic instruments within ACPD. Whether operating as stabilised sources of reputational capital, mechanisms of recalibration, platforms for norm leadership, or narratives of institutional evolution, governance performance shapes how states project identity and negotiate their positions within global anticorruption regimes. ACPD thus emerges not merely as a diplomatic practice but as a relational process through which domestic legitimacy is translated, contested, and strategically mobilised internationally. Ultimately, the diplomatic value of integrity lies in its capacity to be continuously enacted and socially recognised, allowing states to convert governance effectiveness into sustained influence, normative engagement, and adaptive positioning within evolving international environments.

7.4 Designing National Repertoires of ACPD

The comparative inquiry shows that ACPD initiatives are strategically organised to generate recognition and influence in global governance settings (Nye, 2011). They support broader objectives of international positioning and influence aligned with national interests and reflect how state preferences are shaped and reformulated in normative environments

(Wendt, 1999), such as that surrounding anticorruption. Integrity, however, is not internationally projected in a uniform manner. Through ACPD, governance resources are translated into distinct national repertoires shaped by strategic priorities, institutional traditions, and diplomatic cultures (Nye, 2011). Analysing how these repertoires are constructed provides insight into the organisational logics through which states convert domestic governance capacity into sustained diplomatic engagement within evolving global integrity regimes.

Strategic Design

The strategic design of ACPD varies. ACPD is a flexible instrument through which states interpret and mobilise resources in response to evolving international expectations and normative environments. Distinct national goals, ranging from normative diffusion to reputational consolidation, are associated with socialisation processes through which norms acquire stability and legitimacy (Finnemore & Sikkink, 2001). These variations reflect underlying national interest structures.

Denmark illustrates a design oriented towards norm diffusion through financial leverage and cooperation. A defining feature of its ACPD is the strategic funding of international bodies, networks, and research centres dedicated to curbing corruption. In parallel, Denmark promotes development cooperation, technical assistance, and export financing schemes that foster social learning and shared expectations among actors (Adler, 2005). These initiatives sustain the institutional infrastructure that reproduces and stabilises the anticorruption norm. This reflects a preference for influencing international targets through financial incentives with high reciprocity potential. Its effectiveness, however, depends on continued social recognition of Danish moral claims, as diplomatic influence remains contingent on external validation (Adler & Pouliot, 2011). ACPD thus supports Denmark's long-standing objective of maintaining international credibility while safeguarding national interests in an increasingly complex global environment.

In contrast, the United States presents a strategic design characterised by the explicit integration of ACPD into foreign policy. Anticorruption engagement is systematically linked to national security priorities, regulatory projection, and the shaping of international institutional architectures. Through coordinated policy planning and the promotion of transnational compliance regimes, ACPD becomes part of a deliberate effort to structure global governance in ways that reflect American legal norms and market expectations. This constitutes a process of norm entrepreneurship aimed at institutionalising preferred standards of conduct (Finnemore & Sikkink, 2001). ACPD initiatives operate as instruments of agenda-setting, consistent with the capacity of a leading state to frame issues and define policy priorities within international regimes (Nye, 2011), reinforcing the country's role as a central normative entrepreneur.

New Zealand's strategic design is rooted in relational engagement. ACPD is advanced through regional cooperation platforms, development assistance initiatives, and multilateral engagement. It relies on sustained dialogue and partnership-based governance to advance its objectives. This approach aligns with its broader diplomatic culture, which prioritises trust-building and mutual learning as pathways to influence (Bjola & Kornprobst, 2018). In this context, ACPD reinforces New Zealand's position as a credible and responsive actor within regional governance networks.

South Korea presents a reform-driven strategic design shaped by the dual imperatives of domestic transformation and international recognition. Anticorruption initiatives are structured around targeted policy programmes, technological innovation in public administration, and capacity-building efforts aimed at sharing reform experiences with partner countries. Through this design, ACPD supports both the consolidation of internal legitimacy and the projection of developmental competence abroad. It thus becomes a strategic narrative of progress through which the country communicates reform trajectories and renegotiates its role identity within international society (Wendt, 1999). Consequently, South Korea is able to reposition itself as a reforming state capable of contributing practical solutions to shared challenges.

Across these configurations, the strategic design of ACPD reveals a common pattern: states deploy integrity initiatives not only to address governance concerns but also to shape their positioning within global governance arenas. Whether through cooperative diffusion, regulatory integration, relational engagement, or programme-based projection, ACPD reflects how governments interpret the diplomatic value of anticorruption in light of evolving geopolitical dynamics. Strategic design therefore constitutes a key dimension of national repertoires, structuring how states coordinate resources, actors, and instruments to sustain influence within international normative environments (Nye, 2011) while shaping both the direction and the intensity of ACPD.

Institutional Leadership and Coordination Patterns

Institutional leadership structures the translation of strategic intentions into diplomatic practice, coordinating authority, representation, resources, and capabilities (Hocking, 2005; Nye, 2011). The organisation of institutional functions reflects broader administrative cultures, distinct foreign-policy traditions, and historically embedded role expectations within international society (Wendt, 1999). This results in variations in authority, coordination capacity, and operational visibility. The effectiveness of ACPD, however, depends not only on institutional leadership but also on how initiatives are coordinated across institutional structures and policy domains, as diplomatic influence emerges from the strategic alignment of actors, instruments, and resources.

Coordination patterns shape the degree of coherence, adaptability, and continuity in anticorruption engagement. They influence how integrity objectives are translated into diplomatic practice through routinised interactions that stabilise expectations and enable norm diffusion (Adler-Nissen, 2023; Finnemore & Sikkink, 2001). Comparatively, the cases reveal significant variation in the extent to which ACPD is institutionalised as an integrated policy process or pursued through more situational and ad hoc initiatives that rely on episodic mobilisation and relational diplomacy.

Denmark illustrates a pattern of distributed institutional leadership and networked coordination, where ACPD is conducted through horizontally structured interactions among multiple institutions involved in development cooperation, export promotion, and foreign affairs (Melissen, 2005; Zaharna, 2013). Authority is dispersed across governance levels and coordinated through shared policy frameworks and established traditions of inter-institutional trust. Development agencies, export-credit bodies, foreign affairs institutions, and diplomatic missions jointly contribute to the projection of integrity initiatives, enabling ACPD to be embedded flexibly across diverse policy domains (e.g. development cooperation and trade). These institutionalised yet adaptive practices stabilise expectations, facilitate norm diffusion, and reinforce a model that privileges flexibility, partnership-based engagement, and normative credibility. In this configuration, coordination itself becomes a source of diplomatic influence (Nye, 2004), reflecting Denmark's broader administrative ethos of institutional autonomy, sustaining attraction-based forms of influence grounded in perceived governance legitimacy.

The American case features a centralised multi-agency leadership combined with integrated coordination mechanisms. Although ACPD is implemented by a wide range of actors, including diplomatic services, regulatory and law-enforcement agencies, it is strategically guided by overarching federal policy frameworks, with the Department of State establishing priorities and ensuring alignment across institutional domains. Coordination operates through a hybrid model that combines hierarchy with interagency integration, supported by formal reporting requirements, strategic planning cycles, and institutional communication channels. These mechanisms enable the alignment of diplomatic messaging, enforcement practices, and development initiatives through a smart power design integrating resources, instruments, and policy objectives (Nye, 2011). Notably, anticorruption objectives are embedded within broader national security and economic strategies, enhancing the coherence and operational visibility of ACPD. This institutional density strengthens the country's capacity to promote anticorruption norms globally, reinforcing its role in shaping governance architectures and international standards of appropriate conduct (Finnemore & Sikkink, 2001). In this configuration, coordination becomes a mechanism of strategic projection and institutional leverage, enabling the orchestration of regulatory, diplomatic, and security instruments.

In New Zealand, leadership assumes a situational and practice-oriented diplomatic character, closely intertwined with informal coordination patterns rooted in relational governance. ACPD initiatives are typically driven by diplomatic missions, development practitioners, and regional engagement platforms rather than by specialised anticorruption authorities. They are embedded within broader diplomatic strategies without highly formalised coordination or centralised institutional authority. This configuration reflects a preference for adaptive and context-sensitive diplomacy, where leadership emerges through relational credibility, interpersonal networks, and shared norms. Coordination unfolds through context-specific initiatives, particularly in regional settings, facilitating processes of dialogue, mutual adjustment, and social learning (Adler & Pouliot, 2011; Bjola & Kornprobst, 2018; Wendt, 1999; Zaharna, 2013, 2022). This flexible and trust-based approach enhances responsiveness to local governance challenges while sustaining New Zealand's international reputation for integrity and cooperative engagement.

South Korea demonstrates a technocratic leadership aligned with a coordination structure led by its primary integrity agency. The ACRC orchestrates international initiatives, such as training programmes, technological cooperation, and multilateral engagement, within comprehensive policy frameworks that institutionalise reforms and guide their external projection. This concentration of expertise facilitates the international circulation of narratives based on domestic reforms. National plans integrate diplomatic engagement, technological innovation, and capacity-building activities into a coherent strategic agenda, monitored through defined performance indicators. This structured and programmatic approach allows South Korea to connect its reform trajectory with international cooperation objectives, positioning governance innovation as a transferable resource that diffuses across governance contexts (Finnemore & Sikkink, 2001). Technocratic leadership thus becomes instrumental in supporting institutional learning, policy diffusion, and socialisation within evolving governance communities (Adler, 2005), as ACPD operates through the projection and circulation of reform-based knowledge.

These configurations demonstrate how variations in institutional leadership and coordination patterns shape the operational articulation and the symbolic resonance of ACPD. Institutional arrangements influence how diplomatic signals are produced, interpreted, and validated by external audiences (Adler & Pouliot, 2011). Distributed and networked configurations, as observed in Denmark, tend to enhance inclusiveness, adaptability, and normative authenticity; centralised multi-agency systems, as in the United States, reinforce strategic coherence, enforcement credibility, and global projection. Situational and informal arrangements, characteristic of New Zealand, support relational responsiveness and context-sensitive engagement, while technocratic and programme-based models, exemplified by South Korea, promote policy diffusion, knowledge transfer, continuity, and measurable outcomes.

These patterns show that leadership and coordination are more than organisational features; they are constitutive dimensions of diplomatic influence, shaping the degree of policy coherence, international visibility, and capacity to sustain long-term normative engagement. Understanding who leads ACPD and how coordination is structured is therefore essential to explaining how states mobilise integrity as a diplomatic resource, aligning governance performance with strategic positioning in international society. This dynamic reflects broader processes through which institutional arrangements condition the recognition, credibility, and effectiveness of diplomatic action.

Policy Instruments and the Operational Repertoire

The operational repertoire of ACPD becomes most visible in the policy instruments through which strategic interests are translated into concrete diplomatic practice. States deploy a diverse combination of advocacy platforms, compliance frameworks, technical assistance initiatives, and governance innovation exports, reflecting different understandings of how anticorruption can be projected and normalised internationally through norm diffusion dynamics shaped by transnational interaction (Finnemore & Sikkink, 2001). These instruments structure the practical enactment of ACPD.

Advocacy platforms constitute a foundational instrument in all national repertoires. Through advocacy, states seek to influence international agendas by framing governance norms as appropriate standards of conduct (Jakobi, 2013). By participating in multilateral forums, public communication campaigns, expert dialogues, and normative coalition-building initiatives, states promote anticorruption standards as part of broader governance agendas. These platforms enable governments to frame domestic policies as transferable best practices while shaping international expectations regarding transparency, accountability, and regulatory effectiveness. Advocacy thus functions not only as message dissemination but also as a mechanism for agenda-setting and reputational positioning within governance arenas where recognition conditions diplomatic influence (Adler & Pouliot, 2011). It also serves as a primary performative channel through which integrity norms enter international diplomatic discourse.

Compliance frameworks represent a more regulatory-oriented instrument, particularly visible in contexts where anticorruption is linked to transnational economic matters. Export-credit procedures, due diligence requirements, the extraterritorial application of laws, and enforcement cooperation allow states to extend domestic standards beyond national borders, structuring expectations in global regulatory environments (Finnemore & Sikkink, 2001). These tools contribute to levelling competition and protecting market integrity while reinforcing diplomatic narratives of responsible economic engagement and governance credibility (Nye, 2004). In the United States, domestic regulatory standards travel through global infrastructures, thereby expanding the operational scope of ACPD. In this way, regulatory alignment becomes a channel of diplomatic influence.

Technical assistance initiatives further illustrate the cooperative dimension of ACPD. Training programmes, institutional capacity-building projects, and advisory missions enable the diffusion of anticorruption knowledge and practices across governance systems via social learning processes that facilitate norm internalisation (Checkel, 2005). These initiatives often operate within development cooperation structures or regional partnerships, strengthening networks of trust that prioritise mutual understanding and collaborative engagement. By positioning integrity as a shared developmental objective, technical assistance supports both normative convergence and diplomatic relationship-building. In Denmark's case, these cooperative instruments are reinforced by sustained financial contributions to institutions that reproduce anticorruption expertise internationally, allowing the country to exercise influence through infrastructural support consistent with partnership-based diplomatic strategies. Hence, technical assistance transforms governance expertise into relational diplomatic influence.

Finally, digital governance tools have emerged as a distinctive instrument in ACPD. The international promotion of e-procurement systems, transparency platforms, and data-driven oversight mechanisms allows states to communicate reform achievements through technological solutions and performative demonstrations of administrative competence that shape perceptions within international governance communities (Wendt, 1999). Such initiatives are particularly significant in cases where governance innovation forms part of a broader narrative of national transformation, such as in South Korea, enabling it to project administrative competence and policy adaptability as diplomatic assets.

This set of instruments demonstrates that ACPD operates through a multifaceted operational repertoire, fusing communicative, regulatory, cooperative, and technological practices that enable strategic positioning within evolving normative spaces (Bjola & Kornprobst, 2018). The selection and combination of resources reflect national priorities and institutional capacities, determining how integrity initiatives are perceived and internalised through repeated interaction (Checkel, 2005). These processes are further reinforced by relational, collaborative, and communicative capacities mobilised to address shared governance challenges (Zaharna, 2022). Understanding this repertoire is essential for analysing how ACPD moves from institutional design to performative engagement through diplomatic practices that enact identity and influence (Adler & Pouliot, 2011) in global governance arenas.

7.5 Activities and Modes of Engagement

This section shifts the analytical focus to the diplomatic practices through which ACPD is enacted, constructing meaning and identity in interaction with international audiences (Adler & Pouliot, 2011). These modes of engagement show that ACPD operates both as policy implementation and as a performative process that enacts international role identities (Wendt, 1999). By examining listening, dialogical engagement, advocacy, cultural diplomacy, exchanges, and international broadcasting as interconnected practices, the analysis highlights the stabilisation of normative expectations across governance regimes (Checkel, 2005) through socialisation mechanisms that facilitate the circulation of integrity norms. More broadly, these practices are directed at identifiable international audiences, including integrity-focused institutions, donor communities, regional governance forums, and transnational expert networks, within which anticorruption norms are interpreted, validated, and contested. In this way, diplomatic practice becomes the arena in which integrity acquires social and political meaning.

Listening

Before projecting integrity norms internationally, states engage in processes of recognition to interpret external expectations attached to governance standards and identify priorities that may facilitate their positioning in global debates (Adler, 2005). Diplomatic listening emerges as a central mechanism of international socialisation across the four states, enabling them to adjust behaviour and expectations in response to evolving normative surroundings (Checkel, 2005; Cull, 2019). States calibrate ACPD in line with shifting institutional contexts and transnational pressures.

In Denmark, listening is embedded in development cooperation mechanisms and multilateral initiatives. Sustained participation in international forums and technical partnerships gives Denmark a greater understanding of governance challenges faced in partner countries while gaining insight into how integrity norms are interpreted in diverse contexts. This supports the promotion of anticorruption standards through cooperative mechanisms that prioritise dialogue and shared problem-solving, reinforcing normative credibility (Melissen, 2005). Listening underpins Denmark's relational approach to ACPD.

New Zealand demonstrates a strongly relational form of diplomatic listening grounded in regional engagement. Consultations within Pacific networks, collaborative policy dialogues, and context-sensitive initiatives position the country as an interlocutor attentive to local priorities. In this configuration, listening extends beyond information-gathering to become a trust-building practice that enhances the legitimacy of subsequent ACPD and enables cooperative influence (Bjola & Kornprobst, 2018; Zaharna, 2013, 2022). By recognising the perspectives of partner states and non state actors, New Zealand reinforces its identity as a facilitator of inclusive governance processes.

In the United States, listening assumes a strategic orientation linked to the identification of risks, opportunities, and alignment with national interests. Engagement in multilateral negotiations, policy consultations, and intelligence-informed assessments enables the anticipation of trends and the shaping of anticorruption agendas through agenda-setting processes that structure governance priorities within international regimes (Nye, 2011). This illustrates how recognition informs agenda-setting strategies, with listening supporting the design of targeted initiatives that combine normative commitments with regulatory projection.

South Korea presents a technocratic variant oriented towards benchmarking and institutional learning. Participation in global anticorruption regimes, peer-review mechanisms, and specialised policy networks allows comparison between domestic reforms and international standards, fostering policy diffusion and institutional learning (Finnemore & Sikkink, 2001). This engagement enables the refinement of governance innovations and the adjustment of diplomatic messaging in line with evolving expectations regarding transparency and accountability. Listening thus becomes a tool for aligning reform narratives with internationally recognised frameworks of integrity.

Comparatively, these patterns indicate that ACPD begins not with unilateral projection but with mutual recognition, as influence depends on the intersubjective validation of governance performance (Adler & Pouliot, 2011). Listening enables states to interpret how anticorruption norms are understood across different governance contexts, creating the cognitive and relational conditions for effective diplomatic engagement (Martino, 2020). By incorporating external perspectives and adjusting policy approaches accordingly, governments transform anticorruption from a domestic concern into a shared diplomatic language. In this sense, listening constitutes the initial moment of engagement through which states enter processes of international socialisation centred on integrity, shaping identity, expectations, and cooperation.

Dialogical Engagement

Dialogical engagement is a core mechanism supporting ACPD as a process of international socialisation because diplomatic interaction enables the mutual adjustment of expectations and practices among participating actors (Checkel, 2005; Martino, 2020). Sustained dialogue enables meanings attached to integrity to be negotiated, relationships of trust to be cultivated, and shared governance practices to emerge through deliberative processes that construct common understandings of appropriate conduct (Adler & Pouliot, 2011). Across the four cases, dialogical engagement functions as a relational space where anticorruption norms are transmitted and co-produced among state and non state agents. This dynamic is particularly visible in transnational policy networks that facilitate norm diffusion and institutional learning (Finnemore & Sikkink, 2001). Through dialogue, ACPD shifts from transmission to co-creation.

New Zealand exemplifies a strongly relational orientation in dialogical engagement. Engagement within regional governance frameworks and multilateral forums emphasises inclusiveness, reciprocity, and mutual learning. In this context, integrity is framed as a collective objective that prioritises mutual understanding and relational influence within context-sensitive cooperation (Martino, 2020; Melissen, 2005). This relational approach reinforces the country's identity as a facilitator of consensus-building processes and strengthens its credibility as a partner attentive to diverse governance needs.

The Danish model is anchored in structured financial mechanisms. Engagement with international organisations, development partners, and normative communities enables Denmark to participate in deliberative processes that shape integrity standards and implementation strategies within governance communities organised around shared practices and expectations (Adler, 2005). These financial instruments also generate incentives that foster favourable perceptions of Denmark among international partners. Rather than relying exclusively on value-based persuasion, this approach leverages material resources to secure access, influence agenda-setting processes, and sustain Denmark's positioning within global anticorruption governance networks.

In the United States, dialogical engagement often assumes a strategic dimension linked to objectives of regulatory alignment and agenda-setting. Diplomatic negotiations, policy consultations, and participation in transnational enforcement networks provide opportunities to shape how anticorruption norms are interpreted and operationalised across jurisdictions, thereby influencing institutional architectures and governance priorities (Nye, 2011). In this way, ACPD becomes a channel for aligning governance practices with American legal frameworks and market principles. This dynamic reflects processes of normative convergence alongside geopolitical positioning within international society (Bjola & Kornprobst, 2018). American dialogical diplomacy operates through negotiation aimed at structuring global governance expectations.

South Korea presents a functional approach centred on policy exchange, capacity-building cooperation, and the sharing of administrative innovations. Participation in regional initiatives and multilateral platforms allows South Korean institutions to showcase reform achievements while learning from the experiences of other governance systems. Through this process, ACPD facilitates both the external validation of domestic reforms and institutional socialisation into evolving integrity regimes (Checkel, 2005). This pattern supports South Korea's gradual integration into global integrity networks.

Dialogical engagement demonstrates that ACPD is inherently socialising, as repeated diplomatic engagement shapes identities, preferences, and expectations (Wendt, 1999). By creating spaces for negotiation, interpretation, and contestation, this mode of engagement enables states to transform unilateral anticorruption policies into a shared normative enterprise. Trust-building interactions and integrity networks contribute to the stabilisation of expectations, fostering environments in which common standards can be internalised through sustained engagement and behavioural adaptation (Checkel, 2005). In this sense, ACPD operates not merely as communication about integrity but as an ongoing relational practice through which states collectively shape international norms and practices (Adler & Pouliot, 2011), thereby influencing the global anticorruption order.

Advocacy

Advocacy is one of the most visible expressions of ACPD, through which integrity norms are actively articulated and projected in global arenas. It is a performative facet of international socialisation, enabling states to enact role identities and signal normative commitment to shared values, thereby generating attraction-based influence rooted in perceived credibility (Adler & Pouliot, 2011; Nye, 2004) while advancing interests.

Denmark exemplifies advocacy grounded in reputational capital. Recognition as one of the least corrupt countries in the world provides Denmark with the authority to present its governance model as transferable best practice. The country does so particularly through funding of anticorruption programmes and initiatives in countries of strategic interest. This approach combines technical assistance grounded in preference-shaping mechanisms with material leverage (Nye, 2004). Participation in international campaigns and dialogues allows Denmark to frame integrity as a prerequisite for sustainable governance, reinforcing a credibility claim anchored in social trust. Advocacy extends Denmark's normative leadership exercised through cooperative and financial engagement within transnational communities that stabilise governance practices (Adler, 2005). In this context, reputation functions as a key diplomatic resource.

In the American case, advocacy is more structural and normative. Political speeches, policy initiatives, and active participation in international anticorruption regimes enable the United States to shape expectations regarding market integrity, transparency, and enforcement through processes of norm entrepreneurship aimed at institutionalising preferred governance standards (Finnemore & Sikkink, 2001). The country integrates anticorruption discourse into broader narratives of security, development, and democratic governance, thereby constructing normative environments aligned with its legal frameworks and geopolitical priorities. This approach underscores advocacy as a communication strategy and as a form of institutional projection. It thereby contributes to structuring normative expectations in global governance.

New Zealand illustrates a more moderated form of advocacy that privileges credibility and relational sensitivity. Anticorruption promotion is often embedded within cooperative initiatives and diplomatic consultations rather than articulated through highly visible leadership claims. The country contributes to the diffusion of integrity norms through relational mechanisms of international socialisation in multilateral and regional forums that encourage behavioural adaptation (Checkel, 2005), while maintaining a diplomatic style emphasising consensus-building and mutual respect, which facilitates social learning and cooperative influence (Bjola &

Kornprobst, 2018). In this context, advocacy reinforces shared commitments in a more indirect manner.

South Korea demonstrates a reformist advocacy centred on the communication of domestic evolution and governance innovation. Anticorruption reforms are presented as evidence of developmental progress and administrative modernisation through international campaigns, policy exchanges, and institutional outreach. Positioning itself simultaneously as a learner and contributor within global networks, the country enhances recognition of its reform trajectory, while its identity is validated through diplomatic interaction and institutional participation (Wendt, 1999) and supports its aspiration for greater influence in regional and multilateral governance structures.

These cases show that advocacy is a normative practice through which states enact integrity in public diplomatic arenas, contributing to the construction of shared understandings of appropriate governance conduct (Adler & Pouliot, 2011). By promoting anticorruption practices, participating in global regimes, and articulating political commitments to transparency and accountability, governments contribute to shaping collective expectations regarding acceptable governance. Advocacy reinforces diplomatic legitimacy by aligning governance narratives with collective expectations embedded in international regimes (Finnemore & Sikkink, 2001). It further sustains processes of international socialisation through which anticorruption norms shape preferences, identities, and patterns of cooperation (Wendt, 1999). In this way, advocacy contributes to the consolidation of anticorruption as a shared norm.

Cultural Diplomacy

Cultural diplomacy constitutes a symbolic dimension of ACPD through which integrity is framed as a culturally embedded value shaping national identity and international perceptions. Its diplomatic influence depends on recognition by international audiences (Adler & Pouliot, 2011). When recognised, these narratives become sources of diplomatic credibility. Across the four cases, narratives of governance culture, moral responsibility, and institutional ethos are mobilised to communicate anticorruption norms in ways that resonate beyond technical policy discourse. Accordingly, integrity becomes part of broader diplomatic imaginaries linking administrative practice to societal values, generating attraction and normative alignment (Nye, 2004). Cultural diplomacy thus amplifies the interpretive resonance of integrity at the international level.

Denmark exemplifies a cultural framing of integrity grounded in long-standing traditions of social trust and collective responsibility. Anticorruption narratives are often associated with broader representations of the Nordic governance model, where transparency, welfare provision, and institutional reliability are presented as interconnected elements of a cohesive society. Denmark reinforces perceptions of authenticity and moral credibility by projecting a culture of trust in external engagements. In this vein, Danish integrity narratives operate as symbolic carriers of governance authority within transnational communities structured by shared expectations and practices (Adler, 2005). Cultural credibility becomes a quiet but durable source of diplomatic influence.

South Korea centres cultural diplomacy on reform and modernisation. Broader narratives of national transformation, from authoritarian developmentalism to democratic governance, are regularly linked to anticorruption initiatives. Integrity is communicated as a symbol of progress and adaptive capacity through performative demonstrations of reform that contribute to identity renegotiation in international society (Wendt, 1999). Showcasing administrative innovation, digital transparency platforms, and reformist discourse, the country positions itself as a reforming state capable of offering practical solutions to shared challenges.

The cultural diplomacy of New Zealand focuses on fairness, inclusiveness, and relational accountability. ACPD frequently reflects values associated with participatory governance and respect for community perspectives, influenced in part by *Māori* principles emphasising collective stewardship and dialogue. This cultural framing supports a diplomatic style in which anticorruption is presented as an extension of societal norms rather than as an externally imposed policy agenda, enhancing receptivity among regional partners through relational dynamics. Integrity is normalised as a relational expectation within cooperation environments.

The rule of law and institutional checks and balances are central features of American anticorruption cultural diplomacy. ACPD initiatives emphasise constitutional traditions, judicial independence, and regulatory enforcement. Through symbolic references to democratic resilience and legal accountability, integrity is framed as both a foundational value and a strategic instrument in agenda-setting processes aimed at shaping international governance expectations (Finnemore & Sikkink, 2001). The country uses cultural diplomacy to promote stability in international markets and political systems.

Cultural diplomacy illustrates ACPD as a form of symbolic enactment through which diplomatic practices construct meaning and reinforce legitimacy claims (Adler & Pouliot, 2011). By associating anticorruption with narratives of trust, fairness, legality, or modernisation, articulated through both traditional channels (e.g. hosting conferences) and digital platforms (e.g. e-government), governments expand the interpretive frameworks enabling anticorruption norms to be understood and internalised in transnational policy environments (Checkel, 2005). This also reinforces processes of international socialisation by linking governance norms to perceptions of national identity and cultural legitimacy.

Exchanges

Exchanges involve tangible processes of institutional learning and policy adaptation that facilitate the internalisation of norms (Checkel, 2005). Expert missions, training, and capacity-building programmes, as well as the circulation of governance models, enable states to move beyond symbolic projection and engage directly in the co-development of administrative practices within transnational communities that structure shared understandings of appropriate governance conduct (Adler, 2005). In this context, ACPD operates as a mechanism of practical socialisation (Adler-Nissen, 2023; Cull, 2019; Scott-Smith, 2023), facilitating the gradual internalisation of shared standards (Finnemore & Sikkink, 2001) across diverse governance contexts.

In South Korea, exchanges primarily involve the export of policy models. The country has developed training programmes and technical cooperation initiatives to share experiences in technology-based governance tools. This allows it to communicate administrative competence through performative demonstrations of reform that contribute to the recognition of South Korea's reformist identity by foreign partners (Wendt, 1999). At the same time, it positions itself as a developmental partner capable of supporting governance transformation abroad through attraction-based influence grounded in perceived governance effectiveness (Nye, 2004). Hence, reform expertise becomes a vehicle of diplomatic positioning.

In the United States, exchanges often assume a dual function of training and enforcement diffusion. Programmes focused on legal capacity-building, regulatory compliance, and investigative cooperation allow the country to extend anticorruption standards through professional networks and transnational partnerships, facilitating policy diffusion and regulatory convergence (Finnemore & Sikkink, 2001; Zaharna, 2022). By fostering expertise aligned with its legal frameworks, the United States contributes to shaping institutional environments conducive to regulatory harmonisation and market integrity, reinforcing its role in structuring global governance practices in line with its agenda-setting capacities (Nye, 2011). Exchanges therefore become tools for embedding preferred standards within transnational regulatory environments.

Denmark's engagement in exchanges is frequently grounded in development assistance and technical advisory initiatives. Danish representatives promote anticorruption practices emphasising collaboration and contextual sensitivity through financial support for public-sector reforms, transparency, and institutional strengthening programmes. This approach reflects a diplomatic style oriented primarily towards empowerment rather than conditionality, enhancing trust and facilitating the sustainable adoption of governance innovations through partnership-based engagement grounded in normative credibility (Melissen, 2005). Accordingly, cooperation becomes a mechanism of influence.

The New Zealand model is grounded in regional cooperation and peer learning. Capacity-building initiatives within Pacific governance networks prioritise dialogue, adaptability, and the co-production of policy solutions tailored to local administrative realities. By supporting the circulation of policy models through relational mechanisms of international socialisation that encourage behavioural adaptation (Checkel, 2005) rather than hierarchical transfer, New Zealand reinforces its reputation as a responsive partner committed to strengthening collective governance resilience.

Exchanges constitute practical international socialisation, embedding integrity norms within everyday administrative routines and professional interactions that stabilise governance expectations through institutionalised arrangements (Adler & Pouliot, 2011). The circulation of expertise, institutional experiences, and governance tools contributes to consolidating shared expectations regarding transparency and accountability within evolving normative environments (Finnemore & Sikkink, 2001). In this manner, governance expertise functions as a strategic resource shaping influence and international positioning (Nye, 2011). This dynamic complements symbolic communication and normative advocacy, reinforcing the multidimensional character of ACPD.

International Broadcasting

International broadcasting disseminates integrity narratives to broader global audiences through mass communicative practices. States use strategic narrative projection to shape international preferences and expectations at scale (Arceneaux & Powers, 2020; Nye, 2004). Speeches, policy reports, newsletters, and digital diplomacy platforms enable states to project governance achievements, signal normative commitments, and shape international perceptions of credibility and leadership (Arceneaux & Powers, 2020; Cull, 2019). In this sense, broadcasting is more than information transmission; it is a process of discursive consolidation through which states enact identity and legitimacy claims in international society (Adler & Pouliot, 2011), while embedding anticorruption in the symbolic architecture of global public diplomacy.

The United States illustrates a strategic approach to international broadcasting characterised by high visibility. Political speeches, policy documents, and coordinated communication campaigns frequently frame anticorruption as integral to democratic governance, economic stability, and international security. Through sustained messaging across diplomatic and media channels, the country contributes to shaping global narratives that link integrity with institutional order and market reliability. These agenda-setting dynamics influence governance priorities globally (Nye, 2011). Broadcasting thus supports both reputational consolidation and normative leadership by reinforcing collective expectations in international regimes (Finnemore & Sikkink, 2001). Accordingly, mass communication operates as a strategic instrument of influence.

The South Korean model is oriented towards reputational repositioning. Official reports, video content on YouTube channels, and digital outreach initiatives highlight administrative innovation, transparency reforms, and technological solutions to governance challenges. By communicating its transformation into a country actively promoting integrity norms, South Korea seeks to enhance recognition of its trajectory and strengthen its standing within regional and global networks structured by shared practices and institutional participation (Adler, 2005). Through such communicative repositioning, national identity is continuously validated and renegotiated (Wendt, 1999). In this context, international broadcasting becomes a vehicle for signalling reform credibility.

Denmark adopts a more discreet strategy that privileges credibility over visibility. Communication efforts often occur through specialised reports, targeted diplomatic messaging, and participation in multilateral communication platforms. This restrained approach aligns with Denmark's broader diplomatic culture, where reputational authority is derived from identity performance and cooperative engagement that generate attraction-based influence grounded in perceived legitimacy (Nye, 2004). Here, communicative restraint itself reinforces diplomatic credibility.

New Zealand develops a contextualised approach, in which ACPD articulates anticorruption commitments within specific governance contexts, emphasising responsiveness to local and regional challenges and the importance of collaborative problem-solving. Through adaptive messaging and selective participation, New Zealand reinforces its identity as a credible and pragmatic actor that prioritises responsiveness and mutual understanding (Bjola & Kornprobst, 2018), particularly within regional initiatives.

International broadcasting reveals processes of international socialisation through which anticorruption norms circulate, are interpreted, contested, and adapted behaviourally (Checkel, 2005). By framing anticorruption in ways that resonate with foreign publics, states contribute to the consolidation of shared governance expectations while simultaneously competing for reputational recognition in a space where legitimacy and reputation condition diplomatic influence (Adler & Pouliot, 2011; Cull, 2024). It constitutes the communicative culmination of ACPD, linking symbolic performance and institutional practice in the strategic construction of influence (Nye, 2011). Through these communicative dynamics, integrity becomes globally legible as a diplomatic resource.

7.6 Smart Power: Styles of Influence in Anticorruption Public Diplomacy

The comparative evidence indicates that ACPD is an arena in which states convert national resources into influence, combining distinct capacities through different smart power designs (Nye, 2011). These dynamics activate the four modalities of power analysed in this book, reflecting national priorities, governance traditions, and geopolitical positioning. ACPD involves the contextual interpretation of national interests and identities in processes of international socialisation (Wendt, 1999) in which influence depends on intersubjective recognition (Adler & Pouliot, 2011). In this sense, smart power is mobilised to communicate values, embed standards, cooperate, impose constraints, and shape international narratives.

Soft power emerges most clearly where governance performance is perceived as legitimate, generating attraction-based influence (Nye, 2004). This is evident, for instance, in the communicative and reputational capacities associated with New Zealand, South Korea, and Denmark. By projecting governance effectiveness and engaging in inclusive diplomatic practices, these states cultivate attraction-based influence grounded in credibility. Their initiatives rely on the capacity to communicate normative commitments persuasively, engage partners on integrity concerns, and foster environments conducive to voluntary alignment through socialisation dynamics that shape preferences and expectations (Checkel, 2005). In these configurations, influence derives from perceived legitimacy and sustained cooperation.

In Denmark, however, the promotion of attraction and credibility is reinforced by an additional layer rooted in financial engagement. By funding foreign anticorruption initiatives, Denmark deploys soft, hard, and sharp power to support transnational spaces where institutionalised practices stabilise normative environments and facilitate policy diffusion (Finnemore & Sikkink, 2001). In this context, smart power introduces a structural dimension that exceeds symbolic projection alone. Yet this infrastructural influence does not insulate Denmark from reputational fragility, as influence depends on social validation by foreign publics (Adler, 2005). Authority remains strongly tied to external perceptions of integrity consistency; consequently, financial engagement may expand normative reach while heightening the costs of credibility disruption.

Hard power becomes more visible when ACPD intersects with regulatory enforcement, financial conditionality, and sanctions. The United States mobilises investigative cooperation and market access to impose compliance with certain standards. ACPD acquires a coercive dimension when linked to measures that sanction misconduct, restrict financial flows, or condition market participation. This reflects an ability to influence foreign publics by altering incentive structures and constraining behavioural options (Nye, 2011). Importantly, the country's structural position in the international system facilitates its capacity to shape market expectations and regulatory practices (Finnemore & Sikkink, 2001; Nye, 2011). This involves a combination of soft power (influence, attraction), hard power (financial leverage, coercion/inducement), and sharp power (manipulation, imposition, autonomy restriction), with the latter enabling, for instance, the extraterritorial application of American anticorruption laws. This positional leverage amplifies the reach of ACPD beyond communicative channels, transforming anticorruption standards into global requirements.

Sharp power dynamics also surface in contexts where anticorruption discourse is strategically employed in narrative competition, blurring normative boundaries through manipulation, autonomy limitation, or behavioural constraint (Nye, 2021). The American selective framing of integrity concerns and the prioritisation of specific governance agendas, as well as the Danish use of reputational signalling to advance geopolitical objectives, illustrate how ACPD operates within competitive diplomatic environments where states seek to establish moral authority and shape the boundaries of legitimate governance practices (Alexander, 2021). Such dynamics highlight the potential for the manipulation or distortion of normative debates, demonstrating that ACPD unfolds within broader struggles over legitimacy, authority, and agenda-setting.

Collaborative power represents a further modality through which ACPD enables states to shape governance practices through coordination and co-production. New Zealand's regional diplomacy and South Korea's capacity-building programmes in the Asia-Pacific illustrate how ACPD facilitates institutional embedding and policy learning within transnational communities of practice that reinforce shared governance standards (Adler-Nissen, 2023; Adler, 2005; Zaharna, 2022). States exercise influence by cooperating with foreign partners in administrative transformations and supporting the development of shared operational frameworks. Such collaborative capacities reinforce diplomatic relationships while contributing to the stabilisation of anticorruption norms within regional and global networks.

States adapt diplomatic strategies in response to evolving normative and geopolitical contexts (Wendt, 1999). They combine communicative outreach, collaborative programmes, reputational repositioning, and selective strategic signalling. Anticorruption initiatives are mobilised to enhance recognition of governance performance and strengthen international standing. This multidimensional approach reflects the growing complexity of ACPD as states navigate between normative commitment and strategic calculation. These smart power configurations reveal that styles of power in ACPD are not mutually exclusive but interact within evolving national repertoires. States combine attraction, cooperation, constraint, and narrative positioning within competitive diplomatic environments. Through smart power, ACPD facilitates the conversion of national resources into diplomatic initiatives capable of supporting diverse forms of influence (Nye, 2011). Understanding these configurations clarifies how ACPD contributes to the restructuring of power relations in international society through norm institutionalisation and strategic interaction (Finnemore & Sikkink, 2001) within contemporary global governance.

7.7 Patterns of International Socialisation

Recurring patterns illuminate how anticorruption becomes embedded within processes of international socialisation promoted by ACPD. Although each case reflects distinct political cultures, institutional arrangements, and strategic priorities, together they demonstrate that ACPD contributes to the construction of shared governance expectations within transnational communities that stabilise meanings of appropriate conduct.

A first pattern concerns the relationship between domestic anticorruption performance and international credibility. Sustained efforts to strengthen transparency mechanisms, regulatory enforcement, and administrative accountability generate reputational resources that enable a more assertive ACPD abroad. This occurs precisely because diplomatic influence depends on the recognition of governance credibility (Nye, 2004). Whether through Denmark's long-standing institutional credibility, New Zealand's high levels of institutional trust, the United States' legal enforcement capacity, or South Korea's reformist trajectory, the effectiveness of domestic governance is a foundational premise for diplomatic influence. Integrity thus operates as a bridge linking internal institutional legitimacy with external recognition through intersubjective validation processes (Adler & Pouliot, 2011). Domestic performance therefore becomes diplomatically consequential.

A second pattern relates to identity-driven variation in strategic engagement. As state identities are continuously enacted and negotiated through diplomatic interaction (Wendt, 1999), states mobilise ACPD in ways that reflect how they interpret their roles in international society. Denmark's financial leverage, New Zealand's relational diplomacy, the United States' agenda-setting leadership, and South Korea's reform-oriented positioning illustrate how national identities shape ACPD objectives and practices. These identity configurations influence decisions regarding institutional leadership, policy instruments, and smart power strategies, demonstrating that ACPD is embedded in broader narratives of state purpose and international positioning (Nye, 2011). Identity thus structures how integrity is translated into diplomatic practice.

A further pattern concerns asymmetries in anticorruption credibility and enforcement capacity. While all four states project strong anticorruption commitments, they reveal differing degrees of political will, institutional resilience, and exposure to reputational challenges. High-performing integrity systems such as those of Denmark and New Zealand are not immune to episodic controversies that test perceptions of consistency. In Denmark, this tension is especially salient because international influence depends so heavily on reputational authority and on the external recognition of integrity. As a result, even limited enforcement gaps or corporate scandals may carry disproportionate diplomatic consequences. The United States combines normative leadership with selectivity in enforcement priorities, reflecting geopolitical calculations. South Korea's reformist diplomacy coexists with structural vulnerabilities linked to entrenched economic power networks. These asymmetries highlight that ACPD operates within contested legitimacy spaces where norms are not settled; they are continually interpreted, challenged, and renegotiated through international socialisation (Finnemore & Sikkink, 2001). Such dynamics unfold within asymmetrical structures where certain actors possess greater capacity to define legitimate standards of governance (Alexander, 2021). ACPD reflects ongoing struggles over authority and recognition.

A fourth pattern concerns the institutional routinisation of ACPD practice. It becomes stabilised through recurring interactions, programme frameworks, and networks that institutionalise diplomatic practices within governance regimes (Adler & Pouliot, 2011), structuring expectations over time. However, the degree of routinisation and policy integration varies significantly across cases, ranging from highly structured and multi-actor systems to more flexible configurations in which initiatives remain contingent on diplomatic context, leadership dynamics, and relational opportunities. All four cases present continuity in ACPD, whether through participation in multilateral regimes, capacity-building partnerships, or policy coordination mechanisms, thereby transforming episodic engagement into sustained diplomatic routines. As administrative practices and professional exchanges reinforce shared understandings of appropriate conduct, this routinisation favours social learning and behavioural adaptation (Checkel, 2005), contributing to the gradual internalisation of anticorruption norms.

Norm diffusion through practice constitutes a fifth observable pattern, reflecting the circulation of governance standards through performative diplomatic engagement (Bjola & Kornprobst, 2018). Rather than relying solely on formal treaty commitments or normative declarations, anticorruption standards circulate through the performative dimensions of ACPD. Practices of listening, dialogue, advocacy, cultural diplomacy, exchanges, and broadcasting create opportunities for states to demonstrate, adapt, and institutionalise governance innovations. Through these processes, anticorruption norms acquire practical meaning and become embedded across diverse political contexts. Such diffusion occurs across all cases within a relatively structured transnational field of anticorruption engagement populated by recurrent audiences, norm entrepreneurs, and institutional participants shaping governance expectations (Finnemore & Sikkink, 2001), contributing to stabilising the shared diplomatic grammar of ACPD.

Finally, the analysis shows reputational feedback loops shaping the evolution of ACPD as an attraction-based influence that expands or contracts according to perceived governance consistency (Nye, 2004) or the country's reputational security (Cull, 2024). Successful anticorruption engagement enhances international credibility, which in turn creates new opportunities for influence, cooperation, and leadership. Conversely, reputational challenges or perceived inconsistencies may constrain diplomatic effectiveness, prompting further institutional reform or strategic recalibration. This iterative process illustrates how integrity operates as both a resource and a constraint within international socialisation, as diplomatic leverage depends on legitimacy recognition and normative alignment (Adler, 2005; Alexander, 2021). These feedback loops influence how states navigate competitive dynamics in global governance.

These patterns demonstrate that ACPD contributes to the formation of a shared diplomatic language centred on anticorruption, structuring expectations and interaction patterns (Wendt, 1999). By embedding identity narratives within strategic engagement, institutionalising diplomatic routines, diffusing norms through practice, and generating reputational feedback, ACPD shapes the evolving architecture of global public diplomacy. Understanding these dynamics provides a foundation for the integrated analytical model developed in this book, explaining how anticorruption is converted into diplomatic influence, thereby constituting a strategic dimension of international positioning.

7.8 Towards an Integrated Analytical Model

The comparison provides a basis for proposing an integrated analytical model of ACPD, conceived as a multidimensional socialisation process that translates domestic governance performance into internationally valued outcomes. The effectiveness of this process depends on intersubjective recognition within international society (Adler & Pouliot, 2011; Finnemore & Sikkink, 2001). The recurrent sequence of ACPD enactment begins with the consolidation, reform, or strategic recalibration of integrity identity, generating the reputational security needed to sustain attraction-based influence (Cull, 2024; Nye, 2004). This interaction produces reputational feedback loops that expand or constrain diplomatic influence. Over time, these feedback dynamics drive diplomatic repositioning, allowing states to adjust their engagement with the global anticorruption norm in response to evolving opportunities, constraints, and expectations.

Domestic factors such as institutional effectiveness and regulatory credibility shape the reputational resources available to states and their participation in international initiatives. ACPD is thus a structurally embedded modality of influence. Variations in governance performance help explain differences in strategic ambition, institutional leadership, and policy design across national repertoires. The Danish case illustrates that vulnerabilities in domestic integrity may be offset by sustained financial contributions to international anticorruption infrastructures, although such strategies remain highly dependent on external recognition. This reflects compensatory dynamics aimed at mitigating reputational vulnerabilities.

At the identity level, states define the purposes and modalities of anticorruption engagement in ways that reflect their self-understandings and perceived roles within international society. They mobilise ACPD in line with their identities and interests to translate integrity commitments into diplomatic practice, while constructing meanings and structuring expectations (Adler, 2005). Identity configurations interact with strategic interests to produce distinctive styles of influence, ranging from cooperative norm diffusion to regulatory projection and reputational signalling.

The operational dimension captures the performative sequences through which ACPD is enacted. Listening, dialogical engagement, normative advocacy, cultural diplomacy, exchanges, and international broadcasting form a relational continuum that enables integrity norms to circulate and stabilise across governance contexts, in line with public diplomacy processes that prioritise communication and mutual learning (Melissen, 2005). These activities translate abstract commitments into concrete diplomatic practices, reinforcing processes of international socialisation in which standards are recognised, negotiated, adapted, and internalised (Finnemore & Sikkink, 2001). As such, ACPD unfolds through feedback mechanisms linking domestic reform, international recognition, and strategic recalibration. Successful engagement enhances reputational security and expands opportunities for influence, while external expectations may prompt policy innovation or institutional adjustment. This iterative process illustrates how ACPD operates within an evolving environment shaped by cooperation, competition, and normative contestation.

The outcomes of ACPD also depend on the meanings attributed to national resources through "skillful conversion strategies" (Nye, 2011, pp. 99–100). The mere possession of resources does not automatically generate international impact (Nye, 2011). A state may possess deeply embedded integrity values and robust anticorruption legislation aimed at preventing revolving doors, yet international outcomes emerge only when ACPD assigns these elements a socially shared meaning within the international context.

Smart power design considers interests, objectives, contexts, states' positions in the international system, expectations of target audiences and norm entrepreneurs, available national resources, and the power capabilities with the greatest potential for success (Nye, 2011; Vukovic, 2020). Four main types of behaviour, with their respective variants, are employed across the four cases: co-opt and attract (soft power), command economically (hard power), constrain (sharp power), and coordinate (collaborative power), as conceptualised in the literature (Nye, 2004, 2011, 2023; Slaughter, 2011; Vukovic, 2020). The combination of these power styles within the framework of smart power facilitates the integration of national material and immaterial factors into the international anticorruption norm.

ACPD operates as a process through which states enact governance credibility, communicate normative commitments, and negotiate influence within global public diplomacy. By linking structural capacities, identity narratives, national resources, power capabilities, and interaction dynamics, the model developed in this book (Fig. 7.1) provides a

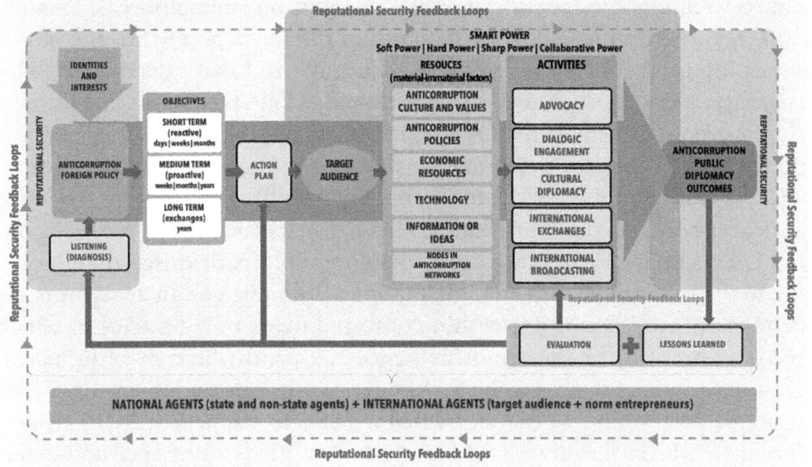

Fig. 7.1 Integrated analytical model of anticorruption public diplomacy. Source: Author's elaboration based on the analytical framework developed in this book

comprehensive lens for understanding how anticorruption initiatives contribute to the restructuring of power relations and governance expectations in contemporary international society. This analytical synthesis integrates the comparative trajectories examined and provides a conceptual foundation for future research on ACPD, particularly regarding reputational security and international influence. As anticorruption continues to gain prominence within global governance agendas, understanding the mechanisms through which it is institutionalised, performed, and contested becomes essential for analysing the evolving practice of public diplomacy in an increasingly interconnected world.

7.9 Synthesis: Anticorruption as a Global Diplomatic Language

This chapter has shown that ACPD is not a marginal extension of governance policy but a structured process of international socialisation through which states communicate, negotiate, and institutionalise integrity in global public diplomacy. Across diverse political cultures, institutional configurations, and strategic priorities, the four cases reveal convergent patterns, with anticorruption operating as a shared diplomatic language linked to intersubjective international recognition (Finnemore & Sikkink, 2001). Integrity thus becomes a common reference point through which states interpret and coordinate expectations in global governance. This language anchors processes of international socialisation by linking domestic governance to identity construction, external validation, and strategic positioning. Through performative practices, states communicate integrity, enact it, frame it, circulate it, and leverage it competitively. Thereby, anticorruption becomes intelligible and actionable across governance contexts, structuring expectations and enabling diplomatic differentiation.

At the same time, this shared language does not eliminate asymmetry or tension. ACPD unfolds within contested fields of legitimacy in which recognition must be continuously negotiated, and where integrity narratives may operate both as vehicles of norm diffusion and as instruments of strategic positioning (Alexander, 2021). The effectiveness of ACPD therefore depends on the alignment between domestic performance and external expectations, as well as on the ethical quality of influence practices. Anticorruption is particularly significant in contemporary diplomacy because of its dual character. It operates simultaneously as a normative commitment and as a strategic resource, enabling states to participate in the consolidation of shared governance standards while advancing interests related to credibility, influence, and positioning. In this respect, ACPD reflects the increasing centrality of governance norms as instruments of both cooperation and competition in international society.

While the comparative framework developed in this chapter identifies recurring ACPD dynamics across four distinct national contexts, it does not claim global representativeness. The cases were selected for their analytical relevance to the study of integrity, public diplomacy, and international socialisation, rather than for their geographical coverage. Consequently, additional trajectories may emerge in other regional settings. In particular, African and Latin American experiences may reveal additional pathways through which anticorruption norms are interpreted, institutionalised, and projected internationally, while regional organisations and South–South cooperation mechanisms may further enrich current understandings of ACPD. Exploring these contexts represents an important opportunity to refine and extend the analytical framework developed in this book.

Ultimately, anticorruption emerges not only as a policy field but as a global diplomatic language through which states make themselves intelligible, legitimate, and influential. By demonstrating how this language is articulated across contrasting national contexts, this chapter establishes a comparative foundation for understanding anticorruption as a constitutive dimension of contemporary public diplomacy.

References

Adler-Nissen, R. (2023). Practice. In S. Goddard, G. Lawson, & J. Sending (Eds.), *The Oxford handbook of international political sociology* (pp. 177–198). Oxford University Press.

Adler, E. (2005). *Communitarian international relations.* Routledge.

Adler, E. (2013). Constructivism in international relations: Sources, contributions, and debates. In W. Carlsnaes, T. Risse, & B. Simmons (Eds.), *Handbook of international relations* (2nd ed., pp. 112–144). Sage. https://doi.org/10.4135/9781446247587

Adler, E., & Barnett, M. (1998). *Security communities.* Cambridge University Press.

Adler, E., & Pouliot, V. (2011). International practices. *International Theory, 3*(1), 1–36. https://doi.org/10.1017/S175297191000031X

Alexander, C. (2021). Hegemony, morality and power: A Gramscian theoretical framework for public diplomacy. In C. Alexander (Ed.), *The frontiers of public diplomacy* (pp. 9–24). Routledge.

Anti-Corruption and Civil Rights Commission (ACRC). (2019). *Annual report 2018.* Retrieved February 9, 2026, from https://www.acrc.go.kr/boardDownload.es?bid=64&list_no=13322&seq=1

Arceneaux, P., & Powers, S. (2020). International broadcasting public diplomacy as a game in a marketplace of loyalties. In N. Snow & N. Cull (Eds.), *Routledge handbook of public diplomacy* (2nd ed., pp. 50–63). Routledge. https://doi.org/10.4324/9780429465543

Bjerregaard, E., & Kirchmaier, T. (2019, September 2). *The Danske Bank money laundering scandal.* Copenhagen Business School. https://doi.org/10.2139/ssrn.3446636

Bjola, C., & Kornprobst, M. (2018). *Understanding international diplomacy* (2nd ed.). Routledge.

Checkel, J. (2005). International institutions and socialization in Europe: Introduction and framework. *International Organization, 59*(4), 801–826. https://doi.org/10.1017/S0020818305050289

Clinton White House. (1997). *International crime control strategy.* Retrieved February 9, 2026, from https://clintonwhitehouse4.archives.gov/WH/EOP/NSC/html/documents/iccs-frm.html

Cooper, A., & Dal, E. (2017). Positioning the third wave of middle power diplomacy: Institutional elevation, practice limitations. *International Journal: Canada's Journal of Global Policy Analysis, 71*(4), 561–582. https://doi.org/10.1177/0020702016686385

Cull, N. (2019). *Public diplomacy: Foundations for global engagement in the digital age*. Polity.

Cull, N. (2024). *Reputational security*. Polity.

Finnemore, M., & Sikkink, K. (1998). International norm dynamics and political change. *International Organization, 52*(4), 887–917. https://doi.org/10.1162/002081898550789

Finnemore, M., & Sikkink, K. (2001). Taking stock: The constructivist research program in international relations and comparative politics. *Annual Review of Political Science, 4*, 391–416. https://doi.org/10.1146/annurev.polisci.4.1.391

Fukuyama, F. (2011). *The origins of political order*. Farrar, Straus, & Giroux.

Hocking, B. (2005). Rethinking the "new" public diplomacy. In J. Melissen (Ed.), *The new public diplomacy* (pp. 28–46). Palgrave Macmillan.

Jakobi, A. (2013). The changing global norm of anti-corruption: From bad business to bad government. *Zeitschrift für Vergleichende Politikwissenschaft (ZfVP), 7*(1), 243–264. https://doi.org/10.1007/s12286-013-0160-y

Jensen, M. (2014). *'Getting to Denmark': the process of state building, establishing rule of law and fighting corruption in Denmark 1660–1900* (QoG Working Paper Series 2014:04). QoG. Retrieved February 9, 2026, from https://pure.au.dk/ws/files/82049568/How_Denmark_got_to_be_Denmark_QoG_Workingpaper.pdf

Martino, L. (2020). The spectrum of listening. In N. Snow & N. Cull (Eds.), *Routledge handbook of public diplomacy* (2nd ed., pp. 21–29). Routledge. https://doi.org/10.4324/9780429465543

Mccoy, J., & Heckel, H. (2001). The emergence of a global anti-corruption norm. *International Politics, 38*(1), 65–90. https://doi.org/10.1057/palgrave.ip.8892613

Melissen, J. (2005). The new public diplomacy: Between theory and practice. In J. Melissen (Ed.), *The new public diplomacy* (pp. 3–27). Palgrave Macmillan.

Melissen, J., & Chandrasekara, G. (2026). Theorising and debating the domestic deficit in IR and diplomatic studies. In J. Melissen, H. Kim, & G. Chandrasekara (Eds.), *Home engagement in diplomacy* (pp. 5–38). Brill. https://doi.org/10.1163/9789004738324_003

Norwegian Agency for Development Cooperation. (2010). *Evaluation of Transparency International: Report 8/2010*. Retrieved February 9, 2026, from https://www.oecd.org/derec/norway/47447924.pdf

Nye, J. (2004). *Soft power*. Public Affairs.

Nye, J. (2011). *The future of power*. Public Affairs.

Nye, J. (2021). Soft power: The evolution of a concept. *Journal of Political Power, 14*(1), 196–208. https://doi.org/10.1080/2158379X.2021.1879572

Nye, J. (2023). *Soft power and great-power competition*. Springer. https://doi.org/10.1007/978-981-99-0714-4

OECD Working Group on Bribery. (2011, October). *Phase 3 report on implementing the OECD anti-bribery convention in Korea*. OECD. https://doi.org/10.1787/f2918556-en.

Pieth, M. (2012). *Collective action and corruption* (International Centre for Collective Action, Working Paper Series 13). Basel Institute on Governance.

Scott-Smith, G. (2023). International exchanges. In E. Gilboa (Ed.), *A research agenda for public diplomacy* (pp. 251–266). Elgar. https://doi.org/10.4337/9781802207323.00025

Slaughter, A.-M. (2011, November 30). A new theory for the foreign-policy frontier: Collaborative power. *The Atlantic*. Retrieved February 9, 2026, from https://www.theatlantic.com/international/archive/2011/11/a-new-theory-for-the-foreign-policy-frontier-collaborative-power/249260/

Transparency International Danmark (TI Danmark). (2012). *Nationalt Integritetssystemstudie Danmark 2011*. Retrieved February 9, 2026, from https://transparency.dk/wp-content/uploads/2019/05/NIS-DK-20120119.pdf

Transparency International New Zealand. (2013). *Integrity plus 2013: New Zealand National Integrity System Assessment*. TINZ. Retrieved February 9, 2026, from https://images.transparencycdn.org/images/2013_NewZealandNIS_EN.pdf

Vukovic, S. (2020). The many faces of power in diplomatic negotiations. *SAIS Review of International Affairs, 40*(1), 45–57. https://doi.org/10.1353/sais.2020.0004

Wendt, A. (1999). *Social theory of international politics*. Cambridge University Press.

White House. (2021, December). *United States strategy on countering corruption*. Retrieved February 9, 2026, from https://bidenwhitehouse.archives.gov/wp-content/uploads/2021/12/United-States-Strategy-on-Countering-Corruption.pdf

Wiseman, G., & Scott, A. (2026). Engaging citizens in a polarised society: The choices for US diplomacy. In J. Melissen, H. Kim, & G. Chandrasekara (Eds.), *Home engagement in diplomacy* (pp. 210–248). Brill. https://doi.org/10.1163/9789004738324_010

Zaharna, R. (2013). Network purpose, network design: Dimensions of network and collaborative public diplomacy. In R. S. Zaharna, A. Fisher, & A. Arsenault (Eds.), *Relational, networked, and collaborative approaches to public diplomacy* (pp. 221–246). Routledge.

Zaharna, R. (2022). *Boundary spanners of humanity*. Oxford University Press. https://doi.org/10.1093/oso/9780190930271.001.0001

CHAPTER 8

Conclusion: Towards a Global Norm of Anticorruption Public Diplomacy

8.1 Reframing Public Diplomacy Through an Anticorruption Lens

Anticorruption public diplomacy (ACPD) has emerged in this book not as a peripheral or derivative policy domain, but as a constitutive dimension of contemporary international relations. In a global environment increasingly structured by expectations of transparency, accountability, and integrity, all of which contribute to reputational security (Cull, 2024), anticorruption is no longer confined to domestic governance agendas. It operates as a transnational normative field through which states position themselves, communicate legitimacy, and negotiate their standing with norm entrepreneurs, state and non state agents, and foreign publics alike.

This book has demonstrated that ACPD is best understood as a structured and meaningful process through which states engage with the global anticorruption norm while simultaneously advancing national interests. It is a dynamic arena in which identity, interests, and norms are continuously co-produced. Through this process, states do not simply project pre-existing values; they actively participate in shaping the meanings, expectations, and practices that define integrity in global governance.

Framing ACPD in this way allows it to be situated within broader transformations of diplomacy itself. As diplomacy becomes increasingly networked, multi-actor, and oriented towards public engagement (Aday,

N. de A. e S. F. dos Santos, *Anticorruption Public Diplomacy*, Palgrave Macmillan Series in Global Public Diplomacy,
https://doi.org/10.1007/978-3-032-28668-0_8

2025; Cull, 2019; Melissen et al., 2023), the boundaries between domestic governance and international projection become more permeable. Anticorruption thus operates as a bridge between these spheres, linking internal institutional performance with external recognition and influence. In this context, the credibility of anticorruption commitments is not given, but constructed through interaction, interpretation, and intersubjective recognition across multiple audiences.

The global relevance of ACPD is further underscored by its growing salience in geopolitical dynamics. From major powers incorporating anticorruption into national security strategies to states seeking international legitimacy through governance reforms, anticorruption has become embedded in the language of international cooperation and competition. Even where it is not explicitly conceptualised as such, many contemporary diplomatic practices reflect its logic, signalling a broader shift towards ACPD.

By advancing an interpretivist and social constructivist understanding, this book positions ACPD as a process of international socialisation grounded in shared meanings and intersubjective recognition. In doing so, it contributes to expanding the analytical scope of public diplomacy and to integrating anticorruption more fully into international relations theory. This reframing highlights not only the strategic value of anticorruption in global affairs but also its role in structuring the normative architecture of the international system.

8.2 Anticorruption as a Socialisation Process

One of the central contributions of this book lies in demonstrating that ACPD is not adequately captured by linear or instrumental understandings of foreign-policy action. It is more convincingly understood as a process of international socialisation through which states enter, interpret, contest, reproduce, and, at times, seek to reshape shared expectations of integrity. This process is not external to state identity or interest formation; it is one of the arenas in which both are constituted, tested, and made intelligible in relation to others. In this sense, ACPD is not simply about communicating compliance or promoting reform. It is about participating in the social production of what counts as legitimate conduct in global governance, with implications for states' reputational security. This understanding is already embedded in the conceptual architecture of the book, which defines ACPD as a process linking identities and interests, objectives, agents, activities, material and immaterial factors, together with ideational elements within a recursive structure of meaning-making and international engagement.

Approaching ACPD as socialisation also reveals that anticorruption commitments do not acquire diplomatic significance automatically. Domestic laws, institutional reforms, rankings, administrative routines, and integrity narratives only become internationally meaningful when they are recognised, interpreted, and rendered meaningful by relevant external audiences. What matters, therefore, is not merely the existence of anticorruption resources, but their conversion into socially intelligible signs of responsibility, competence, and trustworthiness. This conversion depends on interaction.

States communicate, foreign publics respond, international organisations codify expectations, and transnational networks reinforce or contest reputational claims. ACPD operates precisely within this intersubjective space, where governance performance is translated into diplomatic meaning and where external recognition feeds back into domestic self-understandings. The socialising logic identified in Chap. 2 and comparatively refined in Chap. 7 makes clear that ACPD is cumulative and recursive: identities shape interests, interests orient strategic conduct, conduct generates recognition or contestation, and these responses, in turn, affect future positioning.

Seen from this perspective, ACPD operates through more than one mechanism. It has a cognitive dimension because it frames how integrity-related resources are perceived and interpreted internationally. It has a normative dimension because it is embedded in a broader regime of conventions, benchmarks, and standards that define appropriate conduct. It has a relational dimension because trust, legitimacy, and cooperation are sustained through repeated engagement with domestic and foreign actors. Additionally, it has an ethical dimension because anticorruption claims can reinforce integrity norms but may also conceal asymmetries, strategic selectivity, or moral performance detached from substantive commitment (Alexander, 2021). Domestic controversies, conflicts of interest, and perceptions of institutional capture may further complicate the credibility of such claims, illustrating the contingent character of normative authority. These mechanisms show that socialisation in ACPD is not reducible to norm internalisation alone, as it also involves contestation, adaptation, performative enactment, and strategic repositioning within a field structured by unequal capacities and differentiated forms of recognition.

Socialisation through ACPD is neither uniform nor normatively innocent. States enter the global anticorruption field from different positions and for different reasons. Some mobilise anticorruption from positions of high reputational security; others use it to compensate for vulnerability, to seek legitimacy, or to signal reformist intent. Yet across these differences, the comparative analysis reveals a common processual grammar. Anticorruption becomes a medium through which states make themselves legible to international audiences and through which they seek to stabilise desirable interpretations of their conduct. In doing so, they help reproduce the global anticorruption norm even when their primary motivations remain strategic. The significance of ACPD therefore lies not in the purity of state motives, but in the fact that anticorruption has become a widely intelligible language of diplomatic interaction, one through which power, legitimacy, and identity are increasingly negotiated in world politics.

8.3 Comparative Insights Across Political Contexts

The comparative analysis developed in this book demonstrates that ACPD operates across diverse political, institutional, and strategic contexts while retaining a recognisable processual grammar. Denmark, New Zealand, the United States, and South Korea differ significantly in governance traditions, geopolitical positioning, and institutional architectures. Yet despite these differences, their engagement with ACPD reveals convergent patterns in how integrity is mobilised, communicated, and recognised internationally.

A first key insight concerns the relationship between domestic governance performance and international positioning. States with consolidated integrity systems tend to operate from positions of reputational security, allowing them to project anticorruption as a credible and stabilising element of their international identity. In such cases, anticorruption functions as a form of diplomatic capital that reinforces trust and facilitates participation in norm-setting arenas. Comparative evidence also shows that reputational security remains contingent upon the perceived consistency between external advocacy and domestic governance practices. By contrast, states facing internal challenges may mobilise anticorruption more strategically as a means of signalling reform, managing external perceptions, or enhancing international legitimacy. In both configurations,

ACPD remains anchored in the interplay between domestic performance and external recognition.

A second insight relates to the degree of strategic articulation guiding ACPD. While some states adopt explicit, centralised strategies with clearly defined objectives and institutional coordination, others rely on more diffuse and implicit configurations in which multiple actors contribute to a loosely structured but nonetheless coherent repertoire. This variation does not necessarily determine effectiveness. Rather, it reflects differences in political culture, administrative organisation, and strategic priorities. What remains consistent across cases is the presence of a coordinating logic, whether formalised or not, that aligns anticorruption initiatives with broader foreign policy objectives.

A third comparative pattern concerns the role of actors and institutional configurations. Across all cases, ACPD extends beyond traditional diplomatic institutions, involving a wide network of state and non state agents operating at multiple levels. Ministries, regulatory bodies, development agencies, law enforcement institutions, and diplomatic missions interact with private sector entities, civil society organisations, and international partners. This multi-actor configuration reinforces the idea that ACPD is not monopolised by foreign ministries but is instead embedded in broader governance ecosystems. The diversity of actors also contributes to the credibility and reach of anticorruption initiatives, particularly when non state agents function as carriers of expertise and perceived neutrality.

A fourth insight emerges from the patterns of activity through which ACPD is enacted internationally. Across the cases, there is a clear predominance of dialogic engagement and advocacy, supported by practices of listening, exchange, cultural diplomacy, and, to a lesser extent, broadcasting. These activities enable states to participate actively in shaping the global anticorruption norm while also responding to the expectations of international audiences. At the same time, the analysis reveals that ACPD is not limited to consensual or cooperative forms of engagement. In certain contexts, more assertive practices may be employed, reflecting the strategic use of influence in response to specific geopolitical or economic considerations.

Finally, the comparison highlights the strategic mobilisation of resources and capacities. States combine material resources, such as funding and technology, with immaterial elements, including policies, institutional practices, and reputational assets. These are further shaped by ideational factors that determine how resources are interpreted and deployed. The capacity to integrate these dimensions effectively is central to the success of ACPD, as it enables states to align their actions with both domestic priorities and international expectations.

These comparative insights demonstrate that ACPD is both context-sensitive and structurally patterned. While national trajectories vary, the cases examined in this book reveal recurring dynamics that transcend individual contexts. At the same time, they do not exhaust the diversity of ACPD practices globally. Alternative trajectories may emerge in regions such as Africa and Latin America, where anticorruption reforms, regional governance initiatives, and South–South cooperation arrangements may shape distinctive pathways of norm diffusion, socialisation, and international engagement. Exploring these contexts represents an important next step in refining, testing, and expanding the analytical framework proposed here. This dual character reinforces the argument that ACPD constitutes a distinct and analytically meaningful domain within contemporary international relations.

8.4 Towards a Theoretical Framework for Anticorruption Public Diplomacy

Building on the comparative analysis, this book advances the foundations of a general theoretical understanding of ACPD. The findings point to a structured set of recurring dynamics that together define the process through which states engage with the global anticorruption norm. These dynamics can be organised into four interrelated analytical dimensions: strategic structuring, actor configurations, modes of action, and the resource–power nexus. Taken together, they provide the basis for a theoretical framework of ACPD as a patterned yet context-sensitive process of international socialisation.

A first dimension concerns strategic structuring. Across cases, ACPD is consistently guided by a coherent orientation that links anticorruption initiatives to broader foreign policy objectives. This orientation may be explicitly codified in national strategies or emerge implicitly through institutional practice, but in all instances, it reflects the alignment between integrity-related engagement and national interests. The presence of a coordinating authority, whether located in foreign ministries, central governments, or specialised agencies, further indicates that ACPD is not a diffuse or accidental phenomenon, but is organised around identifiable centres of strategic direction. At the same time, the analysis shows that formal planning, while beneficial, is not a necessary condition for effectiveness. States may achieve significant outcomes through adaptive and evolving configurations, underscoring the flexibility inherent in ACPD.

A second dimension relates to actor configurations and the structure of participation. ACPD is characterised by the involvement of a broad and heterogeneous set of agents operating across domestic and international levels. State institutions remain central, but their actions are complemented and often amplified by non state agents, including private sector entities, civil society organisations, academic communities, and professional networks. International actors, in turn, are not merely recipients of diplomatic initiatives but active participants in shaping the meaning and trajectory of anticorruption norms. The diversity of these configurations highlights the distributed nature of agency in ACPD and reinforces its character as a process of international socialisation rather than unilateral projection. It also reveals the variability of representation links, ranging from formal institutional mandates to voluntary and network-based forms of engagement.

A third dimension concerns the modes of action through which anticorruption is enacted diplomatically. The analysis demonstrates that ACPD operates through a repertoire of practices that combine communicative, relational, and operational elements. Among these, dialogic engagement and advocacy emerge as predominant, reflecting the importance of interaction and persuasion in shaping international expectations. These are complemented by practices of exchange, cultural interaction, and message dissemination, which contribute to the circulation and consolidation of anticorruption norms across different contexts. Importantly, the findings also indicate that ACPD is not limited to consensual or cooperative forms of engagement. Under certain conditions, states may employ more assertive or constraining measures, reflecting the strategic adaptation of diplomatic conduct to specific challenges. This plurality of modes underscores the versatility of ACPD as a form of influence that operates across a spectrum ranging from attraction to constraint.

A fourth dimension is the resource–power nexus. The effectiveness of ACPD depends on the capacity of states to mobilise and integrate material, immaterial, and ideational resources in a coherent manner. Material resources, such as financial means and technological capabilities, interact with immaterial elements, including institutional frameworks, policies, and administrative competences. These, in turn, acquire diplomatic significance through ideational factors (smart power) that assign meaning and guide their strategic use. The combination of these elements reflects a multidimensional conception of power, in which soft, hard, collaborative, and sharp power capabilities are not mutually exclusive but dynamically articulated. This integrated approach enables states to translate domestic governance features into internationally recognisable forms of influence.

Underlying these four dimensions is a broader relational dynamic linking identity, interests, and norms. ACPD does not simply reflect pre-existing state characteristics; it actively contributes to their redefinition. Through engagement with ACPD, states simultaneously shape and are shaped by the expectations of international society. This bidirectional process highlights the co-constitutive relationship between agency and structure in ACPD, situating it within a constructivist understanding of international relations in which meaning, recognition, and interaction are central.

The general theory that emerges from this analysis does not seek to eliminate contextual variation. On the contrary, it recognises that ACPD is inherently adaptive, shaped by differences in political systems, institutional capacities, and strategic environments. Its value lies instead in identifying a common analytical grammar that makes it possible to understand how diverse empirical manifestations relate to a shared underlying process. In this sense, ACPD can be theorised as a distinct modality of international engagement through which states navigate the intersection of governance, legitimacy, and influence in contemporary world politics.

8.5 Implications for Theory and Practice

The findings of this book carry significant implications for the theoretical development of public diplomacy and for the practical design of foreign policy. By conceptualising ACPD as a structured process of international socialisation, the analysis expands existing understandings of public diplomacy, power, and global governance, reinforcing the notion of reputational security (Cull, 2024), while also offering concrete insights for policymakers navigating an increasingly norm-driven international environment.

From a theoretical perspective, this study demonstrates that public diplomacy cannot be fully understood solely through the lenses of communication, image projection, or soft power attraction. Instead, it must be situated within a wider framework that incorporates governance performance, norm dynamics, and intersubjective recognition. ACPD exemplifies this shift by revealing how domestic institutional arrangements become central to international influence, not merely as background conditions but as active components of diplomatic engagement and reputational security.

In doing so, the book also contributes to constructivist approaches in international relations by empirically grounding the co-constitutive relationship between identity, interests, and norms. Anticorruption emerges as a domain in which these elements are continuously negotiated through practice, rather than predefined or static. This reinforces the view that international influence is not simply a function of material capabilities, but of the capacity to generate and sustain shared meanings within global governance frameworks. At the same time, by incorporating the strategic use of diverse power modalities, the analysis bridges constructivist insights with broader debates on power, offering a more integrated understanding of how influence operates across normative and material dimensions.

The study further contributes to the literature on global governance by highlighting anticorruption as a structuring norm that increasingly shapes expectations of legitimate state behaviour. By demonstrating how states engage with, reproduce, and strategically mobilise this norm, the book provides a framework for analysing similar governance-centred dynamics in other issue areas, such as environmental sustainability, human rights, or digital governance. In this sense, ACPD can be seen as part of a broader transformation in which global norms become key arenas of diplomatic interaction and competition.

From a practical perspective, the implications are equally relevant. For policymakers, the analysis underscores the importance of adopting a more integrated and strategic approach to ACPD. Effective engagement requires more than the implementation of isolated initiatives. It depends on the alignment between domestic governance performance and international projection, ensuring that anticorruption claims are supported by credible institutional practices. Without such alignment, diplomatic efforts risk being perceived as symbolic or instrumental, thereby undermining their effectiveness.

The findings also highlight the need for coordination across a wide range of actors. Given the multi-actor nature of ACPD, successful strategies depend on the ability to mobilise not only governmental institutions but also non state agents, whose expertise and perceived neutrality can enhance credibility and broaden international engagement. This calls for governance models that facilitate collaboration across sectors and levels (Zaharna, 2022), while maintaining coherence with broader foreign policy objectives.

Moreover, the analysis suggests that policymakers should recognise the diversity of pathways to implement ACPD. There is no single model applicable to all contexts. States may adopt explicit strategies or rely on more adaptive and decentralised approaches, depending on their institutional configurations and strategic priorities. What is essential is the presence of a coherent orientation that links anticorruption initiatives to clearly defined objectives and that enables learning and adjustment over time.

Finally, the book points to the importance of understanding ACPD as a field of both cooperation and competition. While it contributes to the diffusion of shared norms and the strengthening of global governance, it also constitutes an arena in which states seek to advance their interests, shape standards, and position themselves within international hierarchies of legitimacy. Recognising this dual character is crucial for designing policies that are both normatively grounded and strategically effective.

Taken together, these implications reinforce the central argument of this book: ACPD is not only a relevant empirical phenomenon but also a conceptually rich and practically consequential domain that redefines how states engage with the normative structures of contemporary international relations.

8.6 Future Research Agenda

The analysis developed in this book opens several promising avenues for future research, reflecting both the conceptual novelty and the empirical breadth of ACPD. As a field that sits at the intersection of international relations, governance studies, and public diplomacy, ACPD offers fertile ground for further theoretical refinement and comparative exploration. One important direction concerns the expansion of comparative research across a wider range of political systems and regional contexts. While this book has focused on four distinct cases, African and Latin American experiences deserve particular attention, as they were not included among the primary case studies examined here. Both regions provide valuable opportunities for exploring how ACPD develops under different institutional, political, and historical conditions, thereby contributing to the further development and testing of the analytical framework proposed in this study. Future research may also examine the role of regional organisations, anticorruption networks, and South–South cooperation mechanisms in shaping alternative forms of international socialisation and norm diffusion. Such research would help assess whether the analytical patterns identified in this book hold across varying levels of governance capacity, regional integration, and geopolitical positioning.

A second avenue relates to the measurement and evaluation of ACPD outcomes. Given its processual and intersubjective nature, assessing the impact of ACPD remains a complex challenge. Future research could develop methodological approaches capable of capturing reputational effects, norm diffusion, and behavioural change across different audiences, thereby contributing to a more systematic evaluation of diplomatic effectiveness in norm-driven domains.

A third area for further inquiry lies in the role of digital technologies and information environments. As diplomatic practices become increasingly mediated by digital platforms, the ways in which anticorruption narratives are communicated, contested, and amplified are likely to evolve. Investigating how digital tools shape processes of international socialisation, as well as the risks associated with disinformation and strategic communication, represents a particularly relevant and timely research frontier.

Finally, further theoretical work could explore the applicability of the analytical framework developed in this book to other domains of governance-centred diplomacy. Issues such as environmental sustainability, human rights, and global health share similar dynamics of norm construction, identity projection, and multi-actor engagement. Examining these parallels may contribute to the development of a broader theory of governance-based public diplomacy, within which anticorruption constitutes a particularly salient case.

By outlining these directions, this book positions ACPD not as a closed field of inquiry, but as an evolving research agenda. Its conceptual and empirical foundations invite continued investigation into how states engage with global norms, how legitimacy is constructed and contested, and how diplomacy adapts to the complex demands of contemporary international order.

8.7 Concluding Reflections: The Future of Anticorruption Public Diplomacy

This book has argued that ACPD reflects deeper transformations in how states engage with the international system. As global governance becomes increasingly structured around expectations of transparency, accountability, and integrity, anticorruption is evolving into a shared language through which legitimacy is articulated, contested, and recognised. In this context, states are no longer evaluated solely on the basis of material capabilities or geopolitical positioning, but also on reputational security (Cull, 2024), which includes their capacity to demonstrate credible commitments to integrity in both domestic and international arenas.

Looking ahead, ACPD is likely to play an even more prominent role in shaping the contours of international relations. As global challenges become more interconnected and governance failures more visible, the demand for integrity as a condition of cooperation is expected to intensify. This will further embed anticorruption within diplomatic practice, not only as a normative expectation but also as a strategic resource. States will increasingly engage in processes of signalling, benchmarking, and reputational positioning, seeking to align themselves with global standards while simultaneously advancing their own interests.

At the same time, the future of ACPD will be shaped by persistent tensions. The dual character of anticorruption, as both a normative commitment and a strategic instrument, will continue to generate ambiguities. While anticorruption initiatives may contribute to strengthening global governance and fostering cooperation, they may also be selectively deployed to exert influence, shape agendas, or reinforce asymmetries. The challenge, therefore, lies in navigating the boundary between genuine norm promotion and instrumental use, ensuring that anticorruption does not become detached from its ethical foundations.

These dynamics point to a broader transformation in the nature of diplomacy itself. ACPD exemplifies a shift towards governance-centred diplomacy, in which the management of domestic institutional performance becomes inseparable from international engagement. In this evolving landscape, influence is increasingly exercised through the capacity to align internal practices with external expectations and to translate governance credibility into diplomatic capital.

The implications of this transformation are far-reaching. As anticorruption becomes embedded in the normative architecture of international relations, it may contribute to redefining the criteria of legitimacy, reshaping hierarchies of influence, and reinforcing the role of norms in structuring global order. At the same time, it raises critical questions about inclusivity, fairness, and the distribution of authority within global governance systems. Not all states possess the same capacities to perform or project integrity, and the standards by which anticorruption is evaluated may themselves reflect existing power structures.

In this sense, the future of ACPD will depend not only on the actions of individual states, but also on the collective evolution of the global anticorruption norm. Whether this norm develops as a genuinely shared framework for cooperation or as a contested terrain of strategic competition will shape its trajectory and impact. What remains clear, however, is that ACPD has become an integral component of how states navigate the complexities of contemporary international relations.

As this book reaches its conclusion, ACPD can be understood as more than a policy domain or analytical category. It represents a lens through which to observe the changing relationship between power, legitimacy, and governance in the international system. In a world where credibility increasingly depends on the capacity to align values with action, anticorruption emerges not only as a diplomatic practice, but as a defining feature of how states seek to be recognised, trusted, and influential in the global arena.

References

Aday, S. (2025). Introduction to the handbook on public diplomacy. In S. Aday (Ed.), *Handbook on public diplomacy* (pp. 1–6). Elgar. https://doi.org/10.4337/9781803926568.00008

Alexander, C. (2021). Hegemony, morality and power: A Gramscian theoretical framework for public diplomacy. In C. Alexander (Ed.), *The frontiers of public diplomacy* (pp. 9–24). Routledge.

Cull, N. (2019). *Public diplomacy: Foundations for global engagement in the digital age*. Polity.

Cull, N. (2024). *Reputational security*. Cambridge: Polity.

Melissen, J., Du, S., & Goswami, A. (2023). Public diplomacy. In P. James (Ed.), *Oxford bibliographies in international relations*. Oxford University Press.

Zaharna, R. S. (2022). *Boundary spanners of humanity*. Oxford University Press. https://doi.org/10.1093/oso/9780190930271.001.0001

Index

N. de A. e S. F. dos Santos, *Anticorruption Public Diplomacy*, Palgrave Macmillan Series in Global Public Diplomacy,
https://doi.org/10.1007/978-3-032-28668-0